BOOTLEGGERS AND BORDERS

BOOTLEGGERS AND
BORDERS

THE PARADOX OF PROHIBITION
ON A CANADA-U.S. BORDERLAND

Stephen T. Moore

University of Nebraska Press
Lincoln and London

Library of Congress
Cataloging-in-Publication Data
Moore, Stephen T.
(Stephen Timothy), 1969–.
Bootleggers and borders : the paradox
 of prohibition on a Canada-U.S.
borderland / Stephen T. Moore.
pages   cm
Includes bibliographical
references and index.
ISBN 978-0-8032-5491-6 (hardback)
ISBN 978-0-8032-6784-8 (epub)
ISBN 978-0-8032-6785-5 (mobi)
ISBN 978-0-8032-6786-2 (pdf).
1. Prohibition—United States.
2. Prohibition—Northwest, Pacific.
3. Canada—Boundaries—United States.
4. United States—Boundaries—Canada.
5. United States—Relations—Canada.
6. Canada—Relations—United States.
7. Northwest, Pacific—History—
20th century. I. Title.
HV5089.M76 2014
363.4'1097309042—dc23
2014025093

Set in Sabon Next by Renni Johnson.
Designed by N. Putens.

Contents

Illustrations

Preface

THE NATURES OF BORDER

Were it not for the swath cut through the trees, the casual observer might fail to recognize that he or she had crossed a border. Nothing in the natural landscape of the Pacific Northwest—not the lakes, not the rivers, and certainly not the boundless expanse of forest and plain, mountain and valley—provides a clear indication of the forty-ninth parallel. Nature, in this far corner of the West, seems unwilling to recognize such an arbitrary line. The stone and iron obelisks that mark the border, marching in succession from the Atlantic to the Pacific, prove useful in the more heavily populated areas of the East and certainly on the uniform, undulating plains. They are, however, quickly lost in the dense forests of cedar, Douglas fir, pine, and spruce and are dwarfed by the rugged, sometimes precipitous, mountains that stretch to the horizon in the Far West. The Anglo-American boundary commission that surveyed the line between 1857 and 1869 determined that the only way to delineate the border was to carve it out of the forest—an expensive, labor-intensive undertaking, but a necessary one.[1] Years later, even with that physical demarcation, it remained common for travelers to be uncertain as to which side of the border they were on.[2]

Perhaps never was the border's ambiguity more propitious, and yet more problematic, than during the United States' noble experiment with prohibition. For over a century, advocates of temperance reform had railed against the evils of liquor. Free of alcohol, they argued, society would be healthier physically, morally, and psychologically. Workers would be more productive; children would be protected from abusive fathers and wives from abusive husbands. By the end of the First World War, most Americans agreed. When the Eighteenth Amendment took effect in January 1920, no longer could Americans make, sell, transport, or import any intoxicating beverage that contained more than 0.5 percent alcohol. They could, however, legally drink it, and thus it was left to the amendment's enforcement mechanism, the Volstead Act, to ensure that they did not have access to it.

Predictably, from the Pacific to the Atlantic, American dollars promptly headed north and (usually) pure, Canadian whisky, south. Canadian distillers, brewers, export houses, rumrunners, and bootleggers were more than happy to assuage the parched throats of their American friends. In the Northwest, hundreds of yachts, steamers, and schooners ran liquor from Vancouver's Rum Row into the Puget Sound. Farther east, at Crowsnest Pass on the British Columbia—Alberta border, McLaughlin "Whiskey Sixes" raced across the sometimes ill-defined border to supply speakeasies and roadhouses in Spokane, northern Idaho, and western Montana. However, what was a boon to the Canadian and British Columbian economies frustrated and exasperated American diplomats and enforcement officials, who sought from their Dominion counterparts help in stemming this illegal torrent of liquor. Between 1920 and 1933 no issue in Canadian-American relations proved more contentious or more intractable.

One might expect to find the reasons for this intractability in the letters carried in diplomatic pouches traveling between Ottawa and Washington DC.[3] If the United States and Canada existed on separate continents, separated by an ocean, such an approach might make the most sense. But these two nations are not, of course, separated by an ocean. Colloquially, it is understood that they share a "special relationship" and that they are nations and peoples divided only by an "undefended" border. Perhaps coincidentally, just as prohibition was beginning to strain the bilateral relationship, Canadians and Americans joined together in September

1921 to dedicate the completion of the sixty-seven-foot-tall marble Peace Arch located on the border between Blaine, Washington, and Surrey, British Columbia. Adjacent to the memorial's inscription, "Children of a Common Mother," American and Canadian Boy Scouts shook hands. Canadian and American members of the Kiwanis Club, including its international president, also gathered at the arch as a tangible symbol of the "Brethren Dwelling together in Unity" inscription carved on the memorial's opposite face.[4] As if to underscore what the Boy Scouts and Kiwanis members already knew, the Canadian diplomat (and later historian) Hugh Keenleyside commented in 1929, "The boundary between Canada and the United States is a typically human creation: It is physically invisible, geographically illogical, militarily indefensible, and emotionally inescapable."[5] If there is any truth to Keenleyside's observations about the border, then what does the border mean and what is "special" about the special relationship? How did these features of the Canadian-American relationship factor into prohibition?

This study contends that the root of the prohibition enforcement problem lay not so much in the diplomatic relations between Ottawa and Washington DC as in the less formal, but more common, everyday borderlands relations between Canadians and Americans generally. A major premise of a borderlands approach in the Canadian-American context is that North America runs more naturally north and south than east and west. People living near the border may pay allegiance to their respective sovereignties but, due to continental geography and shared history, they often have more in common with their counterparts north or south of the border.[6] Along borders, especially in areas distant from the centers of national power, foreign relations operate according to different methods and rules and are managed by different actors, who hold different assumptions and cultural values.

Perhaps nowhere was this more evident historically than in the transnational Pacific Northwest. West of the Continental Divide, inhabitants of British Columbia, Washington, Oregon, Idaho, and western Montana had long interacted without the mediation of their respective sovereignties. Compared to the almost impenetrable natural border presented by the Rocky Mountains, the forty-ninth parallel was often little more than a political abstraction. Indeed, before the belated completion of the Canadian Pacific Railway in 1885, the movement of people, economic goods, and ideas to British Columbia was accomplished most easily, and most often, through the American Northwest. This north-south connection continued well into the early twentieth century. During prohibition, entrepreneurs, temperance workers, tourists, bootleggers, and law enforcement officials often behaved as if no border existed at all. These were the actors in Canadian-American relations and it was this cultural relationship that was at the heart of the problems plaguing the diplomatic relationship. Paradoxically, it was also this long-standing cultural relationship that encouraged resolution of the diplomatic controversy. In contrast to central and eastern Canada, which remained adamantly opposed to cooperation, the Canadian West offered the earliest and strongest support for the American case.[7] Exploring what it was about the nature of the Canadian-American relationship in the Far West that caused British Columbians to support cooperation at a much earlier stage is one purpose of this study.

At the same time, lest one be deluded into an unchecked notion of continentalism—in the Northwest or elsewhere—to argue that the border is sometimes an abstraction is not to argue that it is unimportant or without meaning. Especially to Canadians. With over 75 percent of its population living within one hundred miles of the boundary, Canada is a border nation. The border is a reality of virtually every Canadian's daily life, whether he or she lives in Toronto or Vancouver, Halifax or Calgary.[8] Not only does it define citizenship, it contributes to how Canadians think, what they believe, and how they work. It should come as no surprise that the border is tied very closely to Canada's national identity, the defining of which sociologist Seymour Martin Lipset calls "the quintessential Canadian issue."[9] Even Canadian nationalists—quick to point out that being Canadian means much more than simply being "not American"—concur that the border plays an important role in shaping their identity. One of the English-Canadian writers with the greatest national and international reputation in the 1920s was the humorist Stephen Leacock, who, not coincidentally, found much of his material in the border and Canada's relationship with the United States. He once observed, "By an odd chance the forty-ninth parallel, an astronomical line, turned out to *mean* something."[10] Beyond the ways it informs the Canadian national identity, the border's meaning helps explain the relationship between Canadians and Americans generally. It is central to that relationship.

The border is also important for a different reason. Although the casual observer may see or cross the border without recognizing its significance, academics too often see it as a definitive line. In so doing, they fail to make the valuable comparative discoveries the border offers.[11] Both countries originated from European expansion and evolved from a common, largely English, heritage. Both adopted federal, constitutional democratic systems, place an emphasis on liberal values, and share many social, economic, and historical experiences.[12] As Lipset and the historian Robin Winks have noted, it is because Canada and the United States have so much in common that they help us understand not only the other, but ourselves as well.[13] This commonality calls into question the notion of American "exceptionalism," or at least it forces us to reframe it in a North American context.

Thus, examining the nature of the relationship between British Columbians and Americans during prohibition offers a window into the subtle but important differences in the way Canadians and Americans approach similar problems.[14] While the purpose of this study is not to provide a detailed interpretive history of the prohibition movement in British Columbia, in Canada, or in the United States, the differences in their respective systems have much to say about the nature of the borderlands relationship. Moreover, these differences played a crucial role in the Canadian decision about whether to accommodate American pleas for enforcement assistance and they provided an alternative model for temperance once the noble experiment finally ended. It is for these reasons that British Columbia plays a central and, in some places, a dominant role in the narrative of this story.

The timing of the prohibition story is also important. Few decades were as important in shaping the Canadian-American relationship as the 1920s, for at least two reasons closely related to the prohibition problem. First, beginning in the 1920s, Canadian external affairs underwent a significant transformation. During the William Lyon Mackenzie King administration, the newly created Department of External Affairs made a concerted effort to define a Canadian foreign policy independent of the British Foreign and Colonial Offices. To do so meant the Dominion had to face the United States alone without compromising its sovereignty. As a consequence the diplomatic relationship between Canada and the United States entered a new, formative stage. The second reason is the increasing degree to which Canadians and Americans began to interact with each other in this period. The "undefended" border had always been a porous one. Yet during the 1920s there was an extraordinary increase in the pace and scope of what Marcus Lee Hansen referred to as the "mingling of the Canadian and American peoples."[15] Its chief cause was the automobile and the ease with which travelers were able to cross the border. By the end of the decade, four million American cars and twenty million Americans crossed the border each year. The effect, according to one historian, marked a "turning point" in the cultural history of Canada, as Americans — in pursuit of liquor, scenery, and other things "Canadian" — brought with them other (sometimes less desirable) aspects of American culture.[16] Both of these dynamics, the increased importance of the diplomatic relationship and the increased permeability of the border during this period, help explain the intractability of the liquor problem.

As Canadians and Americans began crossing the border (and "mingling") in ever-increasing numbers, it follows that they spent a greater amount of time thinking about that border and what it meant to their everyday lives. Borders are divides, but they are also meeting points. They separate, but they also bring together. They provide opportunity but also occasional peril. They serve as protective bulwarks but also provide refuge and sanctuary. They are symbols of national sovereignty but sometimes symbols of continental harmony. As scholars have shown in other contexts, these meanings are not exclusive to the prohibition era.[17] Nonetheless, one means of exploring the cultural fabric of the prohibition-era relationship is to explore how the multiple and shifting meanings of an increasingly permeable border factored into what would have otherwise remained merely a diplomatic problem and to ask whether the border reinforced or interrupted natural historic, social, and cultural patterns. In short, the central paradox of prohibition in the Pacific Northwest is that the very heritage that enabled smuggling prior to prohibition also supported early cooperation in enforcement efforts against the liquor traffic. Though this presents a seeming contradiction, examining the myriad ways Canadians and Americans interacted, viewed the other, and assigned meaning to the border will show that it is not.

For purposes of this study, the terms *Pacific Northwest* and *Northwest borderlands* will be used interchangeably to refer to the region west of the Rocky Mountains, north from Oregon into British Columbia. While both the American Pacific Northwest and British Columbia are distinct regions in themselves, one need not be a geographical determinist to recognize the innate logic of the Pacific Northwest as a region that transcends national boundaries.[18] Moreover, it is a term Canadians have applied to their Pacific province with few apparent misgivings.[19]

Finally, while I have attempted to test familiar themes of the Canadian-American relationship in a regional setting, sometimes finding them applicable to the Pacific Northwest and sometimes not, I have generally refrained from considering their applicability elsewhere along the border. By focusing on a particular region, rather than on the whole of the boundary, one is able to more fully capture the intricacies of the border's sometimes-compatible, sometimes-contradictory meanings and relationships. Thus, though intended partly as an examination of a microcosm of the larger Canadian-American relationship, this study recognizes that the border separating Canadians from Americans is by no means uniform. There are a number of borderlands regions, each having its own social, cultural, and economic patterns and each having its own history.

Acknowledgments

I t is precisely because the research and writing process can sometimes seem like such a solitary endeavor that I am especially eager
to acknowledge the many who prove it is not.

Numerous institutions and individuals eagerly opened their holdings
and helpfully responded to (sometimes vague) inquiries. These include
the British Columbia Archives, the City of Vancouver Archives, the Eastern
Washington University Library, Glenbow Archives in Calgary, the Gon-
zaga University Library, the Legislative Library of British Columbia, the
College Park and Seattle branches of the National Archives and Records
Administration, the Library and Archives of Canada, the Museum of His-
tory and Industry in Seattle, the Seattle Public Library, the Spokane Public
Library, the Vancouver Public Library, the City of Surrey Archives, the
University of British Columbia Library, the University of Victoria Library,
the Vancouver Maritime Museum, the University of Oregon Archives and
Special Collections, and the University of Washington Library and Special
Collections. While many people at these institutions provided invaluable
assistance, a number deserve special recognition: Kenneth Hager at the
National Archives in College Park; Sue Karren at the Seattle branch of
the National Archives; Lea Edgar at the Vancouver Maritime Museum;
Carolyn Marr at the Museum of History and Industry; and Gary Mitchell
and Kelly-Ann Turkington at the British Columbia Archives. I could not
have completed this work without their gracious assistance.

This book is also the product of generous financial support. The Department of History and the Graduate School of Arts and Sciences at the College of William and Mary in Virginia provided numerous research and conference grants. A research award from the Canadian Embassy in Washington DC provided funds to explore the rich holdings of Canadian institutions, while the Canada–United States Fulbright Foundation enabled me to spend a year in Canada, where, free from distraction, much of the initial writing took place. For the time needed to turn a dissertation into a book, the dean of the College of Arts and Humanities, the Office of the Provost, and the Office of Graduate Studies at Central Washington University provided valuable help in the way of faculty research and sabbatical leaves and travel support.

This book began as a dissertation at William and Mary, and so no acknowledgment would be complete without recognizing the contributions of my graduate committee. Ed Crapol quickly agreed to supervise my project and simultaneously offered both steady guidance and a great deal of independence. I think I wore him out, though, because he retired right after signing off on my project. Like Ed, Carol Sheriff and Judy Ewell also greatly contributed to my development as a historian and teacher, and they did so in ways I am still discovering. It was Mike Green who first suggested there might be something in prohibition and the Pacific Northwest borderlands. Mike has been a mentor, a trusted advisor, and a constant champion ever since my undergraduate days at Eastern Washington University. Who else would donate the use of a cabin overlooking the east shore of British Columbia's Kootenay Lake? Never have I written in such a beautifully distracting place! It is thus an honor for me to include his name here.

This work has benefited enormously from the support of many other individuals as well. Carlos Schwantes generously donated a beautiful fall afternoon in Moscow, Idaho, to discuss my project when it was in its most nascent stage. Likewise, my colleagues in the History Department at Central have given of their time reading and commenting on various elements. Special thanks must also go to Sterling Evans, who, in one of the serendipities of professional life, found something he thought really needed to be published buried deep in an otherwise unsuccessful job application.

As I sit here, feverishly typing, trying to complete all the tasks I never knew were part of writing a book, I would like to thank my editor, Bridget Barry, and her assistant, Sabrina Ehmke Sergeant, for guiding me through the process. Their invaluable suggestions, along with those of Sheila McManus and Robert Campbell, who gave so graciously of their time in reading and commenting on the manuscript, have made this book better than it would otherwise be. I would be equally remiss if I failed to note the contribution of Joy Margheim, whose copyediting made me look like a better writer than I really am. Any errors or omissions that remain are, of course, mine alone.

Finally, to my wife, Jackie, do I owe the greatest debt. Her support has always been unconditional, unquestioning, and unfailing. Her patience never ceases to amaze me. Likewise, my daughters, Sarah and Hannah—babies when this project started but now growing all too quickly into beautiful young ladies—are absolute blessings and constant reminders that there are more important things in life than writing books.

BOOTLEGGERS AND BORDERS

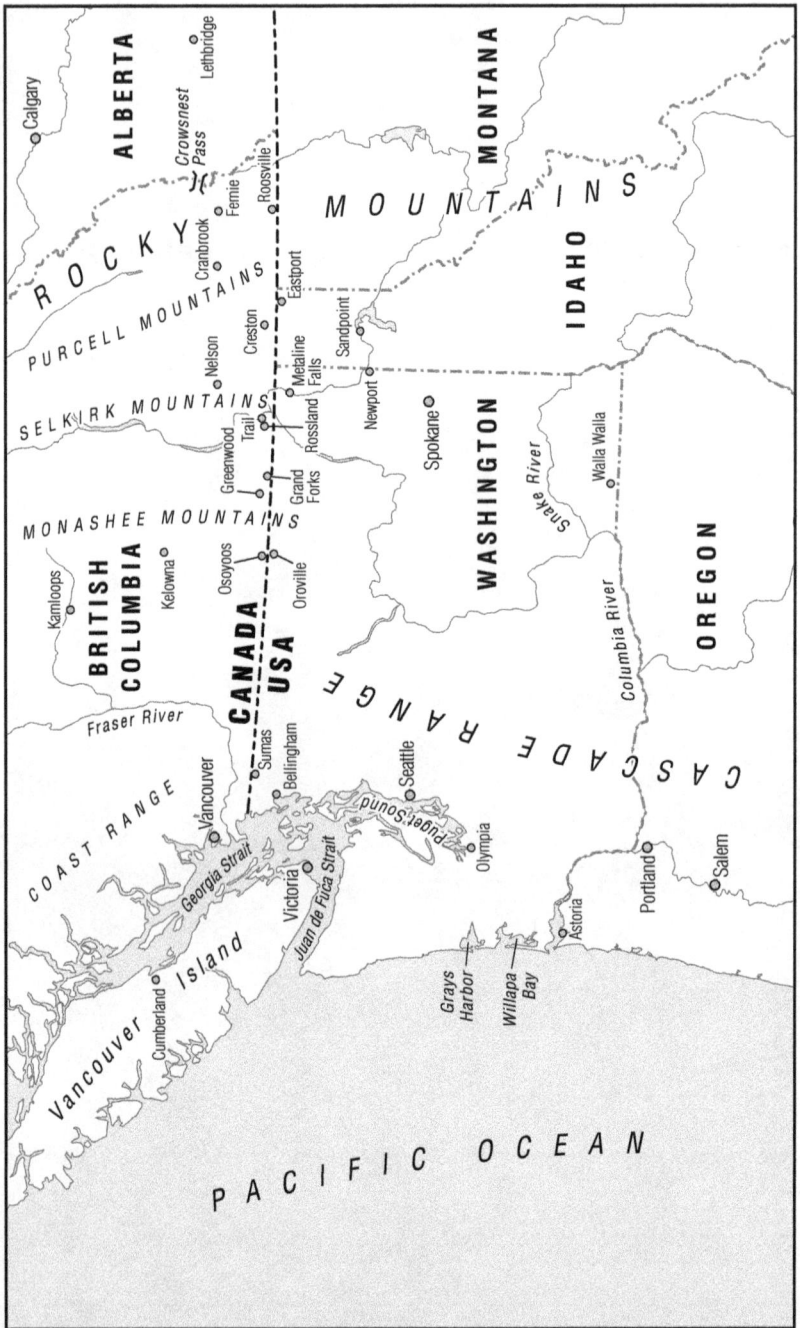

1. The Pacific Northwest borderlands. Erin Greb Cartography.

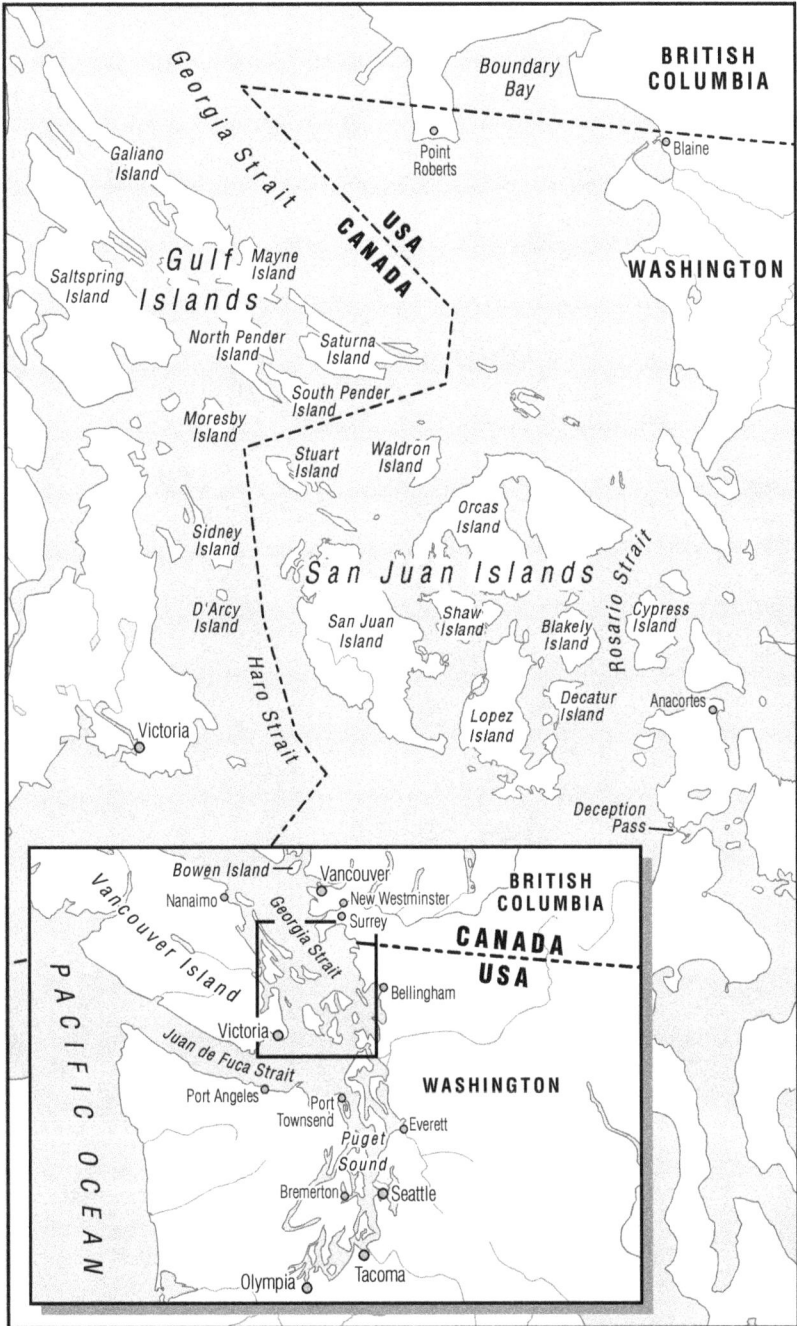

2. The Puget Sound, San Juan Islands, and Gulf Islands. Erin Greb Cartography.

CHAPTER ONE

Creating a Smuggler's Paradise

Ohr ne of the most repetitive themes in the literature of the Pacific Northwest is the relationship between its inhabitants and the natural environment. Early travelers and residents on both sides of the border often commented on the region's beauty and resources. The spectacular natural setting particularly astonished Rudyard Kipling. To those who had not the opportunity to visit, he suggested visualizing "all that the eye admires most in Bournemouth, Torquay, the Isle of Wight, the Happy Valley at Hong Kong, the Doon, Sorrento, and Camps Bay; add reminiscences of the Thousand Islands, and arrange the whole round the Bay of Naples, with the Himalayas for the background." When Frederick Talbot, another early traveler, set out to explore the economic and scenic value of British Columbia, he proclaimed it "a territory upon which nature has bestowed her wealth with so lavish a hand that it is difficult to form comparative estimates." Less descriptive, but no less telling, is the Canadian professor and humorist Stephen Leacock's perspective on the region: "If I had known what it was like, I wouldn't have been content with a mere visit. I'd have been born here."[1] Though booster pamphlets for the Northwest suggested one could "have a decent living . . . simply by eating gorgeous scenery," only occasionally did the harsher reality, that one cannot live on scenery alone, intrude into the regional psyche.[2]

While all raved about the scenery, the Northwest also symbolized opportunity. For those of British persuasion, Vancouver Island was a little piece of England. It had the same climate and was similar in size to Great Britain, while the ocean to the west added a certain mystique and promise of opportunity. "Were I an intending immigrant," Kipling mused, "I would risk a good deal of discomfort to get to the land in British Columbia; and were I rich, with no attachments outside England, I would swiftly buy me a farm or a house in that country for the mere joy of it." For Talbot, British Columbia was the "New Garden," flowing with "enormous riches—agriculture, mineralogical, forestal, industrial—all lying dormant and silently calling for the plucky and persevering."[3] This strong attachment to and identity with the region's natural setting and opportunity gave many Canadians and Americans in the Northwest a common outlook that the natural topography only affirmed.

The historian Jean Barman has commented that any understanding of British Columbia must be firmly grounded in the region's geography. The same must be said of the Pacific Northwest generally, for geography has played a profound role in how Canadians and Americans have thought about themselves, each other, and their relation to their respective sovereignties to the east. Stretching east from the Pacific and west from the Rockies, British Columbia shares a 430-mile land border with the states of Washington, Idaho, and Montana. The province embraces an area as large as France, Spain, Portugal, and the Netherlands combined, while the states to the south encompass a slightly smaller area. Even the interior Kootenay region is significantly larger than most of New England.[4]

As important as size is to the Pacific Northwest identity, so too is its north-south alignment. The region's natural or physiographic boundaries run not east and west but north and south. The Rockies, Purcells, Selkirks, Monashees, Cascades, and Coastal mountains, along with their interlying valleys, dictate that economic and demographic patterns align north and south as well. These mountains confine communities to narrow and inaccessible valleys, creating cultural and psychological islands that straddle both sides of the boundary.[5]

Perhaps the most important aspect of this north-south alignment was the implications it had for regional identity. Canadians and Americans in the Pacific Northwest interacted with little regard for the international border. The first Euro-American settlers of the region were fur traders, bent on exploiting the lucrative potential discovered by American and European maritime explorers in the late eighteenth century. Americans and Canadians formed companies, sometimes jointly, to exploit the region's furs, caring little whether the pelts they trapped were "British" or "American." The cultural residue of these fur empires, which carried over to the missionaries, settlers, and merchant capitalists who followed, was a frontier spirit of individualism and detachment from nationality. Despite the formal division of the Northwest along the forty-ninth parallel, and even despite British Columbia's confederation with Canada in 1871, the border was largely ignored in practice well into the twentieth century.[6]

A lack of transportation nullified whatever illusions British Columbians or Canadians had about early political union. Until the completion of the Canadian Pacific Railroad in the late 1880s, geography determined that British Columbia would look to the neighboring states rather than to eastern Canada.[7] Without a transcontinental railroad, or even a transprovincial line, trade with Canada remained difficult at best, and so the province's trade aligned more with the United States, Great Britain, Australia, Latin America, and Japan. British Columbia's access to eastern North America and Europe remained dependent initially on Pacific sea lanes and then on the American Central Pacific rail line.[8] Not until November 1885 did Canadian Pacific Railway officials drive the last spike at Craigellachie and bring British Columbia into the railway age.

In 1921 the newly completed Pacific Coast Highway opened to traffic, connecting British Columbia with Washington, Oregon, California, and Mexico. At its inaugural ceremonies, speakers proclaimed it a symbol of "100 years of peace between the British Empire and the United States."[9] More practically, it greatly improved western British Columbia's access to the States and to the eastern portion of the province. Since most British Columbians lived within easy driving distance of the border, the typical traveler drove south before picking up an east-west road in Washington State. The Associated Boards of Trade of Eastern British

Columbia, recognizing this peculiarity, annually reiterated its plea for the completion of a transprovincial highway. To accommodate the travel and tourism boom that occurred after the First World War, British Columbia did make a concerted effort to invest in its transportation infrastructure. As *Maclean's Magazine* pointed out, however, road construction in British Columbia was twenty times more expensive per mile than in other provinces.[10] Consequently, the province's roads remained primitive at best. In the 1940s a couple journeying from Vancouver to Lillooet—a two-day, 130-mile trek—commented, "Part of the road was built on cribbing and it looked as though you were hanging over the side of a cliff. Actually, in some places, you were."[11]

Given north-south transportation patterns, it is not surprising that American labor and capital played significant roles in the economic development of British Columbia. Mining accounted for the origin of many British Columbia towns and the United States for many of the miners. The Fraser River gold rush of 1858 and 1859 brought perhaps thirty thousand Americans from California and the rest of the United States into the Fraser Valley. By 1864 fully three-fourths of the fifteen thousand miners in British Columbia were Americans and half of all business establishments were American. These Americans remained until they had made their fortune or acquired the so-called Fraser River humbug. After passage of the Sherman Silver Purchase Act in 1890 promised an increased demand for silver, thousands of American prospectors again found their way to British Columbia, only to leave just as quickly when Congress repealed the act three years later. By 1899 Rossland had become home for the largest Western Federation of Miners local outside the United States.[12] Reflecting the international idealism of North American labor, one British Columbian miner declared, "There is no 49th parallel of latitude in Unionism. The Canadian and American workingman have joined hands across the boundary line for a common cause against a common enemy."[13]

American investment in British Columbia timber was no less significant. The virgin stands of Oregon, Washington, and British Columbia attracted lumbermen from the logged-over forests of the north central

United States. These industrial capitalists brought with them an inexhaustible amount of capital and, in the words of historian Robert McDonald, "made British Columbia their adopted home." So enamored of the profit potential of British Columbia were American investors that by 1909 the province had attracted almost half of all American capital investment in Canada. Not until the turn of the century did eastern and central Canadian capital and business interests find their way in significant numbers to British Columbia.[14]

Communication and cultural patterns closely mirrored the region's north-south transportation and economic patterns. Before the Canadian Pacific Railroad's completion, letters posted in British Columbia—even those destined for eastern Canada—were required to bear American postage.[15] As important, British Columbia's newspapers relied on the United States for news of events outside their region. With the prohibitive cost of telegraphing lengthy messages across Canada, Canadian papers remained dependent on the American Associated Press wire, which they tapped at Boston for the Maritimes, Buffalo for central Canada, Minneapolis for the Prairie provinces, and in Seattle for British Columbia. As a result, the Associated Press provided much of the content for Canadian newspapers. Not until the 1930s did British Columbian dailies begin to rely on the Canadian Press as their primary news source. Even then, the Canadian Press drew the bulk of its material from American sources, editing out only that which was too "American." British Columbia's daily newspapers generally carried the same sports, news, social, and entertainment content as their American counterparts. American stars became Canadian stars, and American heroes, like Babe Ruth and Charles Lindbergh, Canadian heroes.[16] Much of the popular culture British Columbians experienced during the 1920s was American. Even notoriously British Victoria procured two-thirds of its periodicals and 80 percent of its films from the United States. Along with the mainstream press, news organizations with smaller constituencies tended to share information as well. Labor papers in Vancouver, Seattle, Spokane, and Tacoma, for example, established the Western Labor Press in 1914 to share each other's weekly news and cartoons.[17]

With the many geographical factors that tied Canadians and Americans in the Pacific Northwest together, it is easy to assume that the border was inconsequential. Yet a border also obliges the historian to define difference. Though most British Columbians were not strident nationalists, neither were they American. Due partly to a divergence in the way in which British Columbia and the American Northwest were settled and administered, British Columbia had, by the First World War, defined an identity of its own—an identity not completely Canadian and not completely American, but British Columbian.

If it was geographically natural that British Columbians should look to the United States, it was culturally natural for white British Columbians to identify with Britain. While much of Canada revered its British roots, British Columbia was a decidedly British place. As Jean Barman suggests, "British ways were not transplanted into British Columbia simply because they existed elsewhere in Canada. The link was with Britain itself."[18] British Columbia had begun its life as a separate British colony, drew the majority of its settlers from Great Britain, and agreed to confederation only with material allurement—most notably, the promised completion of the Canadian Pacific Railroad. As late as 1918, the British *born* accounted for over 30 percent of the province's population and those of British *origin* accounted for approximately 70 percent.[19] Although the Canadian-born percentage grew significantly during the first decade of the century, until World War II more immigrants continued to arrive from British possessions than from all other parts of Canada.[20]

Many were working-class immigrants who entertained few prospects for opportunity or advancement in the class-ridden British Isles. The plethora of advertisements specifically targeted at prospective British immigrants attracted others. The Victoria & Island Development Association described Vancouver Island as "a bit of England on the Pacific," a theme also adopted by the Union Pacific Railroad in its efforts to attract passengers.[21] Descriptions provided by popular British travelers informed readers that the region's climate was "never too hot and rarely too cold," that several English newspapers were readily available, and that many of the local papers regularly printed "London Letters."[22] Stewart Holbrook, an American lumberjack and later journalist who bounced between lumber camps in the early 1920s, found Vancouver no ordinary "Yankee city." Unlike the rest of Canada, except Prince Edward Island, its motorists continued to drive on the left, as in Great Britain. Not until 1922 would British Columbia switch to the right.[23]

The character of the province determined that white British Columbians perceived their neighbors through a British, rather than a Canadian, lens. As Gwen Ronyk discovered in her examination of the Canadian press, the westernmost dailies more often made comparisons between American and British institutions than between American and Canadian ones.[24] As a result, the anti-Americanism that so animated eastern Canadian thought resonated only slightly in the West.

In other ways, being British distinguished quite starkly the outlook between Canadians and Americans on the Pacific coast. The First World War exemplifies this. British Columbians were among the most enthusiastic participants on behalf of Great Britain when war exploded in 1914 and reportedly provided more soldiers per capita than any other Canadian province.[25] By contrast, America's belated participation—occurring only after years of Canadians fighting and dying in vermin-infested trenches—seemed to many British Columbians a grievous offense, an offense made more stinging by President Wilson's repeated proclamations of neutrality. This seemed to imply that Great Britain and—by extension—British Columbia were equally at fault for the war as the other belligerents.[26] When Hollywood later compounded the insult by repeatedly portraying the idea that one or two American doughboys had held off the entire Prussian Guard, it only increased the bitterness felt by many north of the border. As Stewart Holbrook discovered, "No matter the complete idiocy of these films, they did not endear us to a people who thought of American soldiers as arriving at the front a full two years late."[27] Virtually all Canadians resented the way Americans portrayed America's role in the war. However, because

British Columbian participation was disproportionately high, British Columbian opinion of the United States suffered disproportionately as well.[28]

Even geographically there remained an important point of contrast between the images of the region north and south of the border. As Carlos Schwantes notes, "If in time British Columbia became the New Eldorado, Washington became the New Eden, a veritable farmer's paradise."[29] The establishment of the boundary at the forty-ninth parallel did not uniformly distribute the Pacific Northwest's natural resources. Because so many of the mountain ranges converge in British Columbia, and because of its northerly latitude, much of the land not right along the province's southern border is unsuited for agricultural production. As a result, British Columbia tended to attract a different population than Washington. Whereas the fertile valleys of Washington and Oregon attracted homesteading families with promises of free land, British Columbia relied on the region's timber and minerals. The types of persons employed in these extractive pursuits tended to be single, male, and highly transient.[30] It was a population notoriously opposed to prohibition, as temperance workers would later learn to their dismay.

Although both the Canadian and American governments, along with chambers of commerce, local immigration boards, and railroads, aggressively promoted the region, American and Canadian immigration policy fundamentally differed. In contrast to the national origin–based policy of the United States, Canada utilized a process based on literacy, capital, and aptitude. In 1921 the British Columbia Bureau of Provincial Information recommended that intending settlers should write to the bureau for authentic information and not rely too heavily on the colorful descriptions that emanated from unofficial sources. The agency indicated that "the class of immigrant whose chances of success are greatest is the man of small or moderate means, possessing energy, good health, and self-reliance, with the faculty of adaptability to new surroundings. He should have at least $2500 to $3000 on arrival in the Province, sufficient to make his first payment on his land and support himself and his family while awaiting returns."[31] The province hoped that by attracting a stable class of immigrants, the resulting high standard of living would help minimize population loss to the south.[32]

Perhaps the most important reasons for the different immigration policies were the divergent attitudes held by Canadians and Americans about the frontier generally. As Ken Coates points out, "The periphery had a valued place in the American psyche: it was synonymous with richness, potential, and personal opportunity. . . . But the frontier held no mythical place in the Canadian mind."[33] Accordingly, the histories and cultures of British Columbia and the old Oregon Country differed significantly. In the American West, statehood followed the pattern established over a century earlier in the Northwest Ordinance. There, settlement preceded, and was a prerequisite for, the establishment of government. Americans tended to be aggressive and innovative in the pursuit of opportunity but also more independent and less subject to civil authority. On the other hand, the region later encompassed by British Columbia was from the start governed by the Hudson's Bay Company, under license of the British Crown.[34] After the Treaty of Oregon established the western border between the United States and British North America in 1846, Great Britain assumed this role, creating first the Colony of Vancouver Island. Then, in 1866, as a result of the Fraser River gold rush, the Crown united the island and mainland territories by creating the Colony of British Columbia. As a consequence, the region north of the border enjoyed effective government prior to widespread settlement. This had significant consequences, not least of which was the movement of the North-West Mounted Police into the region. According to William Robbins, the Mounted Police had the effect of undermining "the rampant individualism and disrespect for authority that existed in the western United States." As Robbins concludes, "Canadians moved with greater prudence and caution."[35]

The belief in greater prudence is a cultural attitude historically shared by many Canadians, and British Columbians are no exception. Many contrasted the sleepy, orderly growth of Victoria and Vancouver with the raucous, hustling growth of Seattle.[36] "Peaceableness" was the characteristic most often pronounced to attract settlers to the province. "The mining camps of British Columbia are as orderly as English villages," asserted the *Guide to the Province of British Columbia for 1877–78*.[37] By contrast, some regarded the region south of the border as one of relative lawlessness. One commented that there were "saloons and gambling dens galore ... all out of proportion to the size of the place."[38] Another, revealing his cultural biases, added, "In the Queen's dominions an infringement of the law was really a serious matter, & not a sort of half joke as in California."[39]

The belief in British Columbia as a place of order and the United States as one of disorder continued to influence attitudes, especially those of white British Columbians, about Americans well into the twentieth century. It is not that violence was nonexistent in Canada. However, by deemphasizing violent episodes of their past and by excluding traits thought to be American, British Columbians defined a component of their Canadianism. "Peace, order, and good government," the Canadian national alternative to "life, liberty, and the pursuit of happiness," retained cultural significance in British Columbia as well.[40]

ON THE MARGIN

To point out that British Columbians found it useful to distinguish themselves from their American neighbors does not obviate one central reality: the most pronounced psychological border in the Pacific Northwest remained not the boundary between the United States and Canada but the long-impenetrable barrier posed by the Rocky Mountains. The Rockies did more to separate Canadians and Americans from their respective countrymen in the East than the forty-ninth parallel did to separate British Columbians from Americans in the Northwest. The western continental divide placed the Pacific Northwest on the margin and left many on both sides of the border feeling less a part of any nation than part of a shared colony or hinterland.[41]

One of the major reasons for the lack of national identification is the ethnic makeup of the region's population. As noted previously, it was not until after the completion of the Canadian Pacific Railroad that Canadian immigrants arrived in numbers sufficient to challenge the British character of British Columbia. Even then, it was not that American and British influence diminished but that Canadian influence strengthened. In 1931 the percentage of American-born, or those of non-Canadian parentage, remained greater in the three western provinces than in the rest of Canada. Whether attracted to free land south of the border or the economic opportunity available north, many drifted freely back and forth, ignoring boundary and nationality in the pursuit of opportunity. At times the movement was northward, at others, southward; whatever direction, it was movement enough for Marcus Lee Hansen to speak of the "mingling of the Canadian and American peoples."[42]

For either of these peoples, Canadian or American, the Pacific Northwest was the end of the line, figuratively and literally. Thus the region attracted a different mix than Canada or the United States generally. Rudyard Kipling noticed the many "Sikhs and Punjabi jats," while Frederick Talbot observed "furrow-eyed Italians, fair-complexioned Scandinavians, sullen-looking Russians, stolid Germans, raw-boned Americans, husky Canadians, big-built Irishmen, brawny Scots, and devil-may-care English, all rubbing shoulders."[43] Few overlooked the significant Chinese population that gave Vancouver the largest Chinatown on the West Coast next to San Francisco (but only slightly larger than that found in Seattle). The significant Chinese population gave non-Asian Canadians and Americans a common problem.[44] Unifying other nativists were the many ethnic groups who carefully guarded their cultural identities and traditions in urban enclaves. Most significantly, the ethnic variety in British Columbia accentuated a similarity with Americans south of its border while it constituted a point of difference with the rest of Canada.[45] As two historians point out, nationality only vaguely concerned the majority of settlers: "They were settlers who crisscrossed the international boundary looking for the ideal place . . . [and who] regarded national identity as something for city folks or politicians . . . . National identification with either country came slowly . . . not as a single act of Congress or Parliament but as a slow accumulation of responsibilities and benefits of political customs, and above all, from long-term residence on one side or the other."[46]

With few settlers of eastern Canadian origin, there existed in the Northwest very little of the United Empire Loyalist tradition that has historically furnished the tinder for anti-Americanism in other parts of Canada. British Columbians had learned to live with American proximity; for most, it was not that traumatic. As one young woman visiting Seattle for the first time in 1911 noted, "It is not so very different from our own country except that one sees the American flag flying everywhere and the ladies wear hats to the theatre and one can buy shoes for half the price and one uses gold and huge silver dollars instead of bills."[47] Most found Americans generally kind and hospitable.[48]

Historians have pointed out that sentiment in Canada for annexation to the United States was usually a chimera, used by economic elites for selfish interests. If annexation of any part of Canada were to occur, however, it would have included British Columbia.[49] The province had numerous American-born inhabitants, had important trade and communication links with the States, and was geographically closer to the United States than Canada. As the *London Times* pointed out in 1870, the Rocky Mountains were "nature's veto" upon a union between British Columbia and the Dominion. To the contrary, the paper concluded that if British Columbia had any inclination to join the United States, Great Britain should "place no obstacle in its way."[50] Even the faraway *Chicago Tribune* noticed the degree of annexationist sentiment in the Pacific province and the American consul in Victoria repeatedly assured Washington DC, speaking to the desires of many Americans, that British Columbians were "restless and dissatisfied and thus ever for annexation."[51] Although this spirit probably resonated among only a minority, especially north of the border, it nonetheless signified the many geographic, economic, and cultural ties that existed in the Northwest.

Whether annexationist sentiment was overblown or not, the argument for confederation with Canada paled in comparison. Dr. John Sebastian Helmcken, one of the most prominent residents of British Columbia, argued that confederation would create a confederacy on paper only, since no means of communication with the eastern provinces existed. "Our trade," he commented, "was either with the United States or

England—with Canada we had nothing to do."[52] Although Helmcken opposed annexation, he did wish that the colony be left outside the Dominion. Even British Columbia's most ardent proponent of confederation, Amor de Cosmos, proclaimed himself a British Columbian first and a Canadian second.[53] Some British Columbians regarded eastern Canadians as "North American Chinamen"—thrifty, poor, slow, mean people, "who compared very unfavorably with the Americans and our American element."[54] As Joseph Pemberton, the province's colonial surveyor and occasional poet, explained in 1870,

> True Loyalty's to Motherland
> And not to Canada.
> The love we bear is second-hand
> To any step-mama.[55]

When the rail link that had been promised by eastern interests hoping to sway British Columbia into joining the union failed to materialize, the protests against confederation became louder.[56] Helmcken, in a March 1870 debate, argued, "No union between this Colony and Canada can permanently exist, unless it be to the material and pecuniary advantage of this Colony to remain in the Union. It is absurd for us to ally ourselves with a people with whom we have, and can have, no communication."[57] Unlike the Maritimes, which had accepted political union partly because they perceived a security threat from the States, British Columbia did not need the Dominion for protection.[58] Indeed, although the province did organize militia companies in several border communities, these companies were more social and community organizations than a response to any perceived threat, be that from Indians, Pacific invaders, or Americans.[59] In sum, it seemed that confederation offered few benefits but many frustrations.

Succinctly reflecting the marginalization many felt, British Columbians liked to complain that it was "2,500 miles from Vancouver to Ottawa, but 25,000 from Ottawa to Vancouver."[60] Much of eastern Canada knew little about the West, only that it did not want the province to fall into American hands. Likewise, British Columbians were not well acquainted with Ontario or the Maritimes, and they knew even less about Quebec. British Columbian concerns were not those of eastern Canada. British Columbians thought little about the War of 1812 or the Fenian raids. They found irksome distinctions made between Canadians and Americans in the East to be comparatively meaningless in the Northwest. The nationalistic aims of policymakers in Ottawa, Toronto, or Montreal never seemed particularly pressing or relevant on the Pacific coast.[61]

Finally, British Columbia recognized the disproportionate strength that central Canada, especially Ontario and Quebec, exercised in the Dominion. In exchange for its long-sought railway, the province had relinquished over thirteen million acres of valuable timber and mineral lands to the Canadian Pacific. Their return was a crushing economic burden and a case of absentee eastern ownership. Even the National Policy, Prime Minister John A. Macdonald's 1878 effort to promote Canadian development by countering the American economic presence, was not much better. It quickly became suspect as a means for eastern Canada to exploit western wealth. Many British Columbians recognized that, in their improvident bargain for confederation, they had only traded one dependency for another.[62]

This sense of marginalization was no less significant south of the border, even if it might have been felt less tangibly. Americans did not receive their mail bearing Canadian postmarks and their news generally came from American, not Canadian, sources. However, the American Northwest's dependence on the Northeast and Midwest—as a source of capital and as a market for agricultural and resource exports—remained, and remains, one of the region's most repetitive themes. The Northwest had lived in relative isolation for a hundred years after that isolation had ended on the Atlantic seaboard.[63]

This remoteness, combined with its role as supplier of raw materials for eastern markets, made the region acutely aware of its colonial status and its vulnerability to forces outside the region and beyond its control. Americans in the region regularly compared themselves to other colonial societies. Their place was a hinterland to New York, to Chicago, to Boston, and even to San Francisco. They chafed under prices established by eastern-owned and eastern-operated railroads, grain eleva-tors, and bankers.[64] And they chafed against a government they saw as being complicit in the relationship between exploitive capitalism and American politics. Chafing against the government was made all the more easy when one considered that the region had very little represen-tation in Congress, at least until statehood, and what representation it did have had not existed long enough for the region to have acquired significant political clout.

Accordingly, late nineteenth-century populist movements were very much a reflection of a deeply ingrained sense of marginalization south of the border. Populist issues such as the monetization of silver, regula-tion of railroads, and attempts to break the stranglehold of monopoly found fertile soil in the region. It is perhaps no surprise that in 1892, the first year in which the Populist Party was on the presidential ballot, it received 30 percent of the votes cast for president in the states of Wash-ington, Idaho, and Oregon. In Idaho alone this number was 54 percent.[65]

Grievances centered on perceptions of marginalization sometimes took different forms north and south of the border. However, the fact that both Americans and British Columbians shared similar grievances provided an important point of commonality that transcended a national border. They were, in this way, peoples of one region, even if they were also peoples of two nations.

A SMUGGLER'S PARADISE

Although many welcomed the definition of an international boundary, most Americans and British Columbians were less amenable to restric-tions on their trade. For years they had traded freely along the Strait of Juan de Fuca and along the forty-ninth parallel with little thought of the border or its customs duties. Before establishment of the territorial boundary in 1846 there were no significant restrictions on trade. As soon as Washington became a territory, trade fell subject to duties and the United States established a customshouse at Port Townsend. Still, disputes over possession of the San Juan Islands remained, precluding effective control over regional commerce. There were no customs duties between San Juan and Victoria because both were supposedly British. There were no customs duties levied between San Juan and Washington Territory on account of both being American. Not until arbitrated by Kaiser Wilhelm in 1872—when the islands were ceded to the United States—would jurisdictional disputes disappear. Smuggling, however, did not.[66]

Smuggling flourishes wherever there are outright prohibitions or high duties on imported goods—the duty saved being clear profit to the smuggler. In the Northwest, many even smuggled nonprohibited and low-duty goods simply to avoid the hassle of reporting to out-of-the-way customs stations. Yet smuggling occurred for reasons beyond the expense and inconvenience. Geographically isolated from trade with the Dominion, British Columbians had a great need for products produced south of the border. The province was eager to exchange its rum, wool, and silks—goods much in demand south of the border—in return for Yankee cotton and tobacco, which the province did not produce. Conversely, with few exceptions, it had very little need for commercial protection. When Ottawa established tariff schedules—to which British Columbians were subject—it kept in mind not the needs of British Columbia but the protectionist interests of Ontario, Quebec, and the Maritimes. This left many British Columbians believing that the Dominion knew or cared little about the daily realities of life in its Pacific province.[67]

Since smugglers trafficked primarily in complementary, not competing, goods, most settlers were sympathetic to the contraband trade. Residents overlooked smuggling as "a species of law-breaking over which the Ten Commandments have no jurisdiction."[68] Those who smuggled were not criminals or pariahs but members of "the profession" or "importers of contraband goods." Indeed, there was a certain romantic aura connected with the intrepid smuggler who plied rough waters in an open craft, cached merchandise on secluded beaches, transmitted coded messages by lantern light, and rendezvoused with compatriots late at night—all the while remaining beyond the dogged pursuit of "revenuers." The region had no lack of those willing to take the risks incident to the traffic. Many more were willing to purchase the contraband once it arrived at their doorstep.[69]

Consequently, few chose to assist the enforcement officer at the smuggler's expense—it was rare indeed for settlers to lodge complaints with authorities. Instead, some residents complained that customs officers regularly overcharged, while others took offense that officials worried about petty smuggling instead of the more frowned upon traffic in Chinese immigrants and narcotics. Even Benjamin Ure, one of Skagit County's most prominent pioneers and a one-time customs officer, harbored smugglers on his island near Deception Pass.[70]

One historian has commented that one's view of smuggling depended on one's distance from the border.[71] It is also true that acceptance depended on the type of article being smuggled. Two cargoes particularly frowned upon were Chinese immigrants and narcotics, which did not enjoy the public approval or enabling that liquor later would.[72] After the 1882 Exclusion Act prohibited Chinese immigration into the United States, human cargoes became the contraband of choice. Having arrived from Asia, the recently completed Canadian Pacific Railroad, or the region's mines, Chinese congregated in British Columbia, where they waited to pay $100 or more for the privilege of being smuggled into the promised land. Driving a load of aliens forty or fifty miles was a lucrative business for the smuggler, who could get as much as twice the market value of his eight-cylinder automobile. It was, alternatively, a dangerous business for the Chinese. If intercepted by a patrol vessel on open seas, it was an easy matter for the unscrupulous smuggler to throw the cargo overboard in weighted burlap sacks and present an empty vessel for inspection.[73]

Residents particularly frowned upon the opium trade, not coincidentally because many incorrectly believed the Chinese to be the chief market for the narcotic.[74] Only four years after enacting an antiopium law in 1914, the American government began complaining of the traffic from Canada. Not prohibited in British Columbia—which became the gateway to the entire United States—opium that cost fifteen dollars a tin north of the border was commonly known to fetch forty-five to the south.[75] The drug was not particularly difficult to smuggle undetected. It arrived through the mail, under the clothes of attractive women and in the false bottoms of steamer trunks, inside walking canes, umbrellas, hatbands, and railroad ties, and in floating containers thrown from arriving ships, to be picked up later by a waiting accomplice.[76] One of the more macabre methods was to send opium across the border in coffins. Smugglers were secure in the knowledge that customs officers would be reluctant to check the contents thoroughly.[77]

Problems of the region's geography did not escape the attention of federal officials who recognized that conditions for evading the law were especially favorable in the Northwest.[78] Indeed, the Pacific Northwest proved an inviting environment for the smuggler. The Puget Sound and the Georgia and Juan de Fuca Straits offered secluded islands, bays, coves, inlets, and channels made to order for the smuggler seeking solace from the law. No less inviting was the rugged land border to the east. One correspondent for the *Victoria Chronicle* recognized the challenges when he observed, "The constables here are all on the 'qui vive' . . . but it is of no use; double the number could not properly collect the duty. The country is comparatively open and the smuggler can take his choice of four or five different trails when he wishes to make a break for Uncle Sam's land."[79] President Grover Cleveland, in a fit of irritation, is supposed to have commented in 1885, "The Collection District of Puget Sound has been the cause of more discord and annoyance than all the rest of the Districts in the country put together."[80]

Cleveland's frustration was due, in part, to the ineffectiveness of the region's customs and preventative services. The chief enforcement agency on the American side, the Coast Guard, along with its predecessor, the Revenue Cutter Service, annually claimed success in holding most smuggling in check.[81] One observer optimistically commented that a single organization, "if properly trained and equipped with the authority of the United States back of it could close up the holes and make 'ale'yun [alien] runnin' as rash as suicide or murder . . . and make any form of smuggling a hazardous occupation instead of a merry pastime."[82] Such assertions appeared in either official agency reports written to satisfy

Washington or public commentaries designed to criticize failure in those same agencies—neither had much basis in reality.

The reality was that those in charge of smuggling enforcement faced a daunting, almost impossible task, due primarily to the magnitude of the area to be patrolled and a lack of sufficient funds and resources, as well as a revenue code that made enforcement a subjective endeavor. Both the U.S. Coast Guard and its counterpart in British Columbia found themselves in constant need of additional vessels.[83] It was not uncommon for the Coast Guard to patrol Northwest waters with only two cutters—large, notoriously slow, ungainly vessels clearly outmatched by the more numerous, smaller, and speedier launches used by smugglers. It was not difficult to keep tabs on the few enforcement craft. For every smuggler caught, another twenty, thirty, or hundred slipped by undetected.[84]

Finding and retaining officers in a region abounding with opportunity proved equally daunting. Life was difficult for those who guarded the border. Most served in remote frontier posts, received a meager salary, and enjoyed little time away from official duties. When the Fraser River gold rush exploded in 1858, every man aboard the revenue cutter *Jeff Davis* deserted the vessel to rush off to the mines.[85] One preventative officer, William Carmichael, summed up the plight felt by many when he wrote to request leave: "Before coming here I made enquires as to conditions at this place, and from what information I could procure, found there was no school and probably no accommodations for my family. . . . It will be five years in October since I have had a vacation, and during that time think I can safely say that I have not been away from work for more than two or three days."[86] Two weeks later a reply from Ottawa arrived. His request was denied.[87]

That officials enforced laws along the border somewhat erratically was inevitable. Occasionally it was due to the complex laws and tariff schedules that regulated traffic across the border. American inspectors lost themselves in the myriad complexities of appraisals, bonds, drawbacks, appeals, invoices, registers, licenses, circulars, manifests, vouchers, and abstracts of disbursements. With some literary flair, one commented on the customs officer's guide, *Gordon's Digest of the Revenue Laws*: "I looked into [*Gordon's Digest*] and became satisfied that the Creator had not gifted me with any capacity for understanding that species of writing. For Mr. Gordon, who had digested those laws, I felt a very profound admiration. His powers of digestion were certainly better than mine.... Whenever there was a tangible point to be found, it was either abolished, or so obscured by some other law made in conformity with the progress of the times that it became no point at all."[88] Lacking clear guidelines, customs officers found it difficult to apply the laws uniformly. Further, since many officers served long terms of service at one port—as many as fifteen years for one collector—they were also members of border communities and naturally reluctant to treat neighbors as smugglers.[89]

Of course, where profit existed, so too did outright corruption. The customs service's dependence on the spoils system—in both the United States and Canada—meant that many officials were political appointees, often more interested in personal profit and advancement than in enforcing customs laws. As Roland De Lorme notes in his study of smuggling, the Puget Sound had a particularly poor record in this regard.[90] Although the United States stationed preventative and immigration officers in Vancouver and at other points along the British Columbia side of the border to check smuggling, it was common knowledge that "with some it was said to be made all right."[91] As Herbert Foote Beecher discovered, it was sometimes "made all right" at the highest levels. President Cleveland appointed Beecher as a collector for the Puget Sound region in April 1885 to repay an election debt owed to Beecher's father, the popular minister Henry Ward Beecher. After taking office, Beecher commenced an aggressive assault on the organized opium and Chinese smuggling rings that operated from British Columbia ports. So unusually successful were his initial seizures that he quickly found himself under attack in the Senate by friends of the smuggling combines. Having not yet confirmed his nomination, the Senate ultimately rejected it. Cleveland, however, pleased with Beecher's efforts, immediately bypassed the Senate by naming him a special agent of the Treasury Department for the region—a position that he held until April 1889, when the administration changed.[92]

Even before passage of the Eighteenth Amendment, the Canadian-American Northwest had grown and developed in ways that would make enforcing national prohibition difficult at best. Smuggling had grafted itself not only into the daily life of the Northwest's inhabitants but into the region's politics as well. Moreover, fueled by geographical proximity and necessity, popular convention and apathy, Canadians and Americans in the region operated with little regard for the international boundary. They paid even less attention to regulations and restrictions established by their respective sovereignties to the east. Nevertheless, prohibition would bring to the surface the latent but deeply ingrained cultural attitudes that had helped to shape British Columbia's identity vis-à-vis the United States. The province's response to American prohibition, then, would be a product of both its history and its identity.

CHAPTER TWO

A Cross-Border Crusade

The scene resembled a sporting event more than a prohibition rally. Throngs crowded the streets around Vancouver's Rink Arena on a warm August evening in 1916. Since neither taxis nor special-service streetcars could accommodate the ten thousand eager to see this American wonder, many came on foot. They came to hear the ex–baseball player turned itinerant evangelist Billy Sunday excoriate the evils of liquor. And he did not disappoint them. He climbed on tables and chairs, flailed his arms in outrageous gesture, and much to the crowd's delight, pitched imaginary strikes to emphasize his more dramatic points. Each slide into second base or dive into home plate met with appreciative cheers. "I am a sworn, eternal, irrevocable enemy of the liquor traffic," he started. "I ask no quarter and I give none, and I shall never sheath my sword in the fight against this curse and against the whisky gang until I am put in embalming juice." "Whiskey is all right in its place," he shouted, "but its place is hell and the sooner it gets there the better!" It was, reported the *Vancouver World*, "the largest audience ever addressed under one roof in the Dominion of Canada."[1]

The traffic that Billy Sunday railed against had presented the Northwest with problems long before America nobly experimented with national prohibition. Throughout the nineteenth and early twentieth centuries, independent traders and fur companies, saloon keepers and moonshiners kept the Northwest awash in whiskey, even while missionaries and temperance organizations proclaimed its evils. Like much of the inter-action in the region, reform on one side of the border often mirrored similar reform on the other. The border served as a sort of interface where reformers shared a common goal, as well as the methods and materiel necessary to achieve that goal. Temperance in the Northwest was, from the start, a binational crusade, spread by organizations and individuals, like Billy Sunday, who moved back and forth across the border as if it did not exist at all. By the First World War, prohibition had taken root in both Canada and the United States. However, varying demographics, varying types of federalism, and varying attitudes about the government's role in regulating society contributed to different liquor control systems. These differences, in turn, would have significant implications for Canadian-American cooperation after passage of the Eighteenth Amendment.

"THIS NEFARIOUS TRAFFIC"

The trade in liquor, what one observer called "this nefarious traffic," was not indigenous to the Northwest. The earliest Euro-American explor-ers, traders, and observers in the region were unanimous regarding the Natives' aversion to drink prior to European contact. Washington Irving, in one of his many travels, professed admiration for the Colum-bia region's inhabitants, who, in their abstinence from ardent spirits, "showed superior judgment and self-command to most of their race."[2] Ross Cox, a member of John Jacob Astor's expedition to Astoria, also observed the disgust with which Indians regarded a drunkard.[3]

Through much of the early nineteenth century, liquor was more a commodity than a staple. Fur traders usually offered a dram of liquor with the more traditional trade goods such as blankets, cloth, and vari-ous other sundries. While there was initial difficulty prevailing upon the Indians to accept the liquor, it was not long before a bottle of rum would fetch ten skins. Traders soon recognized that being liberal with liquor was the easiest, cheapest, and quickest means to acquire influence over the Indians. Indeed, it quickly became axiomatic that the best way to trap a pelt was with a bottle.[4] As George Simpson, governor of the

Hudson's Bay Company in the Northwest, noted in 1822, liquor had become the sine qua non of the trade:

> [Liquor] is . . . the grand Stimulus to call forth the exertions of the Indians and I have often heard them reason thus, "It is not for your Cloth and Blankets that we undergo all this labor and fatigue, as in a short time we could reconcile ourselves to the use of skins for clothes as our forefathers did, but it is the prospect of Drink in the Spring . . . that carries us through the Winter and induces us to Work so hard." This I believe is really to be the case, and that if Spirits were withheld it would materially discourage them.[5]

Within two years, however, Simpson had concluded that the introduction of spirituous liquors had been a most short-sighted policy. Liquor had proved counterproductive. After drinking away the value of the furs just trapped, many Indians did not have the faculties or resources to procure additional pelts. Moreover, liquor tended to make Indians less manageable and more insistent in future negotiations. Moral arguments also interjected. To accommodate the demand and to reduce bulk in transport, traders had begun manufacturing liquor themselves. They diluted pure alcohol with salt water, then flavored it to suit the Indian taste using creosote, camphine, and even sulfuric acid, a recipe that only broadly resembled brandy, rum, or whiskey. Herbert Beaver, the first English missionary to the region, criticized the Hudson's Bay Company's approach to liquor, arguing that of the articles the company bartered, "over half may be classed as useless, one quarter as pernicious (ardent spirits), and the remainder of doubtful utility."[6]

In 1823 the Hudson's Bay Company cut the amount of liquor to the fur trade in half, and after 1827 it prohibited the sale of liquor outside the Red River Settlement. Though officials recognized that prohibition might disrupt trade temporarily—perhaps for a year—they thought such a restriction would ultimately prove beneficial to the Indians and, more important, to the company's bottom line. Central to the success of this policy, though, was the adherence to it by the other powers in the region, most notably the fur companies of Russia and the United States.

In February 1825 Dr. John McLoughlin, chief factor of the Columbia Division of the Hudson's Bay Company, negotiated a short-lived agreement with the Russian Fur Company prohibiting the trade of liquor to Indians.[7] The company made similar efforts to negotiate an accord with the American Fur Company, but without any practical success.[8]

Over the next twenty years McLoughlin did what little he could to limit or abandon the trade in liquor entirely. On several occasions he even purchased the entire liquor stocks of vessels trading in the area to keep them out of American, and hence Indian, hands. This also meant keeping it from his officers and servants, so McLoughlin exercised very strong control over the disbursement of liquor to all his subordinates. Nevertheless, although the chief factor remained adamant in his desire to exclude liquor from the fur trade, he remained equally pragmatic. If the Americans or Russians chose to trade liquor, McLoughlin decided, the Hudson's Bay Company must do the same or abandon the fur trade altogether.[9] Simpson agreed. By 1837 the latter had concluded that along the Northwest coast, "Where we have to contend with the Americans and Russians . . . our utmost efforts to check [the liquor traffic] have been unavailing."[10]

If whiskey was important to the fur trade, it was equally a part of the culture of the early Northwest, north and south of the border. The ineffectiveness of McLoughlin's and Simpson's efforts to limit liquor's abundance can be gauged by the perceptions of those who visited or lived in the region. One Scottish immigrant, Robert Melrose, commented in 1854, "It would take almost a line of packet ships running regular between here and San Francisco to supply this Island with grog, so great a thirst prevails among its inhabitants."[11] Under the employ of the Puget Sound Agricultural Company—a subsidiary of Hudson's Bay—Melrose came to Vancouver Island in 1852. His diary remains a testament to his own proclivity toward drink and to that of North-westerners generally. Melrose regularly categorized drunkenness—his own or others'—by degree: "one-quarter," "one-half," "three-quarters," or "whole" drunk. Perusing his diary, it appears that on any given day somebody was at least partly drunk, usually "three-quarters" or more.

One might easily dismiss Melrose's comments as exaggerations were they not corroborated by so many others.

The mining, timber, and railroad camps that made up much of the region were notorious for their heavy drinking and bawdy behavior, existing in what one scholar has described as a Hobbesian state of nature.[12] The small town of Kiona, Washington, located between Yakima and Walla Walla, might have been typical. As described by Norman Clark, "Kiona had only one saloon, and four hundred railroad workers came in every night and all day Sunday to drink. The saloon was so crowded that citizens of Kiona could hear the noise all over town. There was standing-room-only in the saloon, and the dead drunks were thrown in the back yard like so many soggy sacks to retch there in full view of the townspeople."[13] Things were no better north of the border, where, by 1892, statistics suggest that British Columbians imbibed at an annual rate one and a half times that of Canadians in any other province.[14] The *Colonist* reported rampant drunkenness and disorderly conduct in Canadian Pacific Railway camps.[15] One observer of the rail camp at Yale commented that "tattered, dirt-bespattered drunkards rolled about the streets, wallowing in the mud, cursing and fighting, and driving all respectable people into the recesses of their homes, while saloon after saloon was added to the number, already terribly in excess of the needs of the community."[16] When it met in Spokane in 1892, the Presbyterian synod explained the region's intemperance as being the result of a "people living under a high state of pressure in their eager rush after wealth, causing often great nervous depression which calls for the dangerous stimulants supplied by intoxicating liquor."[17]

From the earliest gold rushes on, no social institution proved more prolific, or more important, than the saloon. Reputedly, early Victoria had no fewer than eighty-five licensed public houses and twenty wholesale or "gallon" houses.[18] Emily Carr recalled that in her childhood there were saloons on almost every corner, in the middle of every city block, and every few miles along the roads.[19] In 1884 Shoshone, Idaho, had thirteen saloons but only two churches, and neither church, it seems, had a minister. By 1905 Everett, Washington, had one saloon for every

600 residents, while Walla Walla offered one saloon for every 348 of its (apparently even thirstier) inhabitants.[20]

For many wage workers, the saloon filled a necessary void in the region's otherwise bleak cultural milieu. The saloon was more than a drinking and eating establishment. It was a club for the workingman, a place where one could renew acquaintances, make new ones, keep abreast of daily news—both of the local region and the outside world—and talk in a "democratic" way. The billiards, card tables, boxing matches, magic shows, and stage plays helped ameliorate the dreary existence to which many workers were subject. The saloon served, on occasion, as the community hall or center of charity. During a particularly harsh winter in 1894, the saloons of Spokane fed some five hundred unemployed wageworkers. The saloon sometimes even proved necessary to the orderly administration of small communities. It served as courthouse, meeting hall, or even temporary jail, where prisoners awaited trial or punishment chained to the walls. In 1901, when Snohomish County, Washington, announced the need for additional jail space, it proposed a $100 increase in the saloon's annual license fee. Since there were forty-seven saloons in the county, the increase would easily finance two additional jails.[21]

EARLY TEMPERANCE EFFORTS

One can find the origins of regional temperance in the actions of John McLoughlin. Although the Hudson's Bay Company demonstrated its pragmatic willingness to use liquor when in competition with American traders, most observers credited the company's general ban on liquor and encouragement of missionary activity as being the reason for the region's relative tranquility.[22] Two members of the Methodist Episcopal Church commented, "It is due to say that Dr. McLoughlin seconded the efforts of the missionaries and the friends of temperance, and that the course he has taken in regard to spirituous liquors has done much to preserve the general order and harmony of the ... community."[23]

Among the first to dedicate themselves to the temperance cause in the Pacific Northwest were the missionaries invited by McLoughlin and Simpson, who believed that the best way to preach the gospel was to fight the liquor traffic among a people "being destroyed, soul and body" by strong drink.[24] After the border's establishment in 1846, rarely did missionaries confine themselves to one side. Rather, they circulated freely, depending on local needs and circumstances. When hostilities between whites and Indians erupted in the Washington Territory between 1847 and 1857, for example, the Catholic Missionary Oblates of Mary Immaculate transferred their work from Walla Walla across the border to Esquimalt, British Columbia, where they remained committed to the temperance cause.[25]

What attracted the energy of most temperance zealots was the saloon. To middle-class reformers, the saloon symbolized the most disturbing aspects of the liquor traffic. The pleasures and services it proffered came with a community price. Often open twenty-four hours a day, saloons contributed to the region's high liquor consumption, as men "drank to get drunk, and the quicker the better."[26] They were centers for drunkenness and physical violence and were closely associated with other vices, such as gambling and prostitution, that led men away from family and conjugal fidelity. Also popular were private boxes, or "wine rooms," complete with a couch. Though not publically advertised, what occurred in the private rooms was commonly understood. Even worse, saloons did not always limit services to adults, much to the horror of a Spokane alderman who, in 1888, claimed that seven young boys had enjoyed the atmosphere of one establishment.[27]

By the mid-nineteenth century a disparate group of missionaries, ministers, social reformers, and even labor leaders had united to attack the saloon in a more organized fashion. The Sons (and Daughters) of Temperance, the International Order of Good Templars, the Dashaways, the Woman's Christian Temperance Union (WCTU), and the Anti-Saloon League were but a few of the entities organized specifically to promote the temperance cause. Later even labor organizations like the Industrial Workers of the World became active in the antisaloon movement. It was the saloon, organized labor argued, that robbed the workers of hard-won earnings and made them unfit for the class struggle.[28]

By century's close the antisaloon movement became part of the effort to reform society generally. This progressive campaign included not only temperance but also female suffrage, the amelioration of working conditions for men, women, and especially children, the regulation of trusts, and reform of the local and national political system. So inter-related were many of these issues that it was common for reformers to be active in more than one. Reformers often linked temperance and suffrage, for example, because most thought women were more likely than men to support prohibition at the polls.[29] As an adjunct to its prohibition efforts, the WCTU supported such reforms as sex hygiene, antismoking legislation, and sanitation, as well as the Americanization and Canadianization of recent immigrants. It also supplied literature and other comforts to the lumbermen, railway employees, fishermen, lighthouse keepers, and miners of the Northwest; these populations, reformers contended, were the greatest obstacle to regional temperance.[30]

When the *Washington Standard* proclaimed, "Like a great tidal wave the temperance reform is carrying everything before it, from California to British Columbia," it reflected not only the temperance movement's fervor but the paper's belief that temperance should recognize no bor-ders.[31] Indeed, it did not. Reform on one side of the boundary often mirrored, or cross-pollinated, reform on the other; temperance and prohibition efforts proved no exception. The Sons of Temperance, for example, founded in the United States in 1842, moved into Canada by the end of the decade and pioneered efforts for temperance in both countries. In 1859 a San Francisco mutual-aid organization known as the Dashaways opened a house for the inebriate in Victoria.[32] A decade later the International Order of Good Templars organized the Grand Lodge of Washington Territory and British Columbia, which met annually in cities like Vancouver, Victoria, Seattle, Olympia, and Tacoma. It even had its own temperance organ, the *Weekly Echo*. Unlike all other chapters of the order, which appear to have been organized by province or state, the Pacific Northwest chapter was organized binationally. It seems that, at least initially, this was due to the smaller population of the region. Composed of both Canadians and Americans, the chapter frequently recognized its uniqueness, believing that it, "like the principles of our order, are such that it cannot be contained by national limits." Later, as occasional suggestions were made that British Columbian members form their own chapter, most decided that the international liquor traffic on the Northwest coast could best be countered with a binational temperance organization.[33]

Similarly, the rapid spread of the Woman's Christian Temperance Union across the United States encouraged American leaders to organize a worldwide movement. Canada was the first nation outside the United States to organize a national union when, in 1875, Letitia Youmans founded a chapter in Ontario. Chapters then spread to most states and to all provinces. By 1929 the WCTU had become an international organization, encompassing at least fifty-three nations, and it predicted a "dry world" by 1930.[34]

Francis Willard, the founder of the WCTU, later wrote of the importance of the "Reciprocity Treaty" between Canadian and American temperance leaders, and it was common for the Canadian temperance movement to rely heavily on the United States for arguments and ammunition. The Canadian WCTU imported printed temperance materials from the United States, Canadian newspapers opened their columns to WCTU propaganda from the United States, the *Canadian Woman's Journal* frequently published American advice, and binational conventions frequently occurred.[35] Of course, pro-American sentiment did not always go uncontested. Many Canadian members of the WCTU—though united with their American sisters in the temperance cause—remained suspicious of American cultural penetration, fearing that American materials would surreptitiously "disseminate disloyalty." This concern, however, seems to have been limited to the more eastern provinces, particularly Ontario. Youmans predicted the continued harmony of "women tying together ... the Union Jack and Stars and Stripes with ribbons that are total abstinence badges, while the Yankee eagle soars above and the British lion crouches beneath."[36]

British Columbia, uniquely isolated from the Dominion, remained particularly dependent on assistance from the temperance movement south of the border. Although it was Letitia Youmans who started WCTU chapters in the other provinces, it was the American Frances Willard who founded the British Columbia chapter in 1883. Thereafter, the Washington and British Columbia chapters remained quite close, sharing publications and other support. Young British Columbian girls even became "Willard Y's," members of the province's Young Woman's Christian Temperance Association.[37]

While it was also quite common for itinerant speakers from one country to speak on behalf of temperance in the other, their reception depended largely on whether one was wet or dry.[38] The lumberjack-journalist Stewart Holbrook spoke particularly eloquently for those who retained a certain antipathy against those who would prohibit drink. Years after Billy Sunday's visit, he noted, "The only boredom I can recall was when I sat as a reporter through six endless evenings of the Reverend Billy Sunday's revival orgies in Portland. My only satisfaction was that the big and especially built tabernacle was not once filled to capacity. Being by choice a resident of Portland, this gave me pride in my town. Any place where Billy Sunday could not draw a full house must be more civilized than most."[39]

British Columbia's reception proved equally mixed. Invited by the Provincial Prohibition Association, Sunday was to be the highlight of the 1916 prohibition campaign. Although his rallies proved highly popular—attracting some ten thousand in Vancouver and another seven thousand in Victoria—four of every five members of the audience were women. The *Daily News-Advertiser* consequently decided that his address did "not prove a sensation." More sensational was the debate that raged days before his arrival. The *Daily Province* ran advertisements suggesting, "The blood of every true Canadian and Britisher will boil with indignation at the attempt to stampede the electorate by hysterical outbursts of fanaticism. The British principle is to settle our affairs in the British way, and without outside interference." One letter to the paper's editor declared that Vancouver should be "disinfected" after Sunday's visit.[40] Labor labeled Sunday a "capitalist stooge," and others questioned his support for the war against Germany. In both his Victoria and Vancouver addresses, Sunday denounced these attacks, with some accuracy, as efforts by the liquor industry to prevent him from speaking in Canada.

Nevertheless, many continued to question whether Sunday's way was the Canadian way.[41]

FROM LOCAL OPTION TO NATIONAL PROHIBITION

Early temperance workers initially had sought to reform society by first reforming intemperate souls. The conventional wisdom, offered primarily by the church, was that Christianity offered the most likely solution to problems of vice, intemperance, unemployment, labor violence, and inequality of wealth. Those who believed that society was no better than the sum of its individuals rejected any concept of collective regeneration. Ironically, however, moral reformers soon sought to legislate sobriety when individual temperance failed to produce a temperate society.

With common problems plaguing both sides of the border—and with muckrakers and their shocking exposés circulating on both sides of the border—legislatures in both Washington and British Columbia passed strikingly similar measures between 1890 and 1920. Reformers crafted laws for civil service reform and workmen's compensation, to provide for police and fire protection, to insure pure food and meats, to prohibit habit-forming drugs, and to restrict red-light districts. When women in Washington gained the right to vote in 1910, well before the nation as a whole, suffragettes from the state supported their British Columbian sisters, who also achieved the vote in 1917. Prohibition movements in Canada and the United States were noticeably similar as well.[42]

Before the First World War, local option laws proved to be the most popular form of temperance legislation in both countries. Local option gave the power to prohibit, or limit, liquor to the city, county, state, or provincial governments. The populace would presumably select the form of liquor regulation best suited to its needs, without impinging on the freedom of other localities or the nation. Accordingly, local option helped bridge the widening gap between those who believed that temperance meant moderation and those to whom temperance meant complete prohibition.

In 1878 the Canadian Parliament passed the Canadian Temperance Act, more commonly known as the Scott Act. Based in part on early successes in Maine, Ohio, and Michigan, the purpose of the act was to enable any county or city in the Dominion to prohibit the retail sale of alcohol when approved by a simple majority of the electors. Once adopted, the act would remain in force for three years, after which the populace could again vote to retain or abolish the system. Hoping to replicate the successes of local option, Parliament followed with the McCarthy Act, providing for federal licensing of liquor Dominion-wide. However, as Section 92 of the British North America Act gave provinces the power to license taverns and saloons and to raise revenue, the courts promptly declared the McCarthy Act ultra vires, or unconstitutional. As a consequence, local option in Canada remained protected by constitutional mandate. By 1889 twenty-eight of forty-two counties and two cities in Ontario had adopted prohibition, as had most of the Maritimes. Prohibition proved less popular in French Catholic Quebec, where only six counties had accepted prohibition. Still, by 1907 all provinces operated with some form of local option prohibition, except British Columbia.[43]

For its part, British Columbia put a local option measure on the ballot in a 1909 plebiscite, but the measure failed, as did the public trust in the plebiscite in general when it was discovered that there had been widespread voting irregularities, including both misplaced ballots and an insufficient number of ballots having been printed in the first place. Because the plebiscite was combined with the 1909 general provincial election, and because the government kept no permanent records of the flawed plebiscite, it is difficult to determine whether the failure of the prohibitory measure was a function of the voting irregularities or whether it accurately reflected the sentiments of British Columbia voters on the local option issue.[44]

Many localities in Canada adopted or rejected prohibition based on observations of its operation elsewhere in Canada and the United States. Sometimes those observations were casual accounts taken from the American press; in other cases, they were more systematic. In 1891 the House of Commons appointed a commission of inquiry to examine the operation of liquor and temperance systems throughout North America and to determine the degree to which these systems had curtailed intemperance.

Over the next year, the Royal Commission on the Liquor Traffic held hearings in all Canadian provinces as well as in nine American states. The majority report concluded that license laws, not prohibition, were the most effective remedy for intemperance.[45]

British Columbia remained particularly attuned to both the commission's report and prohibition in the United States generally. Drys extolled conditions in Maine, where the state's personal savings rate had risen by $80.77 since dry laws took effect. The province closely followed news of conflicting trends when votes for prohibition in Oregon failed resoundingly in 1887.[46] Likewise, the eventual victory of statewide prohibition in Washington and Oregon in 1914 attracted widespread interest. When Washington voted for prohibition on November 3, 1914, over 94.6 percent of the electorate voted, making it the largest vote in the state's history—a record that remains unsurpassed.[47] By the time Congress voted by a two-thirds majority for the Eighteenth Amendment and the necessary three-quarters of the states had ratified it, twenty-six states had already adopted state prohibition and three others were on the verge of doing so. Indeed, forty-five of the forty-eight states eventually ratified the amendment, including Washington in January 1919, where the vote was unanimous.[48]

Local prohibitionists in British Columbia obviously took delight in seeing their neighbor adopt statewide—and then national—prohibition. More pragmatically pleased, however, were the province's wets, who recognized the profit potential of the province's contiguity to a dry state. The *Saturday Sunset* of Vancouver commented, "Looking at the question from the point of view of how it will affect British Columbia, it may be taken for granted that prohibition in Washington and Oregon should cause a business revival in this city. . . . It is considered probable that the brewing interests will establish themselves in British Columbia, with a consequent interest in payrolls. Whatever may be said for the moral effect of prohibition, it is certain that the business effect has not been found good [for America]."[49] Nonetheless, most British Columbians found it difficult to visualize Seattle as a dry city. Seattle's population was not very different from British Columbia's. The *Victoria*

Daily Colonist remarked, "In Seattle more perhaps than any other part of the United States, where prohibition has been attempted, legislation against the sale of liquor will receive a severe trial. . . . Those who have watched prohibitory legislation in operation will be greatly interested in observing how our sister city on the Sound deals with it." Reports of social gains began to circulate throughout the Canadian provinces soon after Washington prohibition took effect in 1916. Dispatches from Seattle reported that merchants had sold more eggs, meat, and other foodstuffs in the first seventeen days of prohibition than they had in the previous three months combined.[50]

Though prohibition was secure in Washington, it is unlikely that British Columbia would have gone dry were it not for the First World War. Compared to Seattle, British Columbia's population was even more urban, more male, more transient, and consequently, more attached to its liquor.[51] So concerned about a proposed Prohibition Act of 1917 were the region's miners that, in only four days, they were able to acquire over six thousand signatures against it. Armed with petitions, representatives of the Cumberland local argued that beer was essential to the region's miners, who had to "endure strains of the most arduous and strenuous nature." The robustness of the average British Columbian miner, the delegates contended, "was partly due to reasonable use of beer as a stimulant." Lest this argument prove insufficient, the miners added a not-so-veiled threat: the province should make every effort to avoid labor strife, argued the union, since industrial activity in British Columbia "was made effectual only by the influx of workingmen from 'dry' states across the International boundary line."[52]

Fortunately for drys, temperance efforts were at their peak just as war broke out in Europe in 1914. Prohibition and patriotism instantly became synonymous, especially in a province that sent troops in such great numbers. The war provided irrefutable ammunition to drys. Who could refute that liquor would befuddle the minds of soldiers, making them unfit for the defense of the country? Who could deny that grains used for liquor could be better used as foodstuffs for the troops? Who could deny that it was unfair that young British Columbians fought and died while those at home merrily imbibed in home and saloon? The *Christian Guardian* railed against the brewers, distillers, and saloon keepers who had become, it argued, the "worst pro-Germans we have in Canada today."[53] All the Kaiser's legions were no more menace than "King Alcohol." For British Columbians, to sacrifice their liquor for the benefit of those who fought in the trenches of Europe was no burdensome sacrifice. With these arguments in mind, British Columbian Liberals successfully made prohibition part of the 1916 election campaign and secured a referendum against the sale of liquor on the same ballot. On October 1, 1917, the British Columbia Prohibition Act took effect, prohibiting the sale of liquor except for sacramental, industrial, or medicinal purposes.[54]

As a result of the war, by 1917 the temperance forces had won their battle in each of the provinces except Quebec. There, a modified version of prohibition limited the sale of liquor to light beer and wines. In 1918 the Dominion government passed an Order-in-Council, adding to the provisions of the 1914 War Measures Act, prohibiting the shipment of liquor into any province that forbade its purchase. The order was for the duration of the war and one year thereafter. For a time, then, as Canadian drys liked to proclaim, it was Canada, not the United States, that was the true home of prohibition.[55]

BRITISH COLUMBIA AND THE MIDDLE WAY

The high point for national prohibition in Canada would remain the First World War. Like many other nations around the world, Canada was more interested in watching national prohibition in the United States than in trying it on itself. Over the next ten years, each of the provinces except Prince Edward Island gradually went wet. British Columbia and Quebec were the first, in 1921, followed in short order by the Prairie provinces, then Ontario and New Brunswick in 1927, and finally Nova Scotia in 1930. Neither British Columbia nor the other provinces were choosing to abandon temperance. Gradually recognizing the failures of prohibition to promote temperance, the provinces instead chose a middle way. The answer to the liquor traffic lay not in the extremes of complete control or no control, but in government control. So popular was the idea in British Columbia that, when it was adopted by plebiscite in 1920, early returns showed only two cities, Penticton and Nelson, opposing it. After the final returns, even Nelson narrowly approved. In the larger cities, like Vancouver and Victoria, voters endorsed government control by substantial majorities.[56] Thus the last province to vote for prohibition had become the first English province to abandon it.

Why was British Columbia so quick to abandon prohibition? And why did the rest of Canada gradually follow suit? The answers lay not only in British Columbia's demographics but also in fundamental differences between the federal systems of both countries and in cultural attitudes about government's role in regulating social and individual morality.

Other historians have noted the relative success prohibition enjoyed in regions where the population was rural, homogenous, or middle-class.[57] Demographics account for part of prohibition's abandonment, as most British Columbians did not fit well into any of these categories. When British Columbia voted for prohibition in 1916, it had done so ostensibly on behalf of its many young soldiers in Europe. These soldiers returned home, however, as wet as when they had left. Finding a dry province made them as unhappy about the lack of beer as they were concerned about the lack of jobs. Common among grievances was that prohibition had been "put over" on the army by a group of "busy-bodies." "Slackers" had voted the country dry while patriotic soldiers died, ironically, in a fight for "democracy." After the war, young, male, unmarried, transient wageworkers employed in the region's resource industries continued to dominate British Columbia's population. As late as 1920 a large proportion were foreign born, and many had recently arrived from countries where prohibition had not taken root. Conspicuously absent was the "old-stock" middle class that made up much of the population south of the border.[58]

Religion also played a role in the province's quick abandonment of prohibition. To the degree that temperance was a religious movement, it was dominated by the evangelical denominations—the Methodists and the Baptists, for example—and not by the Anglicans and Roman

Catholics who dominated the ruling circles of British Columbia. Anglicans, for example, accounted for one in four British Columbians in 1911 and one in three a decade later. Although Anglicans did organize a temperance society in 1877, they, like Roman Catholics, generally favored "true temperance," or moderation, rather than total prohibition.[59]

British Columbia also saw in prohibition an effort by eastern Canada to extend its political hegemony to the moral character of the province. Any prohibition legislation created at the Dominion level tended to alienate British Columbians, who already felt marginalized or ignored by the rest of the Dominion. When Parliament passed the Lord's Day Act in 1906, a law to close saloons on Sundays, the common sentiment expressed in British Columbia was, "We don't want any eastern code of morals thrust upon us." Such paternalistic reformism offended many, who argued that it was the moral reformers—those who sought to "do unto others things others do not wish to have done"—who needed reform.[60] In the end, provincial authorities did little to enforce the Sunday-closing law.

Enforcement difficulties proved a hindrance to prohibition in Canada, where the federal and provincial governments shared jurisdiction over the liquor trade. This division, left unclarified even by numerous court decisions, proved confusing at best. While provinces could restrict or prohibit the retail sale of liquor, only the federal government could prohibit its manufacture, its wholesale trade, or its interprovincial trade. Thus, even if British Columbia had continued prohibition, it would have remained vulnerable to the bootleggers whose sources were the distilleries, breweries, and export houses located in the province but beyond the purview of provincial authorities. Although these producers ostensibly produced liquor only for wet provinces or the states to the south, it was well known that much of it naturally seeped into British Columbia. Eventually, as the profit potential of the American market became evident, the Dominion government became even more reluctant to encourage liquor's decentralization. It was common instead for the Dominion, British Columbia, and the other provinces to blame each other for enforcement failures.[61]

In typical Canadian fashion, wet interests took advantage of this fractured federalism, playing one level of government against another in furtherance of self-interest. Protected as they were by federal charter, brewers and distillers proved to be a particularly strong and effective lobby in Canada. Although the liquor industry would have preferred no control to government control, they also recognized the fate of their counterparts to the south, who with national prohibition had become divided and all but extinct.[62] Instead, as A. E. Cross, the president of the Calgary Brewing and Malting Company, learned, the best way to combat the side effects of prohibition was to "educate" the public, broadly defined. He and other brewers spared no opportunity to hammer at public attitudes. They pointed out the large capital investments, the yearly payrolls, the purchases of barley, lumber for barrels, and glass for bottles, and the freight paid to railways. Especially attractive were the taxes paid to provincial and federal coffers. The more liberal provincial or federal governments were, brewers and distillers promised, the greater the share of liquor revenue they could anticipate.[63]

For British Columbia, experience proved the final straw. The province recognized early the difficulties associated with enforcing prohibition. Negligent prohibition commissioners, bootleggers, and doctors who wrote too many prescriptions were the mirror image of future American failures. On January 1, 1920, the day federal prohibition ended, British Columbians once again began importing liquor legally from outside the province. By early 1920 the *Victoria Daily Times* was able to report that there was "no point at which liquor could not be obtained. . . . The prohibition law today is more in disrepute than any other law on the statute books of this Province." As a result, even female suffrage—once tied so closely to the temperance cause—failed to produce majorities for continued prohibition. Defying conventional wisdom in their first access to the polls, women joined most British Columbians in endorsing government control on October 20, 1920.[64]

The last province to vote for prohibition had become the first English province to abandon it. The public that had supported the ideal of prohibition during the war was no longer behind the reality of it. Reforms that had seemed so attractive during the war had, with time, proved hollow. Most British Columbians had tired of ineffective reform and sought some semblance of "normalcy." Although questions about the morality of government control would persist for decades, revenue would—at least temporarily, it seemed—substitute for the dry millennium.[65]

Underlying these differing demographic, political, and financial realities, British Columbians—and Canadians generally—differed fundamentally from Americans in their beliefs concerning the role government was to play in regulating society. Reforms that in the United States carried broad ideological appeal were, for many Canadians, matters to be dealt with by parliamentary action, not by fundamentally altering the foundation of government itself. As Carlos Schwantes points out, "Being citizens of a nation that represented, in a sense, the rejection of the claims of the American Revolution, Canadians were hardly likely to … attempt implementation of broad humanistic goals such as were embodied in the Declaration of Independence."[66] In short, Canadian political culture has been much less utopian than its American counterpart and without any expectation that its politicians would legislate the millennium. Richard de Brisay, a Canadian editor widely followed in both countries, commented that the problems liquor would later present between both countries were the result of fundamental differences in the moral attitudes of Canadians and Americans. "The Americans, as a nation, believe their souls can be saved by prohibitory laws. With Canadians it is not so … ," de Brisay argued. "We do not believe there can be salvation by legislation for anyone, anywhere, any time."[67]

Canadian tradition also dictated that reform should be an individual act of will, not of national policy. Accordingly, the idea of *national* prohibition irritated the sensibilities of those Canadians who believed that moral reform should occur, if at all, at the local or provincial level. These Canadians were quick to point out the irony of the Eighteenth Amendment for the United States. One editor wrote, "Some American states were totally opposed to prohibition, anticipating its abuses and scandals … but had to submit to the situation because a certain number of States decreed it. … Let us felicitate ourselves in the possession of the true liberty which gives the greatest autonomy to each province and does not require any to submit to the influence of others. . . . The Statue of Liberty would be better placed at the entrance of the Saint Lawrence River than in the Port of New York."[68] These general attitudes help explain why Canada's experience with liquor control was so different from that of the United States. They also help explain why Canada would be so reluctant to assist American enforcement over the following decade.

While the border served as a sort of interface between the prohibition movements in both countries, it also helped to distinguish quite starkly the ultimate approach each took to achieve the similar objective of temperance. In the meantime, and only twelve months after prohibition took effect in the United States, the *Seattle Post-Intelligencer* seemed optimistic about its ultimate success. The election of 1920, the paper commented, had dashed the hopes of "unreconstructed wets that some relief from the aridity of the prohibition amendment" would be possible after the election. The paper agreed—along with most prohibitionists—that the longer prohibition continued, the farther away the people would be from any desire to repeal the law.[69] The problem was that many Americans were, in fact, uncomfortably close to a province that had already repealed the law.

CHAPTER THREE

Refugees from Volstead

C. D. Smith, a columnist for the *Victoria Daily Colonist*, called them "refugees from Volstead." He likened American tourists during prohibition to the refugees of Belgium during the war and the Israelites in their exodus from Egypt. But none of these, he wrote, "exceed in sympathetic interest the refugees from Volstead, driven forth by the Eighteenth Amendment." He continued, "Their appearance does not at all suggest privation in the sense of their being starved, hollow-eyed, with haggard faces, torn feet and bleeding hands caused by the dangers and privations of the journey. Neither are they attired in conventional garb of harassed wanderers.... They are mostly clothed in plus-fours and their one look is of assured triumph and anticipation. They have 'got there.' Nothing else matters."[1] Though written with tongue in cheek, and with some exaggeration, Smith's commentary was not far from the mark. With the failure of world prohibition, drys in the United States determined that if they could not protect prohibition elsewhere, at least they would protect it at home. While drys clung determinedly to their new isolationism, however, wets adopted a more internationalist perspective. As wartime prohibition in British Columbia gave way to government control, Americans suffering under the Eighteenth Amendment headed north in droves. For thirsty Americans, just beyond the border lay a wet refuge, a sanctuary from the restrictive shackles of Volstead.

During prohibition, the concept of Canadian-American "relations" invariably brought to the American mind the vague reminder that Canada was sort of a northern extension of the United States, a "delightfully wet place for a vacation."[2] Canada was the one country into which American tourists could drive their own motorcars and, save for a brief examination at a customs station, barely know that a border had been crossed. The American tourist could continue to drive on the same side of the road, speak in English, use American money, buy American magazines, and drink "drinks that were his own once but are so no longer."[3] As the *Literary Digest* pointed out, "The American may well have [had] more trouble getting back into his own country, if . . . he [did] not carry his Americanism on his face."[4]

Nowhere was this more evident than in the Pacific Northwest, where Americans had long viewed British Columbia as a sort of northern playground.[5] Travel pamphlets, newspapers, and other periodicals routinely described the region encompassed by Washington and British Columbia as the "Evergreen Playground." "International Circuit Tours" routinely ferried the tourist between Seattle, the San Juan Islands, the Olympic Peninsula, Victoria, and Vancouver. It was rare to find an American tour company that did not include British Columbia in its itinerary or a British Columbian company that did not include the Puget Sound region. In almost any Sunday edition of the local papers, one could find suggestions for border travel routes, such as the scenic Bee Line Highway that stretched between Banff and Spokane or the Pacific Highway between Seattle and Vancouver.[6]

That Americans viewed British Columbia as a sort of northern extension was no accident. Instead, it was the product of a conscious effort by business and government officials to facilitate travel across the border. Local travel agents and travel pamphlets routinely advertised the lack of "red tape" at the international border. Local boards of trade distributed literature about local cities to tourists arriving in Canada by rail.[7] Agents in British Columbia prominently offered information on attractions in

Seattle, confident that once in Seattle, tourists would naturally find their way to British Columbia.[8] Provincial and state authorities routinely met to discuss uniform motor vehicle traffic laws and enforcement measures, while auto clubs offered reciprocal towing and emergency services. So closely linked were American and British Columbian efforts to promote tourism that in 1916 chambers of commerce in Washington and Oregon united with their counterparts in British Columbia to form the Pacific Northwest Tourists Association. For their part, legislatures in both states and the province, recognizing that their region was in direct contest with California for tourists, promptly agreed to support the association with significant grants. Washington and Oregon contributed $25,000 each and British Columbia half that. This close collaboration between public and private interests on both sides of the border continued for most of the following decade.[9]

The most obvious symbol of the region's cross-border outlook was British Columbia's adoption of driving on the right side of the road in 1922. Brought about mainly through the efforts of local automobile clubs and chambers of commerce, the decision to begin driving on the right was not uniformly popular. As Stewart Holbrook observed, numerous letters to the province's dailies denounced the change as a "traitorous adoption of 'Yankee notions'" and predicted a profusion of collisions and wrecks. Other Canadians, however, knowing that the flood of American tourists was inevitable, decided that it would be safer to accommodate the notoriously reckless — and now inebriate — American driver than it would be to confuse him or her by continuing the traditional British practice of driving on the left.[10]

Prior to the 1920s tourism remained the pastime of the relatively wealthy who could afford to travel by rail. The automobile "democratized" travel, making it possible for those of more moderate means to enjoy travel as well.[11] Businessmen in the western states and provinces recognized the profit to be had in attracting tourists of all social classes and launched vigorous campaigns for road construction. They reasoned that in developing auto travel between the provinces and the states, they would promote closer social and economic ties as well. As the *Spokane*

Daily Chronicle noted in 1929, "The international boundary at 49 [degrees latitude] separates communities under different flags, but with many mutual interests and eager for more frequent association. Sections of poor highways on both sides of the boundary are the real barrier, not the international line." Responding to these concerns, British Columbia added over 250 miles of new trails and over 500 miles of paved roads in 1925 alone, and similar improvements occurred in Washington. The most important north-south connection between British Columbia and the States was the newly completed Pacific Highway, which stretched from California to Vancouver. As the final section was completed between Seattle and New Westminster in 1923, one observer noted simply that the highway was "magnificent."[12]

Government and private business collaborated to offer a range of tourist facilities, from rest areas and automobile campgrounds to bungalow camps (the predecessor of motels) and upscale hotels that would appeal to a broad spectrum of society. By mid-decade it was not uncommon to see long processions of American automobiles inexpensively touring Vancouver and lower British Columbia from Central Park Auto Camp at Burnaby or Hastings Park in Vancouver. For British Columbians touring in Washington, Seattle's Woodland Park offered space for over six hundred cars at a mere fifty cents per day.[13] For the wealthy American tourist, Victoria offered the palatial Empress Hotel for two dollars per night.[14] Americans continued to be particularly intrigued with the quaintness of Victoria, the most British city in British Columbia. The city's most recent addition was the Crystal Gardens, with its heated saltwater swimming pool and artificial ice rink. So enamored of the city was Lucy Robinson, a tourist from Spokane, that in the guest book for the Dominion Hotel she wrote,

> This is Victoria!
> This is that old-world town,
> More English now than England, more American
> Than Iowa itself; born of the mated lands
> Whose frontiers command the western sea.

Ironically, the poem also appeared on the back of the hotel's guest bro-
chure, which also included a list of the liquors available to hotel patrons.[15]

Naturally, then, once British Columbia became the wet oasis in an otherwise dry Anglo-America, thirsty Americans intensified their efforts
to seek recreation and relaxation in the wet province. To be sure, the
spread of the automobile most certainly would have sent American
tourists across the border anyway, if only for the "'foreign' touch which
is part of the joy of travel."[16] Nevertheless, the Eighteenth Amendment
certainly hastened the invasion, and ardent drinkers who lived near the
Canadian border knew exactly what to do. They followed the advice
of a popular refrain:

> Forty miles from whiskey
> And sixty miles from gin,
> I'm leaving this damn country
> For to live a life of sin.[17]

No sooner had prohibition taken effect in the United States than the
Seattle Post-Intelligencer began to joke about the northward migration:
"One thing about prohibition, you don't need surveyors to find the
boundary line of Canada." The trail left by migrating tourists clearly
marked the way.[18] Soon even those who did not live near the border, and
who might never have visited Canada before, found the trek to Canada
irresistible. Americans sought Canada because of the freedom it afforded
them, not only to drink, but to drink without worrying about spies or
"stool pigeons." Tourism and the comforts of tourism—the garages,
filling stations, roadhouses, and snack bars—created a new method of
escape from American temperance run amok.[19]

Historically, Canada has always been a sanctuary of sorts for refugees
fleeing some sort of ill treatment in the United States. In Harriet Beecher
Stowe's *Uncle Tom's Cabin*, Canada was "these shores of refuge" for escap-
ing slaves. Likewise, bands of persecuted Native Americans routinely
fled across the border ahead of pursuing American troops. As Wallace

Stegner describes in *Wolf Willow*, "The medicine of the line of cairns was very strong. Once it had been necessary to outrun your pursuing enemy until you were well within your own country where he did not dare to follow. Now all you had to do was outrun him to the Line, and from across that magical invisible barrier you could watch him pull to a halt, balked, helpless, and furious."[20] Flights of Loyalists after the American Revolution and Vietnam-era draft dodgers are yet more instances in which Canada has served as a sort of relief valve for American social unrest. Thus the tourist during prohibition was merely another example (albeit a less-persecuted example) of an American who found that by crossing the border he or she might avoid, or at least alleviate, the more uncomfortable aspects of being American.[21]

In 1930 the *Literary Digest* reported that more people crossed the Canadian-American border every year than passed across any other international border. Ottawa calculated that some thirteen million Americans visited Canada in 1929, a figure that represented approximately one-tenth of the total American population.[22] One historian has suggested that the number of Americans visiting Canada was even greater. During the depression year 1931–32, John Bartlet Brebner estimates the figure to be closer to twenty million.[23] At the provincial level, some 181,798 cars crossed the border at British Columbia ports of entry in 1929, a reported fivefold increase since 1921.[24] While this figure cannot account for the number that crossed the border without reporting, it was a number sufficient to require the U.S. Customs Department to issue instructions to its officers to discontinue the practice of counting the number of automobiles that crossed into Canada. Their energies were more desperately needed for inspecting incoming traffic.[25] For similar reasons, Canadian officers soon gave up trying to record the license plate number of every American car entering the Dominion.[26]

American entrepreneurs eagerly packed up and moved north to serve their fellow citizens on Canadian soil. As in the earlier gold rushes, these entrepreneurs recognized that the real profits lay not necessarily in liquor sales but in providing comfortable places for Americans to drink. Hotels, roadhouses, and personal residences owned by Americans or financed with American money sprang up all along the international border.[27] H. L. Sawyer was the proprietor of the International Hotel and Bar, located just ten feet north of the border and one hundred feet north of the American customshouse at Eastport, Idaho. As one Treasury agent reported, "Eastport is not a city or town, and can scarcely be called a village. It is simply a point where the railroad crosses the international boundary line."[28] Just as blatant an attempt to circumvent prohibition was the St. Leonard Hotel, located just across the border from Blaine, Washington. Senator Wesley Jones of Washington complained that the hotel was nothing more than a "grog-shop," for no other businesses were located within miles.[29]

Canadian entrepreneurs, hotel proprietors, brewers, distillers, railway officials, boards of trade, mayors, and premiers were likewise eager to pamper the American tourist. As Simon Fraser Tolmie, member of Parliament from British Columbia, noted to his colleagues, "I come from a province where we cater to the tourist trade, and we have tens of thousands of visitors to that part of the country. They leave a lot of money there every year, and we are beginning to think that the work of inducing tourists to come to British Columbia and enjoy themselves is becoming quite an industry."[30] When one dry legislator, hoping to minimize drunkenness, introduced an amendment restricting liquor purchase permits to nonresidents, it was quickly dismissed. When, three months later, the legislature passed a law making liquor permits easier for Americans to obtain, it was wildly cheered. Although American tourists needed to secure a permit before purchasing liquor in British Columbia, the permit cost a mere two dollars and allowed them to buy whatever quantity they desired. The minister of customs at Ottawa even issued instructions to customs officers to assist visitors in making out their tourists permits and to do so free of charge. Prior to this, enterprising individuals had made it a practice to open offices near border points, where, for a fee of fifty cents, they offered to fill out the necessary paperwork.[31]

Finding liquor once north of the border was not particularly difficult. The first thing that greeted Americans as they crossed the border on the Pacific Highway at Blaine, right next to signs indicating provincial speed limits, were large signs advertising the virtue of a particular brand of whiskey or beer. Not coincidentally, pictures of these advertisements that lined the Pacific Highway were widely circulated in the American press, one with a caption that read, "A bit of B.C. scenery that helps one to forget the bad roads."[32] Even the provincial government made sure that it was not too difficult for American tourists to find government liquor stores. One Conservative member of Parliament from New Westminster, William Garland McQuarrie, reflected frustration about this when he noted,

> The first idea that motorists from the other side of the line get is, naturally, that he can buy whiskey, beer and other liquors in British Columbia. . . . He does not have to go very far before he finds a liquor store. We had one at New Westminster, but that was about 18 miles from the border; it was not near enough. Although New Westminster is the first place of any consequence on the road from the border to Vancouver, the government, in order to help the poor individuals from the other side who might feel the necessity for liquor, put in another vendor's place on the south side of the New Westminster Bridge, where there is no population at all. There are perhaps three or four houses in that neighbourhood; practically nobody lives there. . . . The same applies all over the province.[33]

There were many reasons that Canadians so eagerly facilitated the tourist trade. Most, of course, related to economics. First, American tourism in Canada favorably affected Canada's balance of trade with the United States. While Canadian tourists continued to travel to the United States during the prohibition years, their numbers nowhere approached the number of American tourists traveling north, for obvious reasons. Many British Columbians looked upon a journey to the United States with, in the words of the American consul in Vancouver, "about the same enthusiasm as a camel regards a trek across the Sahara Desert. The oases are few and far between—and then the thirst destroyer is mostly ice water."[34]

Between 1922 and 1928, for example, Canada's trade deficit with the United States hovered between $100 million and $300 million annually. But these figures did not include American tourist expenditures, which estimates placed at $140 million to $275 million. Thus tourism was a valuable "invisible export." If Americans spent $150 million in Canada, it was like Canada sending to the United States goods of an equal value. At tourism's high point in 1929, Commerce Department statistics suggest that American tourists spent $300 million in Canada, and Canadian Department of Trade and Commerce figures place that value at an even higher $309 million. By the late 1920s the American tourist trade was so important that it ranked among the top three largest industries in the Dominion.[35] Naturally, the Great Depression had a chilling effect on tourism. By 1932 American spending had shrunk to a relatively meager $183 million and by 1933 to an even smaller $117 million. Still, because Canadian tourists continued to spend lesser amounts in the United States than Americans spent in Canada, tourism continued to favorably affect Canada's balance of trade. It remained, for example, more than twice the value of Canada's wheat exports to the entire world.[36]

The economic value of tourism was not lost on the province. British Columbians considered tourism a "renewable resource." When the province sold $20 million worth of lumber one year, it finished the year with $20 million less timber. On the other hand, after American tourists spent $20 million in the province, the province still had the same scenic resources that had attracted the tourists in the first place.[37] In 1924 city authorities estimated that tourists spent an astounding $40 million in Vancouver alone.[38] Indeed, some of the chief advocates for government control in British Columbia had earlier argued against provincial prohibition on the basis that regulated sale would be a "drawing card" for promoting tourism.[39] Consequently, provincial legislation that made liquor more difficult for American tourists to obtain usually faced stiff opposition from local businesses in British Columbia. No tourist resort would ever vote to dry up its means of attracting patrons. The British Columbia Hotelman's Association long remained one of the chief advocates for the right to sell beer by the glass in British Columbia. It rightly argued that if hotels could not sell beer, Americans would simply chose to stay in auto camps outside town, where they could buy their liquor from conveniently located liquor stores.[40] It is partly for this reason that, in 1925, British Columbia began to license public hotel beer parlors. It is unclear how many additional American tourists hotel beer attracted, but it certainly did not diminish the northward flow.[41]

Thus, when the United States began to plead with Canada to assist in enforcement against the liquor traffic, it came as no surprise that those most sympathetic were Canadian businesses that profited from American tourism. Many British Columbians were concerned that the province's reputation as the center of bootlegging to the United States would so tarnish its reputation that tourists would no longer come, even for a drink.[42] Others were concerned that bootlegging made it unnecessary for Americans to come to the province at all. One Canadian commented, "Even our more mercenary citizens had far rather see an American come up here to get [liquor], spending fifty dollars in hotel bills, ten in souvenirs, a hundred in furs, and whatever may be left in diamonds—than to have night-riders with silent trucks convey it to the American victim in his home town. Then we only get the money for the liquor."[43] In early 1929 the president of the Canadian National Railways echoed this sentiment when he petitioned the minister of railways and canals in a letter that was eventually passed on to the prime minister. "I think our policy should be to assist the Government of the United States in every way to make that country bone dry," he wrote. "The dryer it is the better it will be for us."[44]

Yet aside from economics, there was one other reason why Canadians actively courted the American tourist. Travel had a secondary influence that was more subtle but perhaps more far-reaching in its effects. As one member of the House of Commons noted in 1925, it "builds up the good-will and understanding and opens the eyes of the visitor to the possibilities of the country."[45] Anything that made Americans more conscious of their neighbors to the north was seen as important by Canadians, who had long felt neglected or overlooked by the United States. If Americans left with a greater affinity for things Canadian, so much the better. Thus, one of the reasons why the prohibition era was so important for Canadian-American relations generally was that it gave Americans a view of Canadians that they may not otherwise have had.

Cognizant of the opportunity to make a good first impression, the Canadian Customs Department ordered inspectors to be on their best behavior. A 1928 circular threatened that the officer "who allows his temper to show itself, and acts in a discourteous manner ... will be sent to the freight yards or manifest room where his peculiar temperament will not offend others." In 1929 the department further directed, "When a tourist drives up to a Customs office on the frontier, it is the duty of the examining officer to go outside and interview the visitor. The Department has been advised that at certain offices the Customs officer sits at his desk at waits for the caller to come to him. It need hardly be stated that this treatment savors of discourtesy and must be abandoned forthwith."[46]

THE LIMITS OF HOSPITALITY

American perceptions, such as the American tourist's, that depict Canada as a sanctuary or refuge are one of the few instances in which the American view of Canada corresponds with the Canadian one. As Russell Brown points out, however, this apparent similarity actually arises from an important cultural difference. For Americans, the border has always represented a place across which one may escape when pressures in the United States become too great. For Canadians, on the other hand, the border is what makes Canada a sanctuary from American cultural excess.[47] Northrop Frye has noted that Canada's national identity is characterized by a "garrison state" mentality. While this may seem extreme, the underlying sentiment, that Canada is somehow a shelter from the United States, has always been an important component of Canadianism.[48] During the American experiment with national prohibition, American tourists who saw British Columbia as a wet refuge were often seen by British Columbians with a certain amount of ambivalence. While most British Columbians remained enamored of the profits to be had, many were also wary about the negative effect tourists had on the Canadian social and cultural fabric.

That Americans had to head north for liquor naturally led some

British Columbians to question the farce that prevented Americans from buying the same liquor at home. Many found it mildly amusing that while British Columbians spent their leisure time hiking, playing cricket, or enjoying an afternoon tea, American tourists were usually at a local hotel "guzzling" scotch. British Columbians, unlike their American counterparts, did not have to waste time hunting for liquor or waste brainpower thinking of ways to cheat the government. It certainly reaffirmed the belief that the British Columbian approach to liquor control was manifestly better.[49]

Still, if all American tourist behavior was so benign, few Canadians would have given it much thought. Unfortunately, not all Americans who came north in search of drink were congenial to Canadians of the steadier sort. In one case the *Vancouver Province* reported that sailors from American halibut vessels at port in Prince Rupert were regularly seen "intoxicated" or "semi-intoxicated" and that one had maliciously broken several hundred dollars' worth of storefront glass with a chair.[50] Sir Charles Piers, a contemporary observer, added, "Our American friends coming from a dry country, are perhaps a trifle too much out on the spree, and the nights are in consequence somewhat hectic with their jazz songs, while the water in the early morning resembles a battlefield, so strewn is it with the corpses of dead bottles, all of which have undoubtedly done their duty." Naturally, the *Province* disregarded the fact that sailors on leave, whether Canadian or American, were usually anything but sedate. For his part, Piers failed to allow that many British Columbians quite appreciated American jazz and many other aspects of American culture. Nevertheless, British Columbians often viewed evidence of American misbehavior as a challenge to the "peace, order, good government" mantra that Canadians held so dear.

At times even the economic argument proved less than convincing. Thirsty Americans often made short day trips across the border, purchased liquor, and returned across the border without otherwise contributing to the Canadian economy. Doing so confirmed in the minds of many British Columbians the long-standing belief that Americans were "cheap." Apparently after one too many admonitions to treat American tourists with deference, one customs officer made up a ditty to describe the typical American:

A machine rolls in from the U.S.A. — a family on the trail;
They carry a tent to save on rent, they have extra gas by the pail,
They carry their food, they carry their oil, they have blankets and pots;
They are rarin' to go and will spend their dough on the gratis parking lots.
You open the door, they put up a roar, you hand them a free permit,
They whine of red tape and call you a ape but you mustn't mind a bit;
You dig up their gats from under the mats and insist that they check the rods;
If your temper they try, you mustn't reply, they are tourists and therefore
    gods.[51]

Between Americans being cheap and being mischievous, some British Columbians began to regret the invitation they had extended to the baser elements of the American population.[52]

British Columbians also resented the commonly held assumption that Americans came to British Columbia only for the liquor. Most would have preferred to believe the naive pronouncement made by Assistant Secretary of the Treasury Lowman that "it's not the supposed American thirst but the lure of Canada's beautiful scenery, fine hospitality and good roads" that led Americans to cross the border.[53] British Columbians facilitated tourism because they believed that, in doing so, they were helping Americans to learn more about Canada. In an interesting bit of irony, however, because provincial authorities located liquor stores so close to the border, American tourists sometimes did not need to learn anything about British Columbia at all. One of the more thoughtful observers noted, "The Americans come with plenty of money, and stay at the much-advertised hotels, gulping down the Rockies in predigested doses, then race through in a Pullman car to the next big hotel on the coast. And how can they know anything of the province?"[54]

No more pleased about the migration of American tourists were drys on both sides of the border. The British Columbia chapter of the WCTU constantly railed against the provincial government, which, the temperance organization believed, was in the liquor business only to make money, even if it debauched American tourists in the process.[55] Likewise, the WCTU chapter at Blaine, Washington, angrily protested to the American consul in Vancouver that roadhouses located close to the international border received little attention from provincial authorities.[56] Spokane's two dailies, the *Spokesman-Review* and the *Daily Chronicle*, made informing their readers about the supposedly detrimental effect of British Columbia's liquor system on tourism a regular part of their coverage. In an article headlined "Another Angle on Canadian Booze," the *Chronicle* endorsed the sentiments of one reader who wrote, "I'm not going up to British Columbia for any of the holidays this year. I know many others who will not go because the roads are filled with drunken drivers as the result of the spree over the line. I don't like to go up there because on all the holidays the streets of the 'beer cities' are filled with drunken men."[57] The *Vancouver Daily Province* promptly responded, chastising the Spokane paper for drawing "what is essentially a false picture of government liquor control in this province." It went on to comment, "The *Chronicle* is either a fanatical Dry, or it has some other obscure motive for discouraging people in Washington form visiting us here in British Columbia."[58] Indeed, both Spokane papers were fanatically dry.

Short of revoking the passports of Americans seen drinking in Canada—a policy the still-influential William Jennings Bryan actually advocated—there was little that committed drys or American authorities could do to discourage the flow of tourists northward. As Andrew Sinclair points out, it was "such suggestions of petty coercion" that ultimately ensured the Eighteenth Amendment's demise.[59] In the meantime, Americans continued to head north of the border. Perhaps most important for the path prohibition would eventually take in the United States, American tourists who traveled to British Columbia witnessed the workings of government control. When the failures of American prohibition became more apparent later in the decade, this experience proved an important factor in the effort to repeal national prohibition in the United States. The Canadian system offered a legitimate and realistic approach to temperance.

CHAPTER FOUR

The Halcyon Days of Rum-Running

Roy Haynes, the second U.S. commissioner of prohibition and an astute observer of the border's effect on the liquor traffic, once remarked that it was impossible to keep liquor from dripping through a dotted line.[1] Indeed, there probably was no greater symbolic evidence of the permeability of the U.S.-Canadian border than the success rumrunners and bootleggers enjoyed during prohibition.[2] The border itself provided a lucrative opportunity. For thirteen years, professional rumrunners supplied liquor to thirsty Americans. Collectively, both challenged the vow of John Kramer, Haynes's predecessor, that the law would be obeyed "in the cities large and small" and that liquor would not be manufactured, "nor sold, nor given away, nor hauled in anything on the surface of the earth nor under the sea nor in the air."[3] As Kramer soon discovered to his dismay, rumrunners and bootleggers succeeded precisely because they operated with the support of so many people. The same sentiment that had enabled smuggling prior to prohibition at least initially supported the liquor traffic during prohibition. In the Northwest, the smuggler's paradise became the rumrunner's paradise and the early years of the 1920s the halcyon days of rum-running.

THE RESPECTABLE CRIME

The principal supply of liquor, particularly of unadulterated whiskey, came from Canada, the Bahamas, or the French islands of St. Pierre and Miquelon. Beyond geographical propinquity, Canada enjoyed great advantages as a potential supplier. Canadian brewers and distillers were eager to replace the markets lost when the various provinces and municipalities went dry in the years of and just after the First World War. Accordingly, the Dominion government refrained from banning the export of liquor and chose instead to take full advantage of the lucrative, thirsty, and captive American market. Not until 1930 would Canada make any serious effort to prohibit liquor exports to the United States.[4]

Assuaging the great American thirst quickly adopted the mantle of respectable enterprise, with bootleggers and rumrunners often attaining a social station not generally enjoyed by outlaws. Many a grateful consumer regarded the liquor smugglers as a romantic breed of modern-day Robin Hoods. Few bootleggers were likely to argue with such a characterization. Fraser Miles, one British Columbian rumrunner, considered himself part of an "international drought relief project."[5] Those who supplied liquor were public philanthropists who brought prosperity to British Columbia while providing a valuable service to thirsty Americans. It is, of course, hard for the historian to separate sincerity from the self-rationalization used to justify illicit activities; many rumrunners certainly claimed a greater social conscience than they really had.

Nevertheless, at the heart of these rationalizations were certain truths. Rumrunners liberated the consumer from some of the more perilous domestic alternatives, especially diverted industrial alcohol and moonshine. Following the chemical industry's expansion during World War I, new products like rayon silk, antifreeze, and photographic films required vast amounts of denatured alcohol. As a consequence, the production of industrial alcohol increased fourfold during the 1920s, and it was not particularly difficult to divert it to bootleg channels. To discourage its diversion, the Prohibition Bureau insisted that manufacturers add any one of seventy-six denaturants. Many, like lavender or soap, were harmless; others, such as sulfuric acid, iodine, and wood alcohol, however, were poisonous. These additives did not always deter the less scrupulous bootleggers, who mixed industrial alcohol with caramel and prune juice to make "scotch," then bottled their concoctions with forged labels suggesting it came from England or Canada.[6]

The hazards to public health from this "rot-gut" or "coffin varnish" soon became evident in the rising incidence rates of alcohol poisoning. As the *Post-Intelligencer* commented in 1920, the "trouble with the spirit of the times is that it's often full of wood alcohol."[7] Liquor smuggled from Canada, on the other hand, provided the American consumer closest to the border with the purest, most unadulterated spirits. It quickly became common knowledge nationally that the best brands were available in the upper Puget Sound region due to its proximity to British Columbia.[8]

At least initially, few Canadians expressed any qualms about their role as supplier to the liquor traffic. As one exporter commented, "The people of the United States want whisky and they are ready to pay for it. I see no reason why we should not do business."[9] The Dominion agreed; indeed, it tacitly condoned the rumrunner's activities. So far as Canadian law was concerned, exporting liquor to the United States was legal. In 1920, deciding to take advantage of the market opened by the Eighteenth Amendment, the Dominion levied a special twenty-dollar-per-case export duty on liquor destined for American ports. Thereafter customs officers routinely cleared liquor cargoes to the United States when their receipt was in clear violation of the Eighteenth Amendment. To further assist distillers in taking advantage of the American market, the government reduced the required aging time for distilled spirits from twenty-four months to twelve. As the historian James Gray notes, somewhat playfully, rum-running was at least tacitly accepted in Canada as a legitimate enterprise, if "one that fell somewhat short of an international aid program."[10]

The "respectability" of rum-running also stemmed from the knowledge that many officials were willing to look the other way. It was no secret that the antipathy held by much of the American public toward the Eighteenth Amendment extended to those who legislated or enforced the law. Even many otherwise dry Republicans recognized that the business of rum-running flourished because of popular demand. Unduly vigorous efforts to enforce the liquor laws would, they assumed, threaten party interests. That public officials occasionally moonlighted as rum-runners—including, for example, a member of the British Columbia Legislative Assembly, a former Washington state legislator, and numerous members of the Seattle police—no doubt contributed to the belief in rum-running as an acceptable, if not a truly noble, pursuit.[11]

To be sure, not all British Columbians or Americans endorsed rum-running. Many churches, especially in Baptist and Methodist denominations, equated rum-running with sin. In fact, it was the churches and dry organizations like the WCTU that, in later years, most actively lobbied the Canadian government for cooperation with American enforcement. To dry interests, rum-running was a logical extension of the liquor industry, to be opposed with the same fervor applied to the campaign for prohibition. Nevertheless, many who would not participate in the rum trade directly were more than happy to sell supplies, old boats, or equipment at bargain prices. Only later, as the moral and criminal costs of rum-running became evident, would the general public begin to take a dim view of the liquor traffic.

Put simply, one can attribute the birth of rum-running to an entrepreneurial response to public demand. The end of the Great War hit the Northwest economy particularly hard. As soldiers returned from the front and war-related industry came to a grinding halt, small businesses failed and the number of unemployed in the region skyrocketed. According to one authority, during periods of recession or depression, fisheries had generally served as the "employer of last resort."[12] After the war even this industry faced problems. Newly established regulations prohibited Canadian fishermen from landing their catches in American ports, and the Fordney-McCumber tariff added new duties to fish products. Under these conditions, unemployed fishermen naturally gravitated to rum-running.[13] Later, when the Depression struck the region's resource-dependent economy, asking anyone if he wanted a job was, according to one rumrunner, "as relevant a question as asking the Pope if he wanted to go to heaven."[14]

Even for the lowest of rumrunners, it was lucrative employment. A case of liquor wholesaling for sixteen dollars in Vancouver could fetch as much as eighty dollars in Seattle. Ship captains who before prohibition made between $110 and $175 per month now found themselves netting $500; first officers could expect $350, second officers, $250, and third officers a still-enviable $125.[15] Fraser Miles, who operated on more than one vessel as a third officer, found the pay especially good. Routinely transporting more than eight hundred cases per month, his sixteen-cents-per-case earnings brought "more than a living in 1932 in Vancouver—it was damn near close to prosperity!"[16] Enjoying even more lucrative profits was the independent runner acting as a middleman, who could net as much as eleven dollars per case. A relatively small boat, carrying no more than seventy-five cases, might leave Victoria Harbour at ten one morning and return by ten the next, fetching a tidy $825 in the process.[17] Needless to say, the proceeds from rum-running accounted for more than one of the mansions lining the exclusive neighborhoods of Vancouver, Victoria, Seattle, or Portland.

Despite the legends of flamboyant bootleggers, fast cars, and easy money, most rumrunners personified restrained caution. Flamboyance attracted the attention of the law and so meant a short career. Unfortunately for later historians seeking to tell their story, most rum-runners chose to maintain a low profile instead, remaining unknown to all but their customers. Likewise, cooperation—more than conflict—characterized early relations between rival rumrunners. While violence existed, those involved in the liquor traffic on the West Coast were not Capones, and gangster syndicates never developed in the Northwest to the degree they did in Chicago or New York.[18] Most found it more profitable to divvy up territory than to fight over it. In March 1922, recognizing the feeble efforts of law enforcement, more than one hundred booze runners and wholesale dealers openly convened in a downtown Seattle hotel to establish rules and regulations for their traffic. They adopted resolutions fixing fair prices, condemned narcotics smuggling, and established a code of ethics to guide transactions. Acknowledging that rules could occasionally be broken and prices occasionally cut, the organization expected liquor dealers and rumrunners to stay "within the limits of approved business methods."[19] Indeed, most rumrunners distinguished themselves from the common smuggler, believing they were part of a higher social order. When Johnny Schnarr, an American rumrunner operating from the Canadian side, was offered as much as $25,000 to smuggle dope, he turned it down flat, as he "didn't see it as the same business at all."[20]

There was also a certain unwritten set of rules, or a code of conduct, that guided relations between rumrunners and the police. One of the principal tenets was that so long as rumrunners acted like legitimate businessmen, they were generally left alone. This meant, for example, that the rumrunner should avoid narcotics smuggling and should refrain from stealing cars for transportation or from stealing liquor from legal outlets. This was especially true on the Canadian side, where customs officers often remained on friendly terms with the rumrunners, particularly when those runners were Canadian.[21] Operating "legitimately" also meant refraining from violence if caught. During the first years of rum-running the contest remained a gentleman's game, with law enforcement and bootleggers all "playing by rules under which no one got hurt."[22] Failing to follow this precept often proved fatal. In 1922 Emilio "Emperor Pic" Picariello, a well-liked hotel operator and rum-running kingpin from Fernie, British Columbia, allowed a confrontation with an Alberta provincial police officer to get out of hand. The incident resulted in the officer's death and, following one of Alberta's more sensational trials, Pic and his bookkeeper, Florence Lassandro, were hanged.[23]

THE RUM-RUNNING KING OF PUGET SOUND

Much of the Northwest's reputation for peaceable rum-running can be attributed to Roy Olmstead, generally regarded as the "Rumrunning King of Puget Sound."[24] Olmstead had begun his career with the Seattle Police Department in 1906, at the age of twenty, and quickly rose through the department's ranks. He was a sergeant in the force by 1910 and made lieutenant by 1916, the same year Washington State voted for state prohibition. A keen observer of the fledgling liquor traffic, Olmstead watched the untidy, disorganized operations of two rival rum-running gangs. One was headed by a former policeman, Jack Marquett, the other by two brothers, Logan and Jake Billingsley. Within a few years the futile competition between Marquett and the Billingsleys had led to the arrest and breakup of both organizations and left the liquor traffic in the Northwest in desperate need of consolidation.[25]

Olmstead was thirty-four when national prohibition took effect in 1920. Married, with two daughters, and the youngest lieutenant in the Seattle Police, his future appeared bright indeed. Nonetheless, bored with his career—and cognizant of the lucrative profits to be had under the Volstead Act—Olmstead decided to fill the vacuum left by the demise of the operations of Marquett and the Billingsleys. Certainly by design, the Seattle public heard little about Roy Olmstead for the first few months. In the early morning hours of March 22, 1920, however, just as Olmstead and his associates completed unloading liquor from a boat near Meadowdale, Washington, federal prohibition agents sprang from the woods and began firing wildly at the boat and Olmstead's men. Olmstead himself escaped immediate capture, leaving behind the largest shipment of liquor ever seized in the Northwest. Agents, however, had identified the "baby lieutenant" and apprehended him at his home later the same morning.[26]

While the arrest seemed likely to end Olmstead's short-lived rum-running career, quite the opposite occurred. Dismissed by the police department, Olmstead found that he now was free to pursue his new career full time, unhindered by official duties. He promptly assembled an empire of investors, attorneys, bookkeepers, boatmen, dispatchers, loaders, and salesmen. To avoid the special twenty-dollar-per-case export duty Canada levied on liquor bound for the United States, Olmstead hired ships that loaded in Vancouver but cleared for Mexico. This method allowed Olmstead to undersell his competitors by as much as 30 percent, requiring many to give up the business, resort to piracy, or join Olmstead's organization. In what the *New York Times* called one of the largest rum-running conspiracies in the country, it was a rare month that Olmstead's intricate empire did not clear $200,000.[27]

Olmstead quickly became a fixture of Seattle society and enjoyed a prestige not enjoyed by most other rumrunners. Elaborate parties thrown at his exclusive Mount Baker residence were attended by Seattle's elite.

Yet Olmstead's prominence was due to more than his flamboyance. As the *Seattle Post-Intelligencer* later editorialized, Olmstead's unique code of conduct endeared him to many thirsty citizens. "Roy was a 'good' boot-legger. He prided himself on the genuineness of his labels.... Right or wrong ... he served a social purpose and satisfied an appetite existing in many of the most respectable throats or palates or stomachs."[28] Perhaps more important, especially to the higher social orders, Olmstead oper-ated within the established rules. He never participated in the narcotics traffic, prostitution, or racketeering that characterized the liquor traffic in other large cities. He never allowed his subordinates to arm themselves because he believed that no amount of money was worth a human life. Because of his integrity, many felt that Olmstead was the best thing that could have happened to the liquor traffic in the Northwest.[29]

Olmstead's popularity proved to be his downfall. His very public successes and popularity only served to publicize the prohibition depart-ment's glaring failures, and so that office spared no effort and no expense to bring down his organization. Their labors proved futile until one day in October 1924, when Canadian officials seized one of Olmstead's boats, the *Eva B*, with 784 cases of liquor on board. After the three crewmen aboard the vessel talked, prohibition agents redoubled their efforts. One evening in November they raided Olmstead's home, arresting him, his wife, Elise, and fifteen guests, including two former members of the Royal Northwest Mounted Police. Olmstead's guests had gathered that night to read bed-time stories to Seattle children over the radio station that the Olmsteads operated from their house. Contributing to one of the more delightful myths of prohibition-era Seattle, federal officers claimed that Mrs. Olm-stead's "bedtime stories" were, in reality, cleverly worked-out codes that warned radio-equipped rumrunners in the Puget Sound of the positions of Coast Guard vessels. It is more likely that Olmstead purchased the radio station as a public relations measure. In any case, federal officers were never able to prove their suspicions about the bedtime stories in court.[30]

Although the raid failed to produce liquor, federal agents posing as Olmstead and his wife used the Olmstead's phone to call suspected bootleggers and ask them to deliver liquor to the house. When they arrived, federal officers promptly arrested them as well. Olmstead and his attorney, Jerry Finch, cried foul, convinced that the prohibition office had violated the Olmsteads' civil liberties. Not only had federal agents impersonated Roy and Elise Olmstead, but also, and more importantly, they had tapped Olmstead's phone lines to secure evidence. It was the first time in U.S. history that a federal case had rested on wiretapping evidence. The case quickly became known in the Northwest, then later in the entire nation, as the "whispering wires" case. It promised to be "one of the most sensational cases in the history of Seattle," as well as one of the most important liquor trials under the Eighteenth Amendment.[31]

On January 19, 1925, Olmstead and ninety other defendants were indicted for conspiracy to violate the National Prohibition Act. Many of the defendants, released on bail, quickly retreated to Canada, secure in the knowledge that violations of American liquor laws were not offenses subject to extradition. Others pleaded guilty and testified on the government's behalf. To bolster its case, the prosecution subpoenaed a number of witnesses from British Columbia who could testify about Olmstead's Canadian connections. On March 9, 1926, twenty-three of those who did not flee to Canada, including Roy Olmstead, were convicted and sentenced. Recognizing that they did not have enough evidence to convict Elise Olmstead, a Canadian citizen, immigration authorities instead sought unsuccessfully to deport her. For his part, Olmstead was sentenced to four years hard labor at McNeil Island Penitentiary. Convinced that a higher court would find the use of wiretaps illegal—a sentiment held even by the assistant attorney general of the United States, Mabel Walker Willebrandt—he remained unperturbed.[32]

Olmstead's optimism proved unfounded. When the appeals court failed to overturn Olmstead's conviction, *Olmstead et al. v. United States* proceeded to the U.S. Supreme Court. There, in a five-to-four decision, it met a similar fate. In February 1928, Chief Justice William Howard Taft spoke for the majority when he concluded that wiretapping evidence was admissible. Justices Louis Brandeis, Oliver Wendell Holmes, Harlan Stone, and Pierce Butler dissented, with Holmes calling government wiretapping "ignoble," "a dirty business," and an "odious crime."[33]

For many local residents, the "odious," or "ignoble" methods the Prohibition Department used to combat rum-running contrasted quite unfavorably with the "respectable" methods of Roy Olmstead. Even more endearing to the public was Olmstead's willingness to accept responsibility for his actions. He later commented to one newspaperman from his cell at McNeil, "I'm not complaining, I violated the law."[34] Perhaps most significant was the effect the Olmstead decision had on public perceptions of prohibition generally. Dr. Nicholas Murray Butler, an aggressive participant in the fight against Eighteenth Amendment, called the Olmstead case one of the four "moving influences which hastened repeal."[35] Many residents of the Northwest, disposed toward a favorable view of Roy Olmstead and the service he provided, tended to agree. Although the *Seattle Argus* did not condone breaking the law, it said, "There is but one way to prevent this crime and that is by repealing the law. The attempted enforcement is getting us nowhere."[36]

TIN CORSETS AND LEAKY LUMBER

Wet goods came across the border by every possible conveyance—in automobiles, boats, airplanes, and trains; under loads of coal, scrap iron, or lumber; and in coat pockets, suitcases, hubcaps, and backpacks.[37] Not surprisingly, rumrunners and bootleggers used many of the same methods that smugglers had used for decades. Will Rogers once quipped that there were people "who, if they put in half the time studying on some mechanical invention that they do how to smuggle booze, why they would be as great as Edison."[38] The judge who tried the federal case against Roy Olmstead in 1926 apparently agreed when he admonished, "As to you, Roy Olmstead, I'll say this.... If the same constructive force [and] organizing ability, which was devoted to this enterprise, had been used legitimately, in harmony with the laws, the final result would have been marvelous and you ... would have harvested a big reward."[39]

Only imagination and ingenuity limited the means by which rumrunners and bootleggers transported liquor across the border. One man devised a method he thought foolproof. Fabricating a double-lined tin container shaped like a corset, he filled the considerable space between the two sides full of liquor. Although the tactic worked a couple of times, the inventor one day neglected to fill his contraption completely and, unfortunately, the sloshing of the contents gave him away. Another bootlegger managed to tunnel under the border at Boundary Bay. That, too, was apparently quite successful until "Slim" Cameron, a game warden on routine patrol, accidentally fell through the tunnel's roof.[40] Not to be outdone, a resident of Metaline Falls, Washington, trained his horse to become a booze runner. The owner would ride the horse to Canada, load it up, and then allow it to find its way home. The logic seemed quite appealing: it was doubtful the police would arrest or fine the horse. The *New York Times* even reported that a former American submarine, transferred to the Canadian government and sold as surplus, had been seen bringing large shipments of liquor into Seattle from British Columbia.[41]

Finding new places to hide liquor where inspectors were least likely to look turned into something of a cottage industry. A Mounted Police inspector, examining a refrigerated-car load in 1922, was surprised to find eight undigested bottles of rye whiskey neatly sewn up in hog carcasses. (This, of course, gave a whole new meaning to the term "blind pig.")[42] The Idaho State Police arrested one Albertan when customs inspectors found he had hidden a large quantity of Scotch whisky in the ladies' toilet of the Calgary–Spokane sleeping car. Authorities stumbled upon a much larger find in 1931 when 14,094 bottles were seized near Indianapolis. Apparently, the liquor was being sent by railcar from a distillery in Vancouver to Chicago. Packed tightly in burlap sacks between two-by-fours and other lumber, the liquor attracted the attention of authorities only when the lumber was found "leaking."[43]

This era saw one method of smuggling never before used. Concurrent with prohibition, the 1920s began the golden age of aviation, and it was only natural that a few of the thousands of pilots trained during the war would seek employment piloting an international liquor route. Even as law enforcement cracked down on water shipments, King County, Washington, sheriff Matt Starwich discovered that aerial rumrunners could transport liquor at will. High above inquisitive police and vicious hijackers, the pilot faced only the danger of mechanical failure and a subsequent forced landing. In initial outlay, airplanes usually cost less than the speedboats that plied the Puget Sound. While it was not uncommon for the cost of a small rum boat to exceed $20,000, the cost of an infinitely faster Wright-powered biplane was only $8,500 and the more spacious Hornet cabin plane could be had for as little as $18,000.[44] One of Olmstead's associates, Cecil Langdon, recognized the potential and took leave of his career as a racer and barnstormer to found the Olympic Aeronautic Corporation. Organized ostensibly to provide flight lessons and charter services, Olympic Aeronautic was instead, according to one prohibition agent, simply a front "formed for the clear purpose of smuggling liquor into the United States."[45] Nonetheless, the combined romance of rum-running and airplanes did not escape one journalist, who quipped, "Prohibition and patriotism go, sometimes, hand in hand.... If they seem to be doing a certain violence to the law, still they are keeping alive a craft, so that if China or Guatemala or Switzerland invades us by the air, we shall be ready."[46]

In both British Columbia and the United States, rumrunners benefited from the government's increased expenditures on public roads and highways after World War I. Improvements that facilitated international motor traffic aided not only regional tourism and legitimate commerce but criminal enterprise as well. There was some truth in Will Rogers's joke that bad roads broke more bottles of booze than did authorities. While water routes traditionally proved the most cost-effective form of regional transportation, good roads allowed illicit goods to travel with greater speed and less likelihood of detection. The enlarged network of roads also made it possible for the rumrunner to deliver directly to the consumer, eliminating the costly middleman usually required in waterborne smuggling.[47]

In the early 1920s, it was a poor man who could not buy at least a secondhand Model-A Ford or Chevrolet. The automobile made it possible for even the smallest of rumrunners to take part in the lucrative traffic. Those seeking to conceal the whiskey did so in a spare tire, under false limousine tops, and in double-lined gas tanks. The space available under the cowl of one Anderson-Six, accessible upon removing the speedometer, was capable of carrying fifty or sixty quart bottles. Moving the car's front seat forward eight inches allowed room for three or four additional cases, and a few more bottles lay hidden in a false top.[48]

In practice, those truly serious about the rum-running business made little effort to conceal their loads but relied instead on speed and durability. They required large, powerful automobiles fitted with heavy-duty auxiliary leaf springs. On the trip north, most of these cars carried sandbags so that the car did not ride suspiciously high when empty. They had to be fast enough to elude the persistent, but usually poorly equipped, law officers they sometimes encountered. They also had to be well armored to protect against the bullets of would-be hijackers. Thus, for the rumrunner to invest in a Packard, a McLaughlin Buick, a Hudson-Harmon, or an Anderson-Six was a paying proposition. When modified, the value of these so-called Whiskey-Sixes routinely exceeded a thousand dollars.[49]

While not exclusively so, the actual running of booze across the border was usually conducted by Americans. Adventurous Canadians occasionally drove loads as far south as Utah or Colorado, but the main problem for the Canadian was finding buyers at his destination without running afoul of local authorities. Many preferred to earn a still-profitable two dollars per case to transport liquor to the Canadian side of the border, make the exchange to an American runner, and leave it to the American to incur the risks inherent in getting it across the line.[50]

Rumrunners transporting by auto in the Northwest faced challenges their peers in the prairies did not. One could casually meander across the border in the prairies at any convenient point. On western runs from the British Columbia interior, however, steep mountain ranges funneled roads to a relative few border crossings. Were enforcement officials so inclined and in possession of sufficient manpower, these roads would have been relatively easy to blockade, which would have forced smugglers to portage their goods around border crossings. However, in most cases exporters transferred their loads to American drivers in full view of Canadian and American customs authorities. Canadian authorities were not very interested in duty-paid liquor and it was usual for rumrunners to have paid a "duty" of fifty cents per case to a Canadian export company to "take care" of American customs.[51]

The hospitality and organization offered by Canadian individuals and export companies undoubtedly facilitated the American liquor smuggler. In the coal-mining town of Fernie, British Columbia, one "Mister Big" operated a two-story brick garage that contained not only liquor storage but a repair shop and sleeping area for tired customers. Cars usually began pulling in around three in the afternoon. While the vehicles were loaded and serviced, their drivers spent the afternoon in the pool hall or at a card table playing high-stakes poker with local businessmen. In other cases, ranchers living close to the border made available, for a modest commission, their barns or haystacks, which rumrunners used to conceal caches of liquor. The illicit product could then be smuggled to its final destination at the runner's convenience.[52]

The single most important factor professionalizing and streamlining the liquor traffic in the Northwest was the organization of liquor export companies. In August 1922 sixteen of the largest liquor wholesalers in the province of British Columbia amalgamated in Vancouver under the name of Consolidated Exporters Corporation.[53] Licensed by both the Dominion and British Columbia, the liquor wholesalers decided to merge their activities when the province increased its annual license fees from $3,000 to $10,000. As the largest of the "Big Three" exporters that operated from British Columbia—the others being Manitoba Refineries and Joseph Kennedy Ltd.—Consolidated established export warehouses not only in Victoria and Vancouver but also in Greenwood, Grand Forks, Creston, Cranbrook, and Fernie.[54] Even a cursory examination of a map confirms that these interior export warehouses existed for the sole purpose of smuggling liquor into the United States.[55]

Along with providing liquor at convenient border locations, Consolidated brought to the rum-running trade an organization and efficiency that would have been the envy of any business. With Joseph Kennedy Ltd. and Manitoba Refineries, Consolidated controlled—directly or by proxy—virtually the entire liquor traffic in the Northwest, from its production in the breweries and distilleries of British Columbia to its delivery in the American states. It sent "land agents" to the United States, whose duties, as regional representatives, were to drum up business and to organize the purchase of Consolidated products.[56] The American consul in Vancouver was particularly impressed with this system. He suggested the U.S. government place land agents in British Columbia "with as effective contacts here as the exporters have in the United States" to furnish American authorities with dependable information concerning the movement of illicit shipments.[57]

As the decade progressed, and as the stakes for rum-running increased, Consolidated also created insurance and finance schemes for its rum-runners. If the liquor was seized by authorities en route, Consolidated would replace it. If the rumrunner's automobile was seized, Consolidated would provide the bond required by Customs to get it back. If the rumrunner was arrested, Consolidated would provide bail money and an attorney to represent him in court. The export company also served as lender to rumrunners, since most found securing loans from banks somewhat problematic. When Johnny Schnarr discovered that replacing his first boat would require between $23,000 and $24,000, he went immediately to Consolidated. For a 40 percent commission on every delivery made until the loan was repaid, Consolidated provided Schnarr with the necessary funds. (As a testimony to the lucrative nature of rum-running, Schnarr cleared his debt within the first year.)[58]

Consolidated Exporters facilitated smuggling by water as well as by land. Vancouver and Victoria naturally served as the principal bases for smuggling liquor by water into the United States, but there were significant differences in the functions of both ports. As the largest, Vancouver was the main source of liquor destined for customers in southern Oregon and California. Victoria, on the other hand, because of its more southerly locale, tended to be the staging center for liquor destined for the Puget Sound.[59]

Rum-running by water was usually a three-ship process. At the top of the rum-running hierarchy were the "mother" ships owned by Consolidated Exporters—such as the *Malahat*, the *Stadacona*, the *Quadra*, the *Lillehorn*, the *Coal Harbour*, and the *Federalship*—that could carry a fortune in their holds. Many of these vessels had colorful pasts even before they became the nucleus of the Pacific's "Rum Row." The *Stadacona*, whose name was later changed to *Kuyakuzmt*, had once been the flagship of the New York Yacht Club. Another, the beautiful three-masted schooner *Marechal Foch*, had a large brass plate on the quarter-deck wall proclaiming it the former fishing yacht of Zane Grey. These schooners or steamers routinely left Vancouver with a million-dollar cargo, hovered along the coast of California for days, delivered their load to smaller "contact" ships, and then returned to Vancouver to repeat the process.[60]

The Washington and northern Oregon coastal traffic generally did not use mother ships. To place the largest ships, with their valuable cargo, in American waters was a risky proposition; it was also unnecessary. With Victoria a mere fifteen miles across the Juan de Fuca or Haro Straits from the American market, speed assumed more importance than size. Instead, intermediate-sized vessels picked up loads from Consolidated's export docks in Victoria. They, in turn, distributed their cargoes to even smaller and speedier American vessels for the final run into the sound.

Unable to keep up with the initial demand, the region pressed into service every available boat. Later, as time and profits allowed, rumrunners turned to increasingly sophisticated and speedier vessels capable of eluding the growing number of Coast Guard cutters. Powered by surplus engines that had been used to power fledgling aircraft during World War I, some of these boats achieved astonishing speeds. One rum boat used by Olmstead, the *Three Deuces*, broke the Lake Washington speed record of forty knots using Liberty engines. Soon boatyards were cranking out sleeker and faster vessels to meet the rumrunners' demand. Ironically, it was well known that the Coast Guard procured boats (albeit slower ones) from the very same yards.[61]

Like *Kuyakuzmt*, rumrunners often christened their new vessels—or rechristened old ones—with names intended to confuse Coast Guard pursuers. There was *Ououkinish* and *Kitnayakwa*, *Ouitachouan* and *Taiheiyo*.[62] Schnarr named the *Kitnayakwa* after a river in northern British Columbia, only because "it was a word that I thought people would have a hard time remembering if they only saw it once." His other vessel, *Revuocnav*, would also stymie the observer who might not realize that it was simply "Vancouver" spelled backward.[63]

Rumrunners used other, more creative ways to lessen attention from American or Canadian authorities. For example, vessels that were members of Canadian yacht clubs were not generally required to report to Customs when crossing the border. Most presumed that a reputable yacht club would not keep in good standing members reputed or known to be involved in illicit activities. Taking advantage of this loophole was Frank Turner, a former member of the Victoria police force and member of the Royal Victoria Yacht Club, who profited in retirement with his vessel, *Wandering Lass*. As an alternative to transferring loads on open water, rumrunners made some exchanges using an island cache. They were particularly fond of D'Arcy Island, just northeast of Victoria in the Haro Strait. For most of the 1920s, D'Arcy served as a leper colony and so was avoided by local authorities. The station keeper there was on friendly terms with most rumrunners, probably because he profited by guarding cargoes for more than one.[64]

Consolidated Exporters was particularly important to the waterborne liquor trade. At the most basic level, Consolidated organized the exchange of liquor between vessels. Because the American demand for Canadian whisky far outstripped the supply, it was common for independent rum boats to approach Consolidated "motherships," falsely claiming to have made arrangements for a liquor transfer. To ensure that the liquor was delivered to the proper consignee, who had paid for the liquor in advance, export companies worked out a simple yet very effective arrangement. When a bootlegger from the United States arranged for a shipment from Consolidated, a Consolidated representative would tear in half a dollar bill. On each half was written the amount to be delivered; one half was given to the consignee and the other to the skipper of the rum ship. Only if the two halves matched at the point of transfer was the liquor released. This process nicely eliminated the need for the letter of credentials and not until late in the decade would the dollar-bill method be replaced by wireless-radio release.[65]

When rumrunners pulled up to the Consolidated docks in Victoria or Vancouver, they generally did so in the middle of the day. As far as the Canadian government was concerned, there was no problem exporting liquor to the United States so long as it received the appropriate twenty-dollar-per-case export duty.[66] If exporters wanted to avoid paying the duty, however, they had to prove that the liquor was bound for someplace other than the United States. Accordingly, vessels cleared for Mexican or Central American ports, "lost" their cargo somewhere between Vancouver and California, yet returned with properly made-out papers—signed by Mexican or Central American officials—affirming that the liquor had been off-loaded at Ensenada or La Libertad. One local resident remarked that these were "the fastest boats in the world. They could leave from Vancouver one day and be back the next, and they had the customs stamp to prove it."[67] Even the attorney general of British Columbia found "quite remarkable the facility with which ships can make the trip say from Vancouver to Ensenada."[68]

Land agents for Consolidated Exporters secured these papers, and they did so either by forgery or by providing a trifling *mordita*, or "small bite," to a corrupt Mexican or Central American official. Early on, many American and Canadian officials failed to recognize the true nature of these shipments. Wayne Wheeler, president of the American Anti-Saloon League, believed the liquor actually reached Ensenada. He was concerned only because he thought it was then smuggled north into California. Not until the Royal Commission on Customs and Excise convened in 1926 and 1927 would the full degree of Consolidated's participation in the liquor traffic—and the extent to which its practices defrauded the Dominion of revenue—become evident.[69]

THE COAST GUARD AND OTHER MINOR IRRITANTS

Problems enforcing national prohibition did not take long to become apparent. On January 15, 1920, the day the Eighteenth Amendment took effect, the deputy collector at the border station of Sumas, Washington, wrote to his superior, "Conditions are becoming so bad along the border in this vicinity with respect to the smuggling of liquor that it is deemed advisable by this office to request that another inspector be allowed this port for a period of about six weeks or two months in order to stamp out some of this lawlessness."[70] This collector reflected two sentiments common in early thinking on the rum-running enforcement issue. The first was the surprise expressed at the degree to which the prohibition law would be violated; the second, the misperception of the amount of resources necessary to combat the traffic.

With perhaps some exaggeration, the American consul in Vancouver proclaimed the Northwest "the bootlegger's paradise on the North American continent."[71] The same factors that had long made the Pacific Northwest a smuggler's paradise now made the region a rumrunner's paradise. The protected bays and channels of the Puget Sound afforded the rumrunner ideal locations for concealment and rendezvous, while numerous trails, known by few customs or border patrol officers, criss-crossed the boundary on the rugged land border to the east. With the island-dotted Strait of Georgia adjacent to the similarly adorned Puget Sound, it is unlikely that a rumrunner could have hoped for more than what nature created. The avenues for leakage were so immense that the New York Times repeatedly commented on the region's geographical problems. It finally determined the Twentieth U.S. Prohibition District—the region encompassing Washington, Oregon, and Alaska—to be the most difficult to patrol in the country.[72]

Donald A. McDonald, Washington State's first prohibition director, was one of the few to recognize the problems inherent to enforcing laws against liquor smuggling in the Northwest. In one of his first public pronouncements, he warned, "There are about fifty passable auto and wagon roads crossing the boundary line between this state and British Columbia. In order to watch these highways the federal force in the State of Washington would have to be nearly ten times larger than it is at present. With liquor obtainable in practically limitless quantities in British Columbia ... the task of enforcing the dry law in this state will be one with which the present force will be powerless to cope."[73] Yet the plethora of roads and lack of officers did not seem to concern most observers. To the editors of the Seattle Post-Intelligencer, the outlook was not as bleak as McDonald suggested. Partly tongue in cheek, the paper wrote,

> By placing the officers three feet apart all along the boundary and keeping them there, even the most persistent bootlegger might be discouraged in time. If they decide to dig in on the other side, it will mean a long war, but in the end victory will be with the officers. It is well known that the bootlegger is lacking in patience. It is not his nature to lie low until danger has passed, so that all that is necessary is to bring the entire customs and prohibition forces of the Pacific Coast here and wait until they make a break across the border. The plan may leave the Mexican boundary somewhat unprotected, but it would enshroud British Columbia bootlegging in gloom.[74]

It was partly because of such optimistic but misguided solutions that enforcement faced so many unanticipated obstacles during the early years of prohibition.

At the most basic level, many of the problems officers faced were the result of fundamental flaws in the wording of the Eighteenth Amendment or that of its enforcement mechanism, the Volstead Act. The amendment did not forbid the purchase or use of liquor, only its manufacture, sale, and transport, and it called for the "concurrent power" of the federal and state governments in enforcing the law. Under Volstead, purchasers could not be held for conspiracy; cars, boats, planes, or other vehicles could not be seized if their owner could plead ignorance of their illegal use; and, most importantly, not until the Jones Act in 1929 were the penalties for breaking the law very serious.[75] A number of these deficiencies proved instrumental in undermining the efforts to combat rum-running in the Northwest.

Enforcing a law that soon nearly half of the population did not support placed the police in a contest for public sympathy, a contest they rarely won. Many enforcement officers were no more interested in seeing the law enforced than was the general public. Police attitudes toward "legitimate" rumrunners ranged from reluctant enforcement to tolerance and, eventually, to active participation. Even those who did not actively participate in rum-running were not always opposed to buying liquor from those who did. (Johnny Schnarr even claimed to have once made a delivery to a Coast Guard cutter!) Also hurting police popularity were the occasionally embarrassing, ill-timed seizures that achieved widespread notoriety. In one case, the Coast Guard stopped a suspected rumrunner between Everett and Port Townsend only to find thirty-three coeds from the Washington State College Glee Club whose belongings contained nothing incriminating.[76]

Achieving the cooperation of local authorities was, to most rumrunners, a recognized cost of doing business. Johnny Schnarr remembered that most of the people to whom he delivered had contacts in the police department. Quite often, he was tipped off to impending raids when federal prohibition agents requested assistance from the local police. "There were," Schnarr rationalized, "plenty of people who just didn't believe in the Prohibition laws, even on the police forces, so a guy didn't have to be a crooked cop to help out the bootleggers and rumrunners."[77] Moreover, widely circulated reports that bootleggers offered agents as much as $15,000 to find it convenient to be away from their posts for a few hours made the more unscrupulous officers insistent on some sort of honorarium.[78] As game warden Slim Cameron recalled, "If American [police] weren't getting their cut on everything [then] they didn't play, and a hell of a lot of the B.C. police were the same way."[79]

A local officer unsympathetic to the dry cause generally meant the law went unenforced. Most North Idaho residents knew that Henry Trane, sheriff of Bonner County, opposed the Eighteenth Amendment. Insofar as he was able, complained prohibition agent A. E. McFatridge, Trane afforded "protection" from arrest.[80] In one interview, a resident of Sandpoint alleged that this "protection" required a monthly payoff of fifty dollars. Another interviewee, Nels Nelson, commented that in nearby Newport bootlegging was going on all the time. Although in his second term as sheriff, Trane had never, according to Nelson, "raided a place in that section of the county, nor arrested a bootlegger."[81]

Even without the public apathy or police indifference, law enforcement units charged with enforcing the Volstead Act faced an insurmountable lack of resources. When Congress allocated to the federal government funds for the enforcement of national prohibition in 1920, it did so very conservatively. Without adding to either the Coast Guard or to the number of customs officers, Congress allocated funds sufficient only to create a Bureau of Prohibition with a force of 1,550 agents. As Charles Merz points out, simple math exposes the inadequacy of this meager allotment. Combined, the sea borders of the United States encompassed some twelve thousand miles; the land border with Canada accounted for thirty-seven hundred miles, not including the three thousand miles of the Great Lakes; and another thirty-seven hundred miles defined the southern border with Mexico. Even if the entire staff of 1,550 agents had been relieved of all interior responsibilities and placed along the border, each agent would still have had over twelve miles to patrol.[82] With over one thousand roads bisecting the border between Canada and the United States alone, the inadequacy of the Prohibition Bureau quickly became apparent.[83] As one observer commented, the liquor supply "operated like a garden hose with four outlets. If you put your thumb over one it simply came out the other three with even greater force."[84] On the one hand, drys in Congress opposed allocating more money to enforce prohibition because to do so would suggest that their estimates had been naively low and that the law would not be easy to enforce. On the other hand, congressional wets opposed allocating more because a failure of enforcement meant the failure, and ultimate repeal, of prohibition.[85]

The outlook in the Northwest could be no more optimistic. The twenty agents who composed the Twentieth District of the Bureau of Prohibition were not nearly adequate for a region encompassing over eight hundred thousand square miles. The administrator of the district was the one-time librarian and real estate salesman Roy C. Lyle, who received his post as a patronage appointment of Senator Wesley Jones of Washington. During his decade-long tenure, Lyle had a public image that varied from comical to the pathetic. When asked what he intended to do about rum-running from the air, Lyle replied, in all seriousness, that he was working on a lecture on the topic and would present it in his address to an upcoming convention of sheriffs. To be fair to Lyle, for a number of years he did not even have an automobile for work on land or a boat to patrol the waters of the Puget Sound.[86] As Norman Clark has concluded, there was probably a great deal of truth in Lyle's repeated plea, "We are doing as well as we can." The *Oregonian* found Lyle's plight pitiful enough to conclude that there was "some plausibility to the argument that political capital might be made out of this helplessness."[87]

Indeed, the most repeated pleas heard from the prohibition administrator or those who worked under him were for additional officers, equipment, or increases in salary. The deputy collector at Sumas, Washington, complained about the daily routine, with which those under him were unable to cope. He protested, "Work at this point covers an average period of fourteen hours during which time there are some twenty-seven trains besides the highway and automobile traffic to look after."[88] Agents earned meager salaries that rarely rose above $1,680 per year, and it was not uncommon for them to have to use their own money to secure information from informants. When two prohibition agents, Ballard Turner and Ernest Valsich, were found murdered in Vancouver, Washington, the pleas for assistance only grew louder. A rather alarmed editor of the very dry *Spokesman-Review* asked Senator Jones to station federal troops along the Canadian border. Jones's subsequent request to President Harding, however, elicited the reply, "There are other matters of more immediate importance at the present time."[89]

Like the customs and prohibition agents who worked on land, the Coast Guard also suffered from a severe shortage of resources. When the Eighteenth Amendment took effect, Congress added to the Coast Guard's traditional responsibility—lifesaving and rescue operations—the task of enforcing national prohibition along the nation's coasts. Unfortunately, Congress provided no extra vessels, equipment, or manpower. During the first half of the decade, the entire fleet of the U.S. Coast Guard numbered fewer than one hundred vessels. Most were old Navy-surplus cutters unsuited for the rum war, and not until 1925 would Congress appropriate funds sufficient to modernize the force and make rum-running a risky proposition. Until then the Coast Guard patrolled the waters of the Puget Sound and Pacific with only two tugs, the *Arcata* and the *Scout*. Barely able to make twelve knots, top-heavy, and unseaworthy for the open ocean, they compared quite unfavorably with the much speedier and more numerous rumrunners. Even by 1928 only twenty-two Coast Guard vessels patrolled the Puget Sound.[90]

Surprisingly, the *Arcata* proved fairly successful, due primarily to the ingenuity of its captain, Lorenz A. Lonsdale. Only five feet tall, Lonsdale nevertheless developed a reputation for his tenacious pursuit of Puget Sound rumrunners. Known on both sides of the law as "Grandad," Lonsdale plotted his strategies carefully and followed them up with forceful action. By 1924 he had become something of a local legend, a feat not overlooked by his superiors in Washington, who promoted him to command of a new 110-foot vessel in Baltimore. When Senator Wesley Jones, champion of Northwest dry forces, heard of the plan to transfer Lonsdale, however, he promptly wrote to the commandant of the Coast Guard, "I have been informed that Lonsdale is likely to be transferred to an Eastern Port. If such be the case, the last man in our pay who is wise to rumrunning in the [Puget] Sound will be sent out of the district. Without him our chances of preventing the rum traffic will be nil."[91]

Yet even Lonsdale understood that the Coast Guard was fighting a losing battle in the Northwest. With only two slow enforcement craft to patrol the entire sound, the Coast Guard pursued far more rumrunners than it captured. In one incident, Captain Lonsdale and the *Arcata* commenced pursuit of the rumrunner M-220 in the Juan de Fuca Strait. Unable to keep up, Lonsdale ordered two shots be fired across the M-220's bow. The rum boat's captain, apparently deciding that discretion was the better part of valor, surrendered near Port Townsend. Before Lonsdale caught up to the vessel, however, the crew managed to throw the entire liquor cargo overboard.

This was not an uncommon practice. Without the liquor as evidence, conviction on a rum-running charge was unlikely, so losing a cargo was not a terribly high price to pay. Moreover, rumrunners did not always have to write off the liquor as lost. They often threw their liquor over-board in burlap sacks weighted with enough rock salt to sink to the bottom. Hours or days later, after the salt dissolved, a buoy would pop to the surface indicating where the liquor could be retrieved. In the case of the M-220, without the liquor, Lonsdale was unable to hold the captured crew for more than a day. He later returned to the location of the seizure only to find that independent "bottle-fishers" had been grappling in the vicinity. What liquor he found was insufficient to war-rant the crew's arrest.[92]

In some cases the agencies charged with enforcing the Eighteenth Amendment were the victims of their own success. After prohibition took effect, those charged with liquor violations swamped both police and the courts. Although authorities might arrest a violator, because prior cases clogged the court system, the suspect was usually freed on bail. He would return to the trade, sometimes being caught repeatedly before being tried for the initial violation. As frustrating to officers was the revolving door through which automobiles or boats seized in enforcement of the liquor traffic passed. These vehicles accumulated until political pressure mounted for public auctions. To the dismay of officers, they usually sold for paltry sums, sometimes even to the original owner at a price mutually agreed upon by the rumrunners in advance.[93]

The proximity of the Canadian border did not help matters. Secure in the knowledge that rum-running was not an extraditable offense under any existing Canadian-American treaty, bootleggers simply dashed to the Canadian side when pursued by American officers. This practice left those in pursuit the frustrating choice of breaking off a sometimes lengthy chase or, alternatively, violating Canadian territorial sovereignty. In the latter case, courts usually ruled the seizures illegal and sanctioned the arresting officers. Frustrated by such technicalities, the *Spokesman-Review* concluded, "The sound and right procedure would be to convict them on the unmistakable evidence before the court and then discipline the offending arresting officers if they exceeded their authority."[94]

Finally, hindering enforcement in the Northwest, as in the rest of the nation, was the disorganization of prohibition enforcement. Common sense suggested that a single, unified agency charged with enforcing prohibition would increase overall effectiveness. The reality, however, was that, far from combining and cooperating, many distinct agencies worked at cross-purposes, often spending more time in jurisdictional disputes and deliberate instances of noncooperation than in attacking the liquor traffic. At the federal level alone, the Prohibition Bureau, Customs, the Coast Guard, Immigration's border patrol, and the Department of Justice all fought over resources and responsibilities. Added to this were the far more numerous state and local officers who, according to the Eighteenth Amendment, were given concurrent jurisdiction over enforcing its provisions. Nonetheless, many states decided that it was the federal government and not the state governments that had to enforce federal statutes, especially when the federal agencies seemed to have no interest in cooperating with the states.[95] G.B. Kennedy, the sheriff of Island County, Washington, wrote chidingly to the prohibition agent assigned to his region, "I was very sorry to have missed you last Sunday when you called, partly because you are the first Prohibition Agent that has called on me during my two years in this office."[96]

When, in December 1920, the *Seattle Post-Intelligencer* had made the prediction that few would risk "long chances of punishment" by smuggling liquor across the Canadian-American boundary, the statement was predicated on the belief that American enforcement would present a sufficient deterrent.[97] To the contrary, it seems that the border simply offered too much of an opportunity: it was too porous, enforcement too sparse, and the public too sympathetic. Within only eleven months, the *Post-Intelligencer* had changed its outlook completely. "The American bootlegger is now the best customer British Columbia has," the paper wrote, adding that short of British Columbia going dry, it was likely that "prohibition will continue to be more or less a farce."[98] By the mid-1920s, many in the United States began to consider the possibility that the answer to America's liquor problem was to be found not in its own efforts, but in those of its neighbors to the north.

CHAPTER FIVE

Symbol of Sovereignty

At the very least, borders define citizenship and national sovereignty. Notwithstanding the frequent characterization of the Canada-U.S. border as "undefended," for Canada it has historically stood as a bulwark against American political, economic, or cultural hegemony. Throughout the nineteenth century, the concern for most Canadians centered around maintaining territorial integrity in the face of an increasingly expansive United States. As late as 1911, while debating the merits of the Reciprocity Treaty with the United States, antireciprocity campaigners in Canada received invaluable assistance from blustering Americans who equated trade reciprocity with annexation. Champ Clark, the Speaker-designate of the House of Representatives, proclaimed, "I am for [the Reciprocity Treaty] because I hope to see the day when the American flag will float over every square foot of British North American possessions clear to the North Pole." No less inflammatory were the words of an Illinois congressman who warned his northern neighbors, "Be not deceived. When we go into a country and get control of it, we take it. It is our history and it is right we should take it if we want it and you might as well understand it." Whether annexation weighed voluntarily on the minds of most Canadians or was, as Jack Granatstein argues, a chimera used by elites to maintain their own economic and political power, Canadians have clearly seen the border as serving as the final protector of their sovereignty.[1]

By early 1922 few believed that enforcement of the Eighteenth Amendment could be successful without Canadian assistance. American efforts had proved ineffective, not only because much of the public considered bootlegging a "respectable" crime but also because those charged with enforcing the law were not given the necessary tools to defend the porous, "undefended" border. Barring a change in one or the other, attacking the problem at its source seemed a more promising strategy. Throughout the remainder of the decade, American diplomats made repeated overtures for assistance from the Canadian government. Most were refused. While economics help to explain Canada's lack of interest, achieving Canadian cooperation proved difficult for other reasons as well. Prohibition in the United States, and efforts to persuade Canada to help enforce it, brought to the fore deeply ingrained political and cultural attitudes held by Canadians toward the United States. At a time when Canada was seeking to establish its identity as an independent nation, the border represented the sovereignty so many Canadians sought. Cooperation with the United States would not be a popular option.

EARLY DIPLOMATIC OVERTURES

Initially, the most pressing dilemmas American diplomats faced were the complications that arose when the United States sought to exercise jurisdiction over foreign vessels caught participating in the liquor traffic. Daily, fully loaded ships departed ports in British Columbia in the West, the Maritimes in the East, and the Bahamas in the South, for points along the Pacific, Atlantic, and Gulf coasts. These vendor boats, or "mother vessels," usually remained just outside American territorial waters. From there they transferred their cargoes to the smaller, speedier vessels that assumed the risk of transporting the liquor to land. Because these so-called Rum Rows remained beyond the internationally recognized three-mile limit, nothing they did violated either American or international law. Consequently, any attempts by the United States to enforce Volstead beyond its waters attracted prompt protest from the British and Canadian governments.[2]

To the United States the central objective was to enforce the Eighteenth Amendment by stopping the flow of liquor from Canada. To Great Britain and Canada the issue was more complicated. To the British it was an issue of preserving their rights on the high seas, an issue dear to British governments "from time immemorial."[3] While also concerned about protecting its vessels on the high seas, Canada had even more at stake. Beginning in the 1920s, Canadian external affairs underwent a significant transformation. During the William Lyon Mackenzie King administration, Canada made a concerted effort to define a Canadian foreign policy independent of the British Foreign and Colonial Offices. To do so meant it had to face the United States alone, without compromising its sovereign rights or *amour propre*.[4]

American enforcement required Canadian cooperation on three major fronts. First, the ease with which American boats re-registered as foreign vessels stymied enforcement efforts. Consistent with long-established international practice, American-flagged vessels remained subject to search and seizure by American authorities even on the high seas. Foreign vessels, on the other hand, were subject to this authority only while within three miles of the shore. Realizing this, many American rum boats promptly re-registered as British or Canadian vessels. Second, to prevent the ease with which foreign vessels took refuge beyond the three-mile limit, American diplomats sought to extend that limit to twelve miles. Finally, they hoped to persuade Canada to deny liquor clearances to the United States altogether, on the grounds that liquor exports inherently violated American law. Prohibition Commissioner Roy Haynes believed that if the Dominion agreed to these requests it "would practically control the Canadian border smuggling problem and would prevent the entrance into this country of a very substantial quantity of Canadian liquor."[5]

Accordingly, in June 1922 Secretary of State Charles Evans Hughes petitioned Great Britain and Canada to refuse registry to vessels owned by Americans and requested the extension of the right of search and seizure from three to twelve miles. The first issue did not prove difficult to resolve. Although British and Canadian authorities were initially reluctant to refuse registries to vessels owned by Americans—believing that to do so would place an undue administrative burden on British or Canadian officials—the extent to which American rumrunners abused the protection of the British merchant flag soon awakened their concern. They agreed that a transfer request unaccompanied by a U.S. Shipping Board authorization—which, presumably, rumrunners would be unable to acquire—would place in question the bona fides of those seeking the transfer. In such cases Canadian authorities agreed to forward the requests to the "appropriate" department of the Canadian government. The delay necessitated by this procedure would, in itself, be sufficient to discourage transfer requests.[6]

The second issue proved far more problematic because it threatened to undermine centuries of precedent regarding the rights of search and seizure over foreign vessels. Some Americans, committed to improving the nation's ability to enforce prohibition, believed that the United States should unilaterally extend its right of search and seizure from three to twelve miles. Such advocates pointed out that the significance of three miles was that it had been the distance required for nations to protect their territory against the cannon shot of a foreign enemy. The absurdity of such a policy in 1922—when ships were capable of firing projectiles fifteen to twenty miles—seemed obvious. Nonetheless, Hughes considered the rule, irrespective of origin, "so well established that the United States cannot depart from it, until a general agreement respecting its alteration shall have been reached among the nations of the world." He did concur, though, that exceptions to this policy might be achieved through bilateral agreements with Canada or Great Britain.[7]

When Hughes made such a request in late 1923, Canada immediately recognized the international implications. In light of its desire to act independently on diplomatic issues, it is ironic that Canada chose to defer the issue to Great Britain. However, as Prime Minister Mackenzie King admitted, "We would recognise in a moment that here is something which affects the entire British Empire."[8] Not unexpectedly, the British remained cold to the suggestion. Although Great Britain recognized the obstacles a three-mile limit posed to American enforcement, it was also cognizant that to extend rights of search and seizure to twelve miles—even if limited to vessels involved in liquor trafficking—would "form a precedent for the conclusion of similar treaties until finally the principle would become a dead letter."[9] In the meantime, extending the three-mile limit was out of the question and every questionable seizure by the United States drew immediate protest from London or Ottawa.

Aside from the registry issue and the right of search and seizure, the third issue of most importance to the United States was the Canadian practice of issuing clearances to liquor vessels destined for the United States. Although they intended to violate American law, these vessels broke no Canadian law and so Canadian customs collectors routinely cleared liquor shipments to the United States. Foreshadowing the difficulties this issue would present for the remainder of the decade, the Canadian response to Hughes's request on this matter was prompt and emphatic.[10] Ambassador Sir Auckland Geddes pointed out that, so long as the appropriate duty or bond was paid, the export of liquor broke no Canadian law. Just because the United States prohibited its entry did not warrant the refusal of clearances. To make such a concession would be to imply that it was Canada's responsibility to refuse clearance to any good bound for any port that prohibited its entry. From the Canadian perspective, this would require its customs officers to enforce an American law.[11] Moreover, the Dominion had already instructed its customs officers not to clear liquor except during their official hours and only when it was shipped in bond.[12] As an alternative, the chargé d'affaires at the British Embassy, H. G. Chilton, invited the United States to send a representative to discuss ways Canada might otherwise assist the United States, particularly in the matter of sharing information. Seeing a valuable opportunity to press Canada on other liquor-related issues as well, Hughes agreed to send a representative to Ottawa in November 1923.[13]

Hughes appointed McKenzie Moss, an assistant secretary in the Treasury Department, to lead the American delegation. He instructed Moss to seek Canada's cooperation in a number of areas: first, that the Dominion pass an order-in-council prohibiting the clearance of liquor to the United States; second, that it refuse clearances to all liquor vessels under 250 tons, since (despite claims to the contrary) such vessels were incapable of making voyages to any destination except the United States; and third, short of denying clearances, that Canada notify American officials of all liquor shipments cleared to the United States. On lesser matters, Hughes instructed Moss to secure the right of search and seizure on the Great Lakes, a treaty providing for the extradition of persons apprehended in Canada who were accused of violating American liquor laws, and an arrangement allowing the attendance of Canadian officials as witnesses in American courts.[14]

Hughes understood that the achievement of his goals were unlikely without a concession to Canada. Fortunately, Canada had a concern to which Hughes was willing to concede.[15] Three months earlier Chilton had approached the secretary of state with the request that Canada be allowed to ship liquor across Alaska from Skagway to the Yukon port of Whitehorse. The $75,000 in annual revenue obtained from liquor sales in the Yukon apparently played an important role in financing that territory's government. Under the provisions of the Treaty of Washington of 1871, the United States had conceded to Canada the right to transport liquor into the Yukon via the Yukon River. Since that time transportation from Skagway by land had become a realistic alternative; indeed, at a distance of only twenty-six miles, it had become far superior to the arduous and expensive fifteen-hundred-mile river route.[16] The State Department's initial response had been that it had no authority to grant the Canadian request. As evidence, it pointed to a recent Supreme Court decision, *Cunard Steamship Company, Ltd. v. Mellon*, that prohibited the transport of liquor across any territory of the United States.[17] To Canada, this was a specious argument. Shipment via Skagway, Canada contended, was no different than shipment through the Panama Canal, which the law permitted. Mindful of the validity of this argument, Hughes authorized Moss to offer this concession as a quid pro quo in exchange for Canada's cooperation on the issues important to the United States.[18]

Although Canada was open to the Alaska concession, few of the remaining issues advanced by the United States received a favorable response. Allowing American enforcement officers jurisdiction on the

Canadian portions of the Great Lakes was out of the question, as was the outright denial of all liquor exports to the United States. Chilton saw no point in denying clearances "so long as the American authorities along the border . . . are apparently working hand-in-glove with the liquor smugglers."[19] He pointed out that an already-existing order-in-council prohibited clearances of liquor in vessels under 200 tons and saw little need to increase this limit to 250 tons. On the matter of extradition, the Canadian conferees pointed to a number of difficulties. Not only did American laws denounce as crimes acts that did not constitute offenses under any Canadian law but, more important, most liquor laws in Canada were provincial regulations not subject to Dominion control. Finally, although Canada acknowledged the historical cooperation between customs authorities on both sides of the line, it argued that this collaboration was based merely on friendly relations existing between individual officials and not on any diplomatic arrangement. An agreement mandating cooperation, the Canadian delegation argued, would only place its officers in a difficult position. Since American prohibition began, Canadian officials who furnished information against smugglers had witnessed an increase in attacks against their persons or property.[20] With so little common ground, the conference ended without accord.

Not until the United States reached an agreement with Great Britain in early 1924 did Canada consider concessions of its own. On January 23 British and American representatives finally reached a breakthrough regarding the extension of the right of search and seizure. Although rejecting a twelve-mile limit, Great Britain agreed to raise no objection over seizures beyond three miles provided they were not at a greater distance from the coast than could be traversed in one hour by the rum-runner.[21] As a concession, the United States nullified *Cunard v. Mellon*, thus giving British ships the right to transship liquor to foreign ports through U.S. territory provided that it was kept under seal.[22]

Although the Anglo-American treaty most affected the enforcement against liquor smuggled from the British Bahamas, it also proved significant in that it offered to other nations a precedent for the "one-hour" sailing distance. Most important, it helped to jump-start a Canadian-American agreement. In June 1924 Canada agreed to observe the Anglo-American agreement, with a number of additional provisions. As a concession to nationalists in Parliament, the treaty focused more on commercial smuggling than on liquor. The latter was the United States' problem, not Canada's; both nations, however, had an interest in preventing commercial smuggling. The two nations agreed to share information concerning the clearance of any vessels or vehicles suspected of smuggling; they agreed that clearance would be denied when the vessel in question, regardless of size, clearly could not make the stated destination; they agreed to allow officials from one country to serve as witnesses in official proceedings of the other; and finally, the United States approved the right of Canada to transship liquor across Alaska into the Yukon.[23]

The *Seattle Times* was at once optimistic about the effect this agreement would have on the liquor traffic when it reported, "Puget Sound Booze Fleet Doomed by U.S.-Canada Pact."[24] Few rumrunners spent much time fretting. The only real effect on the liquor traffic was that the treaty required larger vessels to clear from British Columbian ports. Fishermen were happy to pick up the slack with their large fishing vessels, especially during the slow winter months. After these fishing-vessels-turned-rumrunners cleared customs, they simply transferred the liquor to the usual smaller boats. Alternatively, small vessels got around the treaty by carrying shipments ostensibly bound for a coastal port in British Columbia. In these cases, the liquor rarely arrived at the consigned destination. As one rumrunner commented, "I'm sure that if the records for that period were ever examined, places like Bowen Island [British Columbia] would show a per capita alcohol consumption that far exceeded human capability!"[25] Further, the treaty provided little relief for the long land border, which, of course, was not subject to the new "one-hour" limit. As *Maclean's* later pointed out, "No international pact was possible which would push back the jurisdiction of Canadian authority beyond the Dominion's own border."[26] Even more important, the treaty failed to secure the two remaining issues most dear to the United States: that Canada deny all clearances of liquor to the United

States and that Canada agree to extradite those suspected of involvement in liquor smuggling.[27] Although the United States sought to secure these objectives for the remainder of the decade, Canada remained intransigent.

At the heart of this intransigence was the boost the liquor trade gave to the Canadian economy. Because Canada had no legislation curbing rum-running to the United States, and so long as liquor exporters obtained the proper clearance papers and paid the appropriate duties and excise, the Canadian government was willing to look the other way. That the liquor traffic, like tourism, favorably affected Canada's balance of trade was no secret.[28]

It is, of course, impossible to calculate accurately the value of the liquor traffic to the Canadian economy. Smugglers were reluctant to pay the special federal excise of twenty dollars per case on liquor destined for the United States, and so they cleared their cargoes for ports in Mexico, Central America, or South America instead. Thus, even though most of this liquor leaked into the United States rather than going to Latin America, Canadian customs did not characterize it as an export to the United States. Still, from official export figures, one can at least determine the lower limit of Canadian liquor shipped to United States. In 1920 Canada exported only $707,099 worth of alcoholic beverages to the United States. Within only three years, liquor exports increased to $3,178,908, and by 1925, to $11,610,169. These figures continued to increase until, for the last three years of the decade, they routinely exceed $30,000,000 annually.[29]

Benefiting most directly from this trade were Canadian brewers and distillers.[30] Between 1920 and 1929 the number of Canadian breweries increased from fifty-seven to eighty-four and the number of distilleries from ten to twenty-seven. Likewise, the total amount of capital invested in the liquor industry continued to increase significantly throughout the decade. One might attribute the increase to the provinces' abandonment of prohibition during the 1920s in favor of government control. However, the significant increase in production was not matched by a corresponding increase in the apparent consumption of liquor in Canada, which remained essentially flat throughout the decade. Moreover, starting in 1933—the year prohibition ended in the United States—the Canadian liquor industry began to show a significant decline in size and production. The prosperity enjoyed by brewers and distillers, explained the *Daily Province*, was largely due to the "stimulus of the huge liquor trade with Americans."[31]

No less important were the profits reaped by industries providing materials related to brewing and distilling. Throughout the 1920s and early 1930s, the production of Canadian barley, malt, hops, cartons, corks, bottles, barrels, labels, distilling machinery, power, and transportation all experienced growth rates that paralleled the growth of breweries and distilleries. As one example, a burlap dealer in Victoria claimed to have sold over three thousand bags per week to one customer who, like many rumrunners, preferred burlap sacks to wood crates, as the former were much easier to load and unload.[32]

The profits enjoyed by those involved directly or indirectly in the liquor traffic meant that few Canadians were interested in seeing the Dominion prohibit exports to the United States. One Vancouver resident explained, "We have here gentlemen (all Canadians) who have taken up the business of supplying our 'friendly' neighbor with the finest imported liquor at reasonable prices. These men pay customs duties and taxes and in all ways obey the laws of our land besides employing hundreds of citizens of Vancouver where work is sadly needed. Can Vancouver afford to throw away a revenue of this size and incidentally put scores of men out of work to please a few of our narrow-minded bigots and our 'friendly' neighbors who do not even pretend to obey their own laws?"[33] In addition to the stimulus the liquor trade provided to Canadian industry, the Dominion government received considerable income from the liquor traffic. Being one of Canada's largest industries, the distilling and brewing industry paid over $59 million in taxes and duties to the Dominion government in 1929, an amount equivalent to almost one-sixth of federal budgetary revenue.[34] Of that $59 million, over $15 million came from duties and excise collected on liquor exported to the United States. Added to this revenue were the taxes derived from all materials and capital investment that went into the finished product. During the 1920s, as with liquor taxes, customs and excise duties were a particularly important part of the federal government's sources of revenue. Even today they rank behind only income taxes.[35] By cooperating with American enforcement, the Canadian government recognized that it would be undermining the tax revenue the liquor traffic generated.

Prohibition and the liquor industry were also important agents in the expansion of the bureaucratic state in Canada. While most authorities were reluctant to enforce laws that would undermine liquor revenues, they were quick to enforce minor laws that required only the payment of fines — a process that euphemistically came to be known as "licensing by fine." Local municipalities and provincial governments quickly discovered that additional police officers procured additional revenue from such violations. At the federal level, the Dominion added a Preventative Service specifically to attack violations in the liquor trade. Supplementing this agency were the Royal Canadian Mounted Police and customs officers who already combated the traffic. Indeed, more officers at any level meant an increase in net revenue and more opportunities for political patronage.[36]

Both the Dominion and provincial governments refuted persistent attacks claiming that the government was in the liquor business to make as much revenue as possible. They protested in response that revenue was incidental to government policy, not the purpose of it. Nevertheless, it remained the opinion of the American consul in Vancouver that "too much was now at stake from the financial end . . . and that the income derived from the sale of liquor . . . had become part and parcel of the [economy]."[37] Few Canadians failed to recognize that tax revenues collected by the government, though paid by Canadian exporters, originated in the American pocket. In a sense, Americans were subsidizing the Canadian economy. More than one thankful British Columbian enjoyed the irony.[38]

One of the most active opponents of cooperation with the United States was the liquor lobby. Composed primarily of brewers, distillers, and exporters, this lobby tirelessly fought the introduction or passage of any legislation that would have prohibited liquor exports to the United States. The largest liquor exporters in British Columbia, particularly Consolidated Exporters, also sought to minimize the effect of the government's insistence that exporters deposit a cash bond with customs for liquor bound for non-U.S. ports. Although the exporters had no intention of shipping the liquor to the consigned ports, they found the bond an unnecessary hindrance and lobbied aggressively for its elimination.[39]

On occasion American diplomats and enforcement officers sought help directly from Canadian industry. Such overtures usually met with little success, particularly because many of these industries enjoyed close connections to the Dominion government. In one such case in 1927, citing customer confidentiality, the Canadian Pacific Railway refused to provide American customs officers with information on shipments of liquor from Vancouver that landed in the United States. The American consul in Vancouver found the Canadian Pacific's attitude not at all surprising. He predicted that appeals made to the Canadian government to encourage the cooperation of private industry would prove futile. In writing to his superiors, he commented, "The Canadian Pacific Railway is a power in Canada and doubt is expressed if any kind of representation from any official in the Dominion Government on the question of liquor smuggling to the United States would have much weight. This frame of mind is shared to a large extent by many officials in Vancouver whose appointments are more or less political."[40] More than a few advocates of cooperation with the United States wondered whether Canada's staunch attitude against cooperation was the result of large campaign donations that both Liberals and Conservatives received from the liquor industry. Nevertheless, until the full extent of the liquor industry's connection to Canadian politics was uncovered by the royal commission investigation in 1926 and 1927, most Canadians did not feel it was government's role to interfere with what was then considered a legitimate Canadian enterprise.[41]

American efforts to secure British Columbia's cooperation in enforcement also involved federal-provincial political difficulties. Broadly

speaking, the Dominion alone had the authority to prohibit the manufacture or export of liquor, while either a province or the Dominion
could prohibit the sale for local consumption.[42] Consequently, export
houses sprang up all along the British Columbia–U.S. border. Though
the province could raise annual license fees on the export houses, it
otherwise exercised no control over them.[43]

Even local governments worked at cross-purposes with Dominion
and provincial governments. When Dominion and provincial authorities agreed to share in the spoils of the liquor trade, they usually left
local municipalities out in the cold. Unable to derive revenue from
most liquor violations themselves, municipalities were understandably
reluctant to assist in the enforcement of either Dominion or provincial
law. Instead, they chose to prosecute offenders under lesser, municipal
codes. Repeat "first-time" offenders were released with minimal municipal sanction, free to be fined again later.[44] It made no sense to seriously
hinder American rumrunners, who provided a tidy bit of revenue to
local hotels, restaurants, garages, or other establishments.

AFFRONTS TO CANADIAN SOVEREIGNTY

Prior to the mid-twenties, Canadian sentiment toward cooperation
with U.S. enforcement remained fairly uniform across the Dominion.
The profits to be had in the liquor traffic no doubt contributed to this
widespread support. Yet no matter how significant profit was to Canada's
unwillingness to prohibit clearances of liquor and to otherwise assist in
American enforcement, to focus exclusively on economics is to overlook
other factors that were equally important. The Canadian reaction to
prohibition in the United States provides a unique window into how
Canadians and Americans viewed each other and their respective political and cultural systems.

For many Canadians, a primary obstacle to cooperating with the
United States was the Eighteenth Amendment itself. As the decade
progressed, and as each of the other provinces followed Quebec's and
British Columbia's lead in abandoning provincial prohibition in favor
of government control, many Canadians were wont to look upon the

American system with a certain smugness. One letter to the *Victoria Daily Colonist* questioned, "The Dominion of Canada . . . by an overwhelming majority has dropped prohibition and gone wet. Are the people of Canada who made this change one whit less intelligent than the people of the USA?"[45] There were good reasons Canadians had chosen government control. For a moderate, temperate people—a description Canadians often assigned themselves—government control was quite sensible. It spared the public the horrors of complete (or American) prohibition, such as sudden death from poisoned liquor and unpopular, corrupt enforcement officials. As the *Vancouver Sun* observed, "The liquor legislation of the United States is based on the assumption of a morally perfect public. It is based on conditions as they should be, not on conditions as they are. Laws are only enforceable in so far as they reflect the will of the people. Lawlessness occurs when legal evolution gets too far ahead of moral evolution in the individual. Rum-running into the United States has been started because American liquor legislation is more advanced than the average morals of the American people."[46]

The root of America's prohibition problems, according to some Canadians, lay not in the lack of Canadian assistance but in a fundamental deficiency in the American character. America's problems were reflections of its historical tendency to pass laws regulating national morality. To many Canadians, this seemed a foreign concept. "The Americans," wrote the *Canadian Forum*, "believe their souls can be saved by prohibitory laws. With Canadians it is not so. . . . We do not believe that there can be salvation by legislation for anyone, anywhere, any time."[47] Even more incredible, the United States had inflexibly constitutionalized its form of prohibition, rather than leaving it to the people to accept, reject, or modify it according to regional values. Such an approach reaffirmed an attitude already deeply ingrained in the Canadian national psyche, that the Canadian political system was far more responsive to the ebb and flow of public thought than the United States.' The Eighteenth Amendment was an ill-conceived law that was unenforceable from the start.[48]

The *New York Times* was quick to pick up on widespread Canadian sentiment that opposed helping to enforce an unpopular American law:

"Why should Canada, it is asked, concern itself with this purely domestic American problem, and make a crime out of what is now legitimate trading on this side of the line when ... millions of Americans break the prohibition law daily and even men in important official posts seem to show no particular solicitude for it?"[49] The *Toronto Saturday Night* even quipped that "if Canada desires to make herself unpopular with the influential and powerful people of the United States, the 'governing classes' so to speak, the best way to go about it would be to put an embargo on liquor exports to the United States."[50] The basis of rum-running was not Canadian cupidity but American thirst.[51]

The American consul in Victoria discovered widespread local opinion that American officials were only halfhearted in their efforts to curtail the traffic. Canadians understood that Congress perennially appropriated only meager sums for enforcement, that most states and localities rarely shouldered their part of the enforcement burden, and that local customs and attitudes shaped the extent to which prohibition laws were enforced.[52] As the *Ottawa Journal* reported, "Everybody knows—it is part of the record—that prohibition enforcement in the United States has been honeycombed with corruption, with sinister politics, with indifference, with plain crime and with inefficiency."[53] This situation prompted the *Journal* to headline an editorial, "U.S. Enforcement, Like Charity, Should Begin at Home."[54]

Many Canadians were reluctant to expend resources helping the United States because the idea smacked of Canadian enforcement of an American law. It was not Canada's responsibility to help the United States enforce a law that the Dominion itself had refused to copy.[55] Such Canadians bristled at the possibility that Ottawa would give in to American pressure. The *Toronto Mail and Empire* reminded the government in Ottawa that it was in office to administer the laws of Canada, not those of the United States.[56] One British Columbian complained, "Uncle Sam, with his usual greed, having bitten off more than he can chew with his Eighteenth Amendment, is using his influence with our government at Ottawa and getting his work done at our expense."[57] The *Canadian Forum* added, "If they can prove their sincerity by a thorough cleaning up of their own preventative service (whose corruption is notorious), we feel sure they will find our authorities ready to help them by further cooperation to any reasonable extent."[58]

Nevertheless, it seems that at least initially the Dominion made a good-faith effort to at least uphold its end of the 1924 treaty with the United States. Whenever customs officers cleared liquor destined for United States ports, they usually phoned their American counterparts informing them of the names of the vessels and their captains. In the case of shipments by land, Canadian officers often gave American officials information regarding where the smuggled liquor could be confiscated on U.S. territory. Not all American officers were receptive to this assistance. One Canadian customs agent reported to his supervisor that his opposite number on the American side had requested that he stop making phone calls about impending shipments and instead send a report once a week. Whether this was because the American officer was overwhelmed by paperwork or simply wanted to be able to look the other way is unclear. In defense of American officers, many had become somewhat cynical about the information provided. It seems that an inordinate number of the vessels cleared from one border point were named "*Daisy*" and their skippers, "Bill Smith." Whatever the reason, in response to incidents such as these, the ardor of Canadian officials cooled somewhat in the matter of helping their American counterparts.[59]

A Vancouver resident questioned whether, if the situation were reversed, the United States would jump at the opportunity to help Canada enforce an unpopular Canadian law. He saw no reason to treat the United States as a "friendly" neighbor. "Why call a nation friendly," he commented, "that pushed back our boundary from the Columbia River to the 49th parallel, shoved the Alaskan boundary in 30 miles, stole the island of San Juan and worst of all, looked on with indifference while our good men died like flies and, in the meantime, gathered in the shekels?"[60] While this person reflected the most extreme of opinions against cooperation with the United States, particularly in British Columbia, the sentiments he expressed were symbolic of those expressed by many concerned that Canada might bow to the wishes of its domineering, insensitive neighbor.

Not uncommon was it for Canadians to remember the United States' belated participation in the First World War, its unwillingness to support and join the League of Nations, or its characteristic lack of interest in issues important to Canadians.[61] Canadian editors recognized the irony that, while foreign entanglements frightened the United States, it hadn't the "slightest hesitancy in inviting outside nations to get caught up in [its] own barbed-wire of prohibition legislation."[62] As the nationalist *Toronto Mail and Empire* commented, "Canada would show itself to be a simpleton in the family of nations into which it has recently been adopted if it entered into any engagement to help make the United States dry."[63]

Many dry Americans found the lack of cooperation from Canada infuriating. Rum-running, they argued, did not constitute, by any stretch of the imagination, a respectable business, and the fact that the Dominion enabled this traffic was less than neighborly at best, criminal at worst.[64] One editor turned the situation around when he commented on the smuggling of goods north: "Will they be content when we tell them that the violators of their excise laws are innocent under ours and that they cannot expect us to interfere with such activities? We have heard that more than once from Canada ... and thought it a poor plea to come from friends."[65] Playing on the incessant Canadian fear of cultural intrusion, the *New York Times* even suggested an appropriate form of reciprocity: "As Canada bootlegs rum to us, we could bootleg literature to Canada."[66]

At the same time, many other Americans found asking Canada to enforce an American law at least somewhat troubling. If Canada had refused to export liquor to the United States, it is likely that the Dominion would have been deluged by liquor violators as well. It would be more useful, many suggested, for the United States to prevent rum vessels from clearing U.S. ports in the first place. Asking Canada to do what the United States did not do first seemed hypocritical. Fiorello LaGuardia, the feisty congressman from New York, once grumbled that there had never been "a more outrageous, cheap proposition in the history of the world."[67]

The excesses of American enforcement, however, were what united the majority of Canadians against cooperating with the United States. When in 1924 and early 1925 the U.S. Coast Guard seized a number of Canadian vessels under questionable circumstances, it flirted with an easily aroused Canadian nationalism and helped to solidify Canadian intransigence.

On October 24, 1924, the U.S. Coast Guard cutter *Shawnee* seized the *Quadra* as the latter discharged liquor to speedboats off the California coast. The 175-foot, 573-ton Canadian-registered rumrunner had originally served as a lighthouse tender when it arrived from Scotland in 1892. It had later doubled as a fisheries patrol vessel and a survey platform until damaged in a collision with a Canadian Pacific Railway steamer at Nanaimo in 1917. Repaired and purchased by Consolidated Exporters, the *Quadra* then commenced a successful career as a rumrunner. When the *Quadra* departed Vancouver with a forty-thousand-case cargo in September 1924 it had complied with Canadian law by depositing the requisite bond of forty dollars per case, declaring the cargo bound for La Libertad, San Salvador.[68]

The *Shawnee* brought the *Quadra* to San Francisco, where the crew was tried for conspiracy to violate the Eighteenth Amendment. Although most Canadians did not challenge the right of the United States to seize vessels within the one-hour's sailing distance specified in the 1924 treaty, a number of facts regarding the case aroused concern in British Columbia. Apparently, a Rum Row rival of Consolidated Exporters had paid Charles F. Howell, the captain of the *Shawnee*, $20,000 to seize the *Quadra*, regardless of whether it was inside or outside the one-hour limit. Consolidated in turn paid Howell another $20,000 to lie about the incident in court. Howell was eventually court-martialed for perjury and lost his command. Even though the actual position of the *Quadra* at the time of seizure could not be accurately determined, the judge ruled in favor of the Coast Guard and sentenced the *Quadra*'s captain with a fine and two years in jail. Twelve other defendants were given jail time, most of whom jumped bail and returned to Canada.[69]

The story did not end there. As per its usual agreements with its rumrunners, Consolidated Exporters sent Frederick R. Anderson to San Francisco to serve as the crew's lawyer. When Anderson arrived in San Francisco, prohibition authorities promptly arrested him. They contended that Anderson, as counsel for Consolidated, was a party to the alleged crime and was therefore subject to arrest. Locking up a Canadian attorney quickly attracted the denunciation of the San Francisco Bar, and it aroused even greater protests from Canada. Twenty-thousand British Columbians petitioned the action, protesting that Anderson had come to San Francisco to represent his clients and should be immune from this excessive display of prosecutorial exuberance. The premier of British Columbia promptly urged the Dominion government to negotiate no new agreements with the United States pending an apology. In the meantime, Anderson promptly jumped bail himself and returned to Vancouver. Federal judge John S. Partridge cited this as yet "another illustration of the cynical disrespect for the laws of the United States." He then doubled the bail on all of the other defendants in the case.[70]

As with the *Quadra* case, British Columbia's response to another seizure turned not on the legal merits of the seizure but on the subsequent treatment of the accused. In February 1925 the American steamer *Caoba*, with a cargo of lumber and a crew of eighteen, encountered stormy weather off the Washington-Oregon coast. The severity of the storm caused the vessel to ground near the mouth of the Columbia River, driving the crew to take refuge on the vessel's two lifeboats. After laying adrift for two days, the *Caoba*'s crew was spotted and rescued by the rumrunner *Pescawha*, under the command of Robert Pamphlet.

By all accounts, Pamphlet was an agreeable man, well liked by all with whom he came in contact. Unfortunately, neither Pamphlet's amiability nor his rescue of the *Caoba*'s crew meant much to the captain of the Coast Guard cutter *Algonquin*. While searching for a vessel reportedly adrift at sea, the captain later testified, he had sighted the Canadian-registered *Pescawha* heading due westward, still inside American waters. Believing the *Pescawha* to be a rumrunner, the *Algonquin* commenced pursuit and eventually overtook the *Pescawha* approximately sixteen miles off the Washington coast. After discovering 1,073 cases of liquor, the Coast Guard arrested the crew and towed the *Pescawha* to Astoria, Oregon.[71]

The *Pescawha* had cleared from Vancouver in November 1924. Because of its small, one-hundred-ton size, the schooner was ineligible to clear for any but coastwise destinations and so had cleared for Cape Scott on the northwestern tip of Vancouver Island. Instead, it appears that Captain Pamphlet proceeded directly south. In the ensuing two months, the rum-runner delivered liquor to a number of vessels off the Washington and Oregon coasts. After the *Algonquin* seized the *Pescawha*, Pamphlet made no effort to argue that the *Pescawha* had not been in American waters. According to him, the *Pescawha* was en route to Ensenada, Mexico, and had entered American waters only in response to the *Caoba*'s distress.[72]

Evidence suggested otherwise. Food and other provisions found during the seizure were insufficient to last the crew more than two weeks. Portland newspapers found on the *Pescawha* indicated that the vessel, contrary to Pamphlet's assertion, had made contact with land on a number of occasions prior to the seizure. Accordingly, the U.S. District Court in Oregon doubted that the *Pescawha* was bound for any Mexican port. In the end, it found Pamphlet and his crew guilty, fined the captain $10,000, and sentenced him to two years' imprisonment at the federal penitentiary at McNeil Island.[73]

Although circumstantial evidence suggested that the *Pescawha* may have been outside the one-hour limit when the *Algonquin* commenced pursuit, to most Canadians—and to many Americans as well—the vessel's position was irrelevant and soon forgotten.[74] According to the letter of the law, few doubted that Pamphlet's conviction was justified. Yet the matter was more than one of simple legality. The *Pescawha* would not have been seized had it not gone to the rescue of another ship in distress. To a great majority of British Columbians, the special circumstances of Pamphlet's case entitled him to special consideration. Pamphlet had been captured, the *Vancouver Daily Province* argued, not because he was unlucky, unskillful, or inexperienced but because he was "a gallant seaman and a humane man."[75]

Even the vast majority of Americans sympathized with Pamphlet's plight. So outraged was one American after hearing of Pamphlet's treatment that he decried, "I cannot believe that my country could be guilty of base ingratitude."[76] The *Portland Spectator* promptly demanded that Pamphlet be pardoned. On behalf of the crew, the city of Portland awarded Pamphlet a gold watch bearing the inscription, "Captain Robert

Pamphlet, a true sailor, in recognition of his action in rescuing the crew of our *S.S. Caoba* at sea, February 3, 1925."[77] A crew member rescued from the *Caoba* mused with regret, "We cannot help but feel that they are now prisoners because of their humanity to us."[78]

Many, forgetting that Pamphlet was a rumrunner, continued to hold the opinion that he never should have been convicted. Many more believed that, having been convicted, he should have been pardoned. During the four years following the *Pescawha*'s seizure, the Canadian legation at Washington repeatedly agitated for Pamphlet's release. Although admitting that public sympathy for Pamphlet did not in any way mitigate his guilt as a rumrunner, the Canadian minister pointed out that substantial sentiment in the western part of Canada, as well as in the bordering American states, supported leniency for the "heroic" Pamphlet. After the Coolidge administration proved unresponsive to these requests, many held out hope that an appeal by the British Columbia attorney general might convince the new president, Herbert Hoover, to grant Pamphlet executive clemency.[79] Appeals by the province's attorney general and by the Canadian legation in Washington proved futile. Pamphlet served his entire term at McNeil Island before his release in August 1929.[80]

During the early years of the 1920s, most British Columbians seem to have agreed with most Canadians that cooperation with the United States was not in their best interests. Too much was at stake diplomatically, economically, politically, and even culturally to acquiesce to American demands. Canada's newfound sovereignty could hardly be sacrificed at the altar of American interests. While the Dominion as a whole would continue to hold to this philosophy until 1930, British Columbia had reason to question Canada's role in the liquor traffic much earlier. Two events—a particularly brutal hijacking of a British Columbian rumrunner and three months of royal commission hearings—would expose the rotten underbelly of rum-running in the Northwest. British Columbians began to recognize that rum-running profits were not to be had for free. They came with a price that imperiled the otherwise peaceful North Pacific borderlands.

CHAPTER SIX

The *Beryl G* (and Second Thoughts)

It was a clear morning in September 1924 when Chris Waters, the lighthouse keeper for Turn Point, Stuart Island, surveyed the waters from his perch on the American side of the Haro Strait. Scattered around him in all directions were the Gulf and San Juan Islands that dotted the waters between British Columbia and the United States. To the southwest, not more than ten miles distant, lay Victoria. Glancing toward the northeast he sighted a small boat about one-half mile out, drifting on the tide. With the help of William Erickson, the husband of the postmistress at Prevost, a small town on the east side of the island, Waters set off to recover the vessel, suspecting that it was a fishing boat that had broken free of its moorings. As they approached the drifting craft, both men noticed the name, *Beryl G*, painted on its bow. Finding it abandoned, they towed it to Prevost Harbor for closer inspection.

Not until they boarded the *Beryl G* at Prevost did Waters or Erickson suspect something was amiss. Bearing traces of recent habitation, the boat also showed obvious signs that a struggle had occurred on board. Dirty dishes and a frying pan littered the galley and what appeared to be a bullet hole punctured the companionway door. Strewn about the cabin floor were a linen cap, bedclothes, and a recent issue of *Adventure* magazine, each soaked or strewn with congealed blood. Blood stains also marred the lockers, a settee, and the galley stove, as well as the vessel's deck, hatch covers, and starboard bulwarks. From the companionway door a scarlet trail meandered to the bow, where a bloody mass of clothes lay in a heap. Conspicuously absent were firearms, money, liquor, and the ship's anchor. Finding the vessel's papers, Waters discovered that the *Beryl G* was Canadian, registered to one William Gillis of Vancouver.

The vessel was of Canadian registry and its missing crew—Captain Gillis and his seventeen-year-old son, William Jr.—were Canadian. Prevailing winds and tides made it almost certain that whatever had transpired before the empty boat found its way to Stuart Island must have occurred on the Canadian side of the border. With the Canadian elements of the mystery clear, Waters immediately contacted the Coast Guard, who in turn notified the British Columbia Provincial Police.[1]

Although Waters did not yet realize it, what he had stumbled upon would become one of the most sensational murder mysteries in the history of British Columbia. Over the course of the next eighteen months the attention of British Columbians and Americans in the Northwest remained riveted on the case of the *Beryl G*.[2] The criminal investigation, the extradition of the accused from the United States, and the subsequent trial in Victoria would have significant implications, not only for those involved in the case but for British Columbian–American relations as well. The cooperation that British Columbian and American officials exercised during the investigation and extradition phases of the case was characteristic of the day-to-day relations between Canada and the United States—more so perhaps than were the activities of diplomats in Ottawa and Washington DC. Moreover, the case of the *Beryl G* brought into sharp and immediate contrast the Canadian and American justice systems and, along with a customs scandal investigation that shortly followed, forced many British Columbians to rethink their role in a liquor traffic that was quickly spiraling out of control. Rum-running threatened to injure more than Canadian-American relations. It had turned the border region into a dangerous, almost literal, abyss that threatened the fabric of British Columbian society.

When news of the *Beryl G*'s fate reached Victoria, the British Columbia Provincial Police commissioner assigned Inspector Forbes Cruickshank to the case. Cruickshank was a natural choice. Born and bred in Scotland, Cruickshank had served with the Dundee police before arriving in Canada. Sent west with the North-West Mounted Police, he later settled in Vancouver, where he worked in the Criminal Investigative Division of the Provincial Police. For months prior to the *Beryl G* incident, he had worked jointly with American police to break up a narcotics ring operating in the Puget Sound and Gulf of Georgia.[3] He was, as one colleague remembered with some reverence, "a policeman and nothing else."[4]

Cruickshank quickly discovered that the *Beryl G*, though registered as a fish packer, was commonly known to run liquor. Since detectives had found neither liquor, money, nor the crew, Cruickshank suspected this was another hijacking. He had seen them before. So common were hijackings during prohibition that coastal residents routinely awakened to the sound of shots emanating from the surrounding waters. Once robbed of their cargo, most rumrunners were reluctant to file a complaint with police, knowing that the law had little sympathy for a "cheater who had been cheated by a cheater."[5] Their only recourse was armor plating and machine guns, more to protect themselves from hijackers than from police. During the early days of rum-running, the otherwise-legitimate runner had more to fear from the hijacker than he did from all law enforcement efforts combined.[6]

The trail of blood leading to the ship's side in conjunction with the missing anchor suggested that the crew had been killed, tied to the anchor, and thrown overboard. Beyond that, Cruickshank had little to go on. The police had found a camera and an expensive gold-trimmed yachting cap. The latter was not a type common to rumrunners and not one that friends of Captain Gillis remembered him to have worn. The camera's film, with one frame exposed, revealed the *Beryl G* alongside the stern of another vessel, the *M493*. When a search of Canadian registries failed to account for the *M493*'s ownership, Cruickshank decided that the Seattle waterfront was the most likely place to begin. For the next two months he worked in close collaboration with the sheriff of King County, Washington, Matt Starwich.[7] After weeks of fruitless searching, they finally stumbled upon a reference to the vessel in the Lake Union lock records, identifying the *M493* as a fifty-six footer owned by Pete Marinoff of Tacoma, Washington. Powered by twin three-hundred-horsepower Liberty engines, the vessel was obviously involved in the liquor trade. And its owner, as almost everyone knew, was a rumrunner.

Known in the rum-running fraternity as "Legitimate Pete," because he confined his illicit activities to running liquor, Marinoff was to bootlegging in the Tacoma region what Roy Olmstead was to bootlegging in Seattle. He was not particularly hard to find, since rumrunners who broke no Canadian law had nothing to fear from Canadian authorities. Moreover, because of the hazard posed by hijackers, legitimate runners were more than happy (under the right circumstances) to assist the police. When Cruickshank caught up to him, Marinoff confirmed that he had indeed hired the *Beryl G* to buy 350 cases of liquor from the *Comet*, one of the "mother ships" that operated off the west coast of Vancouver Island. The *Beryl G*, in turn, distributed liquor to the even smaller, speedier American vessels like the *M493*.[8]

Marinoff confided that he had arranged for the *M493* to meet the *Beryl G* off Sidney Island, located about fifteen miles northeast of Victoria on the Canadian side, and take the liquor in two loads. According to plan, early on the evening of September 15, 1924, Marinoff's crew met Gillis and his son on the northeast side of the island. For the first load of 110 cases of gin and scotch they paid $28 per case, or $3,080. When the *M493* returned for the second load, the *Beryl G* was nowhere to be found. Beyond this, Marinoff professed to know little about the *Beryl G*'s fate but suggested that Cruickshank talk to one Al Clausen, the owner of an auto repair shop in Seattle.[9]

It turned out that Clausen also owned a boat, the *Dolphin*, which he hired out to rumrunners. Clausen informed Cruickshank that, shortly after the *Beryl G* turned up on Stuart Island, three men had approached him about retrieving liquor at Sidney Island. Clausen identified the three as Owen Baker, Charles Morris, and Harry Sowash. Clausen had not suspected *Beryl G* liquor was involved until the third trip, when Baker bragged that he had stolen it from William Gillis. Baker told Clausen that he had put Gillis and his son ashore on Halibut Island.[10]

Although Cruickshank now had three names, he still had no bodies. A search of Halibut Island for Gillis and his son turned up nothing, as did a month of extensive dragging operations around the island conducted by the British Columbia Hydrographic Department. Without a body or an eyewitness, Cruickshank knew that even proving a murder had occurred would be difficult.[11]

Meanwhile, as Inspector Cruickshank continued his work with Sheriff Starwich in Washington, Sergeant Robert Owen of the Provincial Police uncovered an important clue of his own. A boat builder at Oak Bay reported being commissioned to alter the appearance of the *Denman No. II*, just days after the *Beryl G* appeared at Stuart Island. Considering it a long shot, Owen nevertheless tracked down the *Denman*'s owner, an admitted beer runner from Victoria named Paul Strompkins. Although Strompkins denied any knowledge of the *Beryl G*, or of Baker, Sowash, or Morris, he did not convince Sergeant Owen. Needing someone to contradict Strompkins's story, Owen painstakingly canvassed his contacts and informants among the islands. Eventually he found Thorston Paulson. Paulson admitted knowing Strompkins and confessed that together they had, along with Baker, Sowash, and Morris, sacked liquor at Paulson's home on Moresby Island. When Owen confronted Strompkins with Paulson's testimony, Strompkins confessed. He admitted he had been at Sidney Island when the *Beryl G* was hijacked and that Gillis and his son had been killed. However, the brutal murders, Strompkins claimed, were the handiwork of Baker, Sowash, and Morris.[12]

The police still lacked the bodies, but they finally had a witness. The Washington police quickly found Morris in Seattle and promised to do all they could to facilitate his extradition to British Columbia. Baker and Sowash, however, were nowhere to be found. Rumors circulating along the Seattle waterfront suggested they had fled upon hearing of Strompkins's interrogation. On November 27, 1924, British Columbia issued warrants for Baker and Sowash in both Canada and the United States and posted a $4,000 reward for their capture.[13]

Morris, Baker, and Sowash were likely suspects, each of whom had a criminal record. Charles Morris had the shortest one, having served four months in the Pierce County jail for passing counterfeit coins in 1914.[14] Owen Benjamin "Cannonball" Baker's record was longer. Baker had served time at McNeil Island Penitentiary for violations of the Mann Act, which outlawed white slavery, for assault, and for grand larceny. The latter charge stemmed from a 1921 hijacking of a bootlegger in the south Puget Sound. (Coincidentally, that bootlegger had been none other than Pete Marinoff, who had enough friends among the local authorities to have Baker charged with larceny. Whether Marinoff knew of Baker's involvement in the *Beryl G* hijacking when he talked to Forbes Cruickshank is unknown, but it appears likely that he had his suspicions.) It was at McNeil Island that Baker, before being paroled in June 1924, met Harry Sowash.[15] Sowash, whose real name was Harrison F. Myers, had served in the U.S. Army during the war before being sentenced to his term at McNeil. Although he liked to claim that his imprisonment was for hitting an officer with a shovel, it was really for stealing and selling military aircraft parts. While out on parole, he was arrested again for burglary and confined to the U.S. Disciplinary Barracks at Alcatraz, California. Transferred back to McNeil in October 1921, Sowash was finally released on August 12, 1924, only one month before the *Beryl G* incident.[16]

Finding Baker and Sowash proved easier than Cruickshank and Owen had anticipated. The size of the reward, it seems, proved a stimulus to police everywhere. Baker had fled to New York, where he secured employment on a harbor dredging barge under the alias of George Nolan. In late December 1924, operating on a tip from Seattle police, New York detectives arrested Baker at the South Ferry Hotel. Within days, Inspector W. R. Dunwoody of the British Columbia Provincial Police was in New York to begin the extradition process.[17]

Only by a strange twist of fate did British Columbia police locate Sowash. Far away in New Orleans, in one of their routine roundups of the

French Quarter, police brought in a number of individuals for questioning. Among them was a dapper young man who, showing remarkable nerve, said that he had recently arrived from San Francisco and was on his way to South America. Satisfying the police, who had no reason to hold him, the man casually left the station without further hindrance. Though he could not pin it down, one detective had found something familiar in the face of this man. Deciding to peruse photos in the police circulars that littered his desk, the detective soon discovered that the face belonged to a Harry Sowash, who was wanted for murder in British Columbia. The detectives raced to the New Orleans waterfront just in time to catch Sowash boarding a freighter for Mexico. The British Columbia attorney general promptly ordered Inspector Thomas Parsons to New Orleans to facilitate Sowash's extradition.[18]

Even though rum-running was not an extraditable offense under any Canadian-American treaty, murder and hijacking were. On December 24, 1924, the Canadian government made formal requests for the extradition of Baker and Sowash through the British Embassy. The proceedings proved fairly routine. Though initially vowing to fight extradition to "the last ditch," Baker soon waived his rights to counsel and consented to his return to British Columbia for trial. Already a celebrity when he arrived in Victoria in late February, the infamous "Cannonball" Baker attracted throngs of spectators hoping to catch a glimpse of him at the police station. Though Sowash did not contest his extradition, it followed the same pattern as Baker's. The U.S. marshal at New Orleans released Sowash to Inspector Parsons on February 25 and Sowash arrived in Victoria a few days after Baker.[19] In accordance with the extradition treaty of 1902, the United States billed Canada $68.32 to cover American costs in the Baker matter and $39.50 for Sowash.[20]

Already in Seattle, Cruickshank took the lead in organizing the extradition of the third suspect, Charles Morris. The attorney general of British Columbia appointed Bert Ross, an American attorney, to assist Cruickshank and to represent the Canadian government in the extradition proceedings.[21] Choosing to fight extradition, Morris's defense filed a writ of habeas corpus. It pointed out that an American attorney (not a

Canadian prosecutor) had filed the extradition complaint and that the commissioner hearing the case was a Washington State Superior Court judge (not a federal official) acting in a Washington State (not a federal) court. The Constitution, they argued, did not give Congress the power to confer federal powers onto state courts. Thus the state of Washington had no authority to serve as the extraditing court. Further, that a King County sheriff (not federal officers) had arrested and imprisoned Morris suggested false imprisonment. Although the judge determined that the Canadian government had shown sufficient cause for Morris's extradition and ordered him extradited, Morris's writ required the case be advanced to the U.S. District Court of Appeals. After a second appeal, it went to the Ninth Circuit Court in San Francisco.[22]

As the months passed, prosecutors in British Columbia became increasingly concerned that the delay in the Morris extradition might threaten their cases against Baker and Sowash. The Canadian government made repeated appeals through the State Department requesting that the Ninth Circuit Court expedite the case. While Secretary of State Hughes remained sympathetic to the Canadian position, he nevertheless informed the British ambassador that Morris could not be extradited until the court proceedings were complete. By late spring, having despaired of securing Morris from the United States, British Columbia proceeded with its case against Baker and Sowash by setting a trial date of June 15.[23]

TRIAL AND CONVICTION

The public eagerly anticipated hearing the lurid details of the crime that was quickly becoming the most celebrated of British Columbia's history. They did not have long to wait, for the trial proceeded with a rapidity that startled those not familiar with the Canadian justice system. One American attorney who came to see the trial was shocked when he learned that the jury would be chosen and the trial under way all in one day.[24]

Outside the courthouse, crowds milled about, hoping to find a seat should anyone leave. Inside, in the prisoner's dock sat Baker and Sowash, and on the witness stand, Paul Strompkins, on whom the prosecution's case rested. Strompkins had turned king's evidence in return for a dismissal of the charges against him, and the story he told was a damning one. At numerous times during his testimony, on the verge of hysterical breakdown and overcome by sobs that convulsed his body, Strompkins had to pause. Gathering himself, he presented to the court the details of the events leading to the murders. The story began in early September 1924, when Baker hired Strompkins and his boat, the *Denman No. II*. Baker claimed he had a contract for $25,000 to produce a rum-running film for a Hollywood moving-picture company. The contract required him to secure film footage of rumrunners operating in the Puget Sound. As Strompkins later discovered, the idea of the film contract was simply a blind devised to lure his participation in a less innocent plot: looting liquor caches hidden by rumrunners among the coastal islands.[25]

As Strompkins continued, the scheme that unfolded became increasingly sophisticated. The liquor they intended to steal had not been chosen at random. Baker had enlisted the cooperation of a corrupt Seattle police detective, Sergeant John Majewski. Majewski was to secure information from the British Columbia police regarding the whereabouts of suspected liquor caches among the Gulf and San Juan Islands. His contact in British Columbia, Constable William Hatcher, had intimated knowledge of liquor locations as well as an interest in forming a partnership. Believing that he was dealing with a coconspirator, Majewski agreed to meet Hatcher in early September at the Strathcona Hotel in Victoria. According to Strompkins, when Majewski returned from that meeting on September 7, he held a list noting locations where liquor could be found. What Majewski did not know was that Hatcher was part of a sting operation and that the locations given were false.[26]

The nonexistence of the caches was most unfortunate for the crew of the *Beryl G*. As Baker, Sowash, Morris, and Strompkins futilely plied the waters in the *Denman No. II*, they became increasingly frustrated. Baker, the self-appointed leader of the expedition, decided on another strategy. At numerous times during the previous week, they had observed the *Beryl G* near Sidney Island. Baker knew the *Beryl G* was working for Marinoff. Ever since Baker had been sent to prison on the basis of Marinoff's testimony in 1921, he had waited for an opportunity to settle the score. Hijacking the *Beryl G*, he decided, would be appropriate retribution.[27]

As midnight approached on September 15, Baker, Sowash, and Morris left the *Denman No. II* in a small skiff and quietly rowed to the *Beryl G*, at anchor in a cove on Sidney Island. Morris was wearing a yachting cap embroidered with gold trim and a jacket adorned with gold buttons—a costume designed to suggest to Gillis and his son that they were being boarded by revenue enforcement officers. Strompkins testified that he heard two shots fifteen minutes later. When Morris returned after a few minutes, he told Strompkins, "We had to shoot the old man—we had to shoot him in the arm." As he pulled alongside the *Beryl G* to transfer the liquor, Strompkins discovered the truth. He arrived just in time to see Sowash club the younger Gillis to death. Baker and Sowash then dragged the boy, and the lifeless body of the elder Gillis (obviously shot in more than just the arm) to the vessel's side. They shook hands in mutual congratulation before Baker handcuffed the bodies to the vessel's anchor, slit both bodies open with a butcher knife, and dumped them over the side. Later that night the group cached the *Beryl G*'s liquor nearby and proceeded to Anacortes, Washington.[28]

Both Baker and Sowash adamantly denied Strompkins's version of the story. Knowing that rum-running violated no Canadian law, Baker wisely refrained from denying his participation in the liquor traffic, but he denied altogether any knowledge of the *Beryl G*. For his part, Sowash blamed the deaths on Baker and Morris but otherwise affirmed Strompkins's story. One by one, witnesses called by the prosecution also corroborated Strompkins's testimony. Earl Whitcomb, an Anacortes bootlegger, testified that he had bought five cases of liquor from Baker, each in burlap sacks and marked according to brand with green paint. It was the same burlap and green paint, Thorston Paulson testified, in which he had sacked the liquor with Baker, Sowash, and Morris just days after the *Beryl G*'s hijacking. The sacks contained the same brands of liquor, Pete Marinoff testified, that the *Beryl G* was to have purchased from the *Comet*. Prosecutors tied Baker and Sowash not only to the liquor but to physical evidence found aboard the *Beryl G* as well. After a tireless investigation along the Seattle waterfront, Forbes Cruickshank had finally found Harold Kerrigan, a clothing salesman who testified that he had sold Baker the gold-trimmed naval cap that was found bloodstained on the *Beryl G*'s deck.[29]

On June 19, 1925, after only three days of hearings, the jury found Owen Baker and Harry Sowash guilty and the judge sentenced both to death by hanging. Though the *Victoria Daily Times* immediately proclaimed it the "most sensational trial in the history of B.C.," the case was not entirely finished. Baker and Sowash immediately appealed their verdicts and, since the Court of Appeals would not meet until October, they received temporary reprieves. On October 20 the appeals court affirmed the convictions, leaving the fate of Baker and Sowash to the Supreme Court of Canada.[30] Meanwhile, the Crown's case against Charles Morris proceeded with the same rapidity that had characterized the trial of Baker and Sowash. On June 22 the U.S. District Court at San Francisco finally denied Charles Morris's appeal against extradition and sent him to face a Canadian jury. Over the course of three days in October, the prosecution laid out the same argument it had used against Baker and Sowash and a new jury reached the same verdict.[31]

A crowd of some one hundred spectators came to watch the executions of Baker and Sowash at Oakalla Prison in Vancouver on January 14, 1926. Though the Cabinet of Canada had commuted Morris's sentence to life in prison, the Supreme Court had denied the appeals of Baker and Sowash. The American consul was among the crowd that day; so too were a fair number of American tourists eager to see Canadian justice in action. Public reports alleged that execution passes had been peddled for five dollars each and that there had been no shortage of buyers. The *Beryl G* case ended with the same drama with which it had begun. Muffled by the black cap that covered his head, Sowash's last words to the public hangman electrified the audience: "Step on it, kid! Make it fast!"[32]

THE *BERYL G* IN CANADIAN THOUGHT AND MEMORY

By the time the investigation, extradition proceedings, trial, and executions were complete, the *Beryl G* had laid bare the whole, occasionally rotten structure of prohibition on the Pacific coast. The evidence produced by the Crown portrayed a steady flow of liquor from British Columbia into the Puget Sound. Boats capable of high rates of speed kept up almost scheduled sailings across the border and ensured that thirsty Americans would not lack for Canadian whisky. American prohibition authorities expressed no small interest in the case. Even diplomats in Washington paid particular attention to how the case of the *Beryl G* might strengthen the American hand in negotiating amendments to the 1924 treaty with Canada. Many American officials hoped, and many contemporary observers suspected, that news of hijackings like that of the *Beryl G* would cut down on rum-running generally.[33] More likely correct was the conclusion of the *Seattle Post-Intelligencer*: "Now that Canadian police have swept the reputed hijacking crew of Owen 'Cannonball' Baker from the Sound, the rum-runners' lanes have been freed from their greatest menace, the pirates, and the only enemy of the smuggler now operating is the Coast Guard fleet."[34]

The *Beryl G* offered other lessons as well, not least of which was the value of cooperation exercised between American and Canadian authorities, particularly at the local level. While treaty and convention tied the hands of federal authorities in Washington DC and Ottawa, no such hindrances existed at the state, provincial, and local levels. Local authorities understood that criminals recognized no borders, except to the degree that the boundary served as a sort of refuge. Consequently, provincial police inspectors worked jointly with their counterparts from the states and counties south of the border. Herbert Ross, the American attorney who served as the American liaison for the Crown's case, commented repeatedly on the closeness and importance of this cooperation in the *Beryl G* case.[35] Moreover, except for police testimony, American witnesses provided virtually all the evidence for the prosecution. Because many of them were rumrunners or bootleggers themselves, they were initially reluctant to testify in a Canadian court, fearing retribution by U.S. authorities. An agreement arranged by the British Columbia attorney general, however, assured them immunity from prosecution under the Volstead Act.[36]

Perhaps more important was the role the *Beryl G* played in the region's collective memory. For many years afterward, the hijacking of the *Beryl*

G remained the defining incident of the rum-running era in the Pacific Northwest. While contemporaries recalled the specifics of the *Beryl G* with varying degrees of accuracy, common to all recollections was that Baker and Sowash were Americans. For many Canadians, the incident seems to have served as something of a national catharsis. They could point to the *Beryl G* as proof of American debauchery and of Canadian superiority. They could point out that the criminals were Americans against whom Canadian officers were tireless in pursuit.[37]

One of the first attempts to connect the *Beryl G* to what many British Columbians believed was an American tendency toward lawlessness and moral laxity was made by the *Vancouver Sun* shortly after Baker's and Sowash's execution. In a mid-January editorial, the *Sun* castigated American newspapers for enfolding Sowash and Baker "in the mantle of tinsel heroism, to ascribe to them a philosophical depth, to sermonize about them and raise them to a level they do not deserve. . . . Any sentimental effort to make cheap heroes out of them is now to insult the very basic laws of life."[38] Making heroes out of criminals seemed a uniquely American trait, and western Canadian dailies had regularly criticized the United States for its high crime rate and the apparent inability of its judicial and law enforcement agencies to do anything about it. A common complaint was that Americans coddled their criminals too much or did not make them serve full sentences.[39] In the case of the *Beryl G*, they had a strong argument, for Baker had been paroled early by the governor of Washington.[40]

Yet the root of the American problem, many Canadians asserted, went much deeper. The United States was, almost by definition, a nation that revered disobedience to law. As the *Calgary Albertan* contended, "A nation born in rebellion can only with difficulty exalt obedience for law as among the highest of national virtues. . . . Whatever the cause, the whole history of the United States is marked by lawlessness—whether it is one of the two-gun days of the pioneer Southwest, the numerous Indian uprisings in the Northwest, crime and corruption in Philadelphia, or near-anarchy in Chicago."[41] By contrast, many Canadians believed that that disobedience to law did not exist in Canada because the Canadian or British system of law was patently better. Even in its early stages, Canadian law had extended westward before settlement. Since that time, a high regard for law and order had remained central to the Canadian identity. With such varying histories, it was only natural to many Canadians that the hijackers of the *Beryl G* were American.

The reputation for swift justice in Canadian courts seemed to resonate on both sides of the border. Most American criminals, it seems, usually felt their chances of evading the penalties of crime were not so good north of the international boundary and so confined their activities to the area south. Common was the belief that Canadian jurors were likely to be harder on American criminals than on Canadians. As the *Argus* saw it, Baker had made two crucial mistakes: his first had been committing murder; his second, committing murder on Canadian soil.[42] One American who had the misfortune of being tried in Nanaimo, British Columbia, just after the Sowash-Baker conviction discovered this bias firsthand. The presiding judge almost certainly had the *Beryl G* slayings in the back of his mind when he issued a particularly harsh sentence:

> The people of Canada are determined that Canada will not become a happy hunting ground for criminals. . . . Criminals over here, or in any other country may be sure that, if they come to British Columbia and commit crimes there will be no sparing of money to secure evidence against them and no sparing of money to bring them back within our jurisdiction. After conviction takes place, after such a fair trial, then the courts of British Columbia intend to deal drastically with would-be murderers—not that we seek vengeance, but that we intend to demonstrate than in Canada, law is respected. . . . Canadian sentiment will see to it that the punishment is such as will act as a deterrent to the perpetration of this sort of thing, which, I regret to say, has become so common, namely, the organization of bands of criminals from the United States who come to our country to perpetrate murder.[43]

The *Seattle Argus* apparently agreed when it commented, "Criminal justice works in Canada."[44]

During the early halcyon years of rum-running, most British Columbians believed that the prosperity associated with the liquor traffic came without significant cost. Many had no problem with rum-running or with those who practiced the trade. To some, rumrunners were nice people involved in an honest trade that happened to conflict with a foolish American law.[45] Even if some did not entirely approve of the trade, they could still take a certain amount of delight in the stories of intrepid rumrunners outwitting the noble but notoriously under-equipped law enforcers. Consequently, whichever category they best fit, most British Columbians, like most Canadians, were reluctant to support American requests for enforcement cooperation, especially when those requests came more from Washington DC than they did from Washington State.

Nevertheless, the story of the *Beryl G* had a much darker side that threatened to overshadow whatever nationalistic exuberance certain Canadians felt. One island resident later recalled, "When they started this sort of hijacking business, that wasn't funny."[46] The *Beryl G* incident made it abundantly clear that the prosperity associated with rum-running came at a price. The border was more an abyss than the impenetrable and protective barrier many thought it to be. It could not protect British Columbia from the disorder that emanated from the American side. It could not protect the staid Victorian order that British Columbia held so dear. Just as important, the liquor traffic imperiled the neighborly relationship most British Columbians enjoyed with their counterparts south of the border. In later years, as the province considered cooperating with American enforcement, the *Beryl G* would remain one of its most compelling arguments.[47] Equally compelling would be a customs scandal uncovered only months after Sowash gave his final instructions to the executioner.

CHAPTER SEVEN

Customs Scandals
(and More Second Thoughts)

To a British Columbian public still reeling from the *Beryl G* incident, an impending customs scandal added even more fuel to the fire. A long-overdue investigation of the Canadian Customs Department lasted for a year and a half. It occupied the attention first of a parliamentary commission and later a rare royal commission. It even temporarily unseated the Liberal administration of William Lyon Mackenzie King. Perhaps even more significant, the customs scandal confirmed first in the British Columbian mind, and later in the Canadian mind, that the time had come to cooperate with the United States against a liquor traffic that was spiraling out of control.

H. H. STEVENS AND THE PARLIAMENTARY COMMISSION

The origins of both the Stevens customshouse inquiry—as the parliamentary commission soon became known—and the subsequent Royal Commission on Customs and Excise grew out of a concern that smuggling along the forty-ninth parallel had increased to startling proportions since the beginning of American prohibition. Most Canadians at first ignored American complaints that smuggled liquor undermined prohibition in the United States. But smuggling was a two-way street. The minister of revenue, W. D. Euler, commented in 1929 that "it is impossible to have wet and dry countries adjacent to each other without a flow from the wet to the dry."[1]

As profitable as smuggling liquor was, it could be made even more lucrative by smuggling American commercial goods back into Canada. It was not long before U.S. textiles and other goods were flooding Canadian markets. American cigarettes, for example, proved particularly attractive to the northbound smuggler. Since taxes on tobacco were much lower in the United States, cigarettes could be sold north of the border at a price that undermined the legitimate Canadian market. Canadian tobacco interests claimed that fifty million cigarettes were smuggled into Canada at annual loss of some $5 million. Not only did this hurt Canadian industry, it also put many Canadians out of work.[2]

So concerned were central Canadian manufacturers and local boards of trade that they organized the Commercial Protective Association (CPA) in 1924. The CPA hired a staff of criminal investigators to find ways to stop smuggling into Canada and to publicize abuses of the customs and excise laws of the Dominion. This was, of course, a job the Customs and Excise Department should have been doing on its own. The customs officer was the first line of defense on Canada's "defended" commercial border, and customs and excise duties were important sources of Dominion revenue during the 1920s. As an official history of Canadian Customs and Excise points out, however, the public reticence toward liquor smuggling seems to have infected the Customs Department as well. With the tacit approval of the department's administration, Customs grew alarmingly lax during American prohibition.[3]

It fell to R. Percy Sparks, president of the CPA and a clothing manufacturer from Ottawa, to convince the Dominion government that it was in its best interest to halt smuggling from the United States. It proved a difficult task. In an early 1925 report to the prime minister, Sparks presented a few of the association's findings. As one example, the CPA alleged that professional smugglers were driving Canadian textile firms into bankruptcy by flooding the Canadian market with lower-priced American textiles. Combined with other commodities smuggled northward, some authorities estimated the total loss of revenue to be greater than $50 million annually.[4]

CPA operatives posing as smugglers gathered even more shocking evidence of lax or corrupt customs officials who kept expensive cars and threw "champagne parties" at elaborate summer homes. Sparks complained particularly about the chief customs officer at Montreal, J. E. A. Bisaillon, whom he accused of theft, perjury, and complicity with the smuggling fraternity. Bisaillon, it seems, actively participated in the smuggling traffic from his farm, which conveniently straddled the boundary between Quebec and Vermont.[5]

As disturbing as these accusations were, they failed to elicit action by the Liberal administration of William Lyon Mackenzie King. Twice Sparks wrote to King to offer evidence against Bisaillon; in neither case did Sparks receive assurance that the Liberal government would investigate the matter. This inattention seems indicative of the aloof, laissez-faire, and sometimes even hostile attitude the Mackenzie King administration took toward the smuggling issue early on, especially regarding liquor smuggled to the United States.[6] One Alberta customs officer stationed at Wild Horse noted in his diary that Ottawa had ordered "hands off liquor being smuggled to the United States." Likewise, the officer in charge of the border station at Roosville, British Columbia, later recalled, "It was not the rumrunners who corrupted us, but the Canadian politicians, federal, provincial, and municipal."[7]

Despairing of attention from the Liberal government, Sparks turned the results of the CPA's investigation over to H. H. Stevens, a front-bench Conservative from Vancouver Centre. As a former minister of Trade and Commerce, Henry Herbert Stevens proved to be a wise choice. In many ways, Stevens's career reflected many of the industrial and progressive changes that characterized British Columbia during the early decades of the twentieth century. In 1887, at the age of nine, he emigrated from Bristol with his family, settling first in Hamilton and then in Peterborough, Ontario. Henry's father, finding Ontario a difficult place to make a go of the grocery business in the depression-racked 1890s, gathered his family and headed to the Far West. Over the next twenty years the younger Stevens accumulated an eclectic background. He worked as a fireman on the Canadian Pacific Railway and as a stagecoach driver to the booming mining town of Grand Forks. Seeking more exciting pursuits, Stevens traveled to Seattle in 1899 to join the transport section of the U.S. Army. The army shipped him first to the Philippines and later to China as part of the force sent to quell the Boxer Rebellion. In 1901 Stevens returned home to the Kootenay region, where he staked claims for a New York mining syndicate and joined the local chapter of the Western Federation of Miners. Ironically, it was here that Stevens defined his conservative political philosophy. It seems that he found his own political views incompatible with those of the left-wing socialists and radicals who composed the Western Federation of Miners. Disillusioned, Stevens returned to the security of the family grocery business before later founding a brokerage and insurance business. He even managed to serve as a Methodist preacher and Sunday school teacher before being elected to Parliament in 1911.[8]

Along with his religious background, Stevens's experience in China may have been the most formative in defining his views on the liquor traffic. Although he participated in no fighting, Stevens did operate the ambulances that picked up American casualties, most of whom, he claimed, were alcoholics. He later recalled, "If that's what booze does to a man, no more booze and I left it alone."[9] Indeed he did. He committed the remainder of his public life to cleaning up British Columbian society as a staunch advocate of prohibition. Stevens became one of the first Canadians to endorse cooperation with American enforcement of prohibition, primarily out of his belief that the provincial and Dominion governments operated hand in hand with the liquor industry.[10] Although a Conservative, Stevens was probably in agreement with some of his more liberal-minded colleagues, believing that "private interests must be subservient to the public good." Still, as his biographer has commented, Stevens was a "Conservative Methodist rather than a radical Protestant." He was more interested in remedying the ills of the system than in changing it. His investigation of the Customs Department fell nicely in line with these philosophies. But politics motivated Stevens's actions as well.[11]

By January 1926 the Liberal government of Mackenzie King was under attack. Before the federal election held the previous November, King's Liberals controlled more than twice the number of seats held by the Tories. Though Conservatives did not win the majority needed to gain power directly, they did acquire a 46.5 percent plurality, leaving the Liberals with a mere 40.1 percent and the Progressives with the remaining 14 percent. The election proved a stunning victory for Conservatives; for the Liberals, it was a serious repudiation. Just as unsettling to the Liberals, the prime minister and five members of his cabinet lost their seats in the election.

King did not automatically resign as prime minister. Constitutional precedent allowed him to remain in office until the House withdrew its support by a vote of no confidence. Deciding to wait until a new Parliament convened in early 1926, he used the interim to insure that Parliament would remain in Liberal hands. This meant convincing western Progressives, who held the balance of power, to align themselves with the Liberals. Likewise, the Tories viewed the interim period as an opportunity to consolidate Progressive support for a Conservative government.[12]

Stevens and Conservative leader Arthur Meighen believed the growing customs scandal to be the issue that would seal a Tory victory. Of the three major parties in the House, the Progressives were the least likely to condone corruption. Indeed, one of the Progressives' chief platforms in the previous election had been that only they had the "moral courage and idealism" necessary to reinvigorate Canadian politics.[13]

It was in this atmosphere that Stevens made his damaging accusations public in February 1926. He made the thinly veiled implication that Liberals were trying so hard to remain in power precisely because they hoped to mask the scandal. There probably was some truth to this charge. Stevens's accusations did not come as a complete surprise, at least to Mackenzie King. Ever since Sparks had made his disclosures to King the previous February, the prime minister had recognized the need for a full-scale investigation of the Customs Department. He had quietly and conveniently retired the customs minister, Jacques Bureau, to the Senate just days before the election. A few days afterward he finally ordered the dismissal of Bisaillon. Still, this was the extent to which the Liberals had sought to reform the department. The changes could hardly be called sweeping.[14]

Under the pressure of Stevens's disclosures, Liberal political survival depended even more on Progressive support for a coalition government. Consequently, Liberals agreed to the appointment of a special committee to investigate Stevens's charges. Placated by this concession (as well as by an offer of a cabinet position for a western Progressive), the Progressives agreed to back a Liberal government. A Liberal member from Prince Albert, Saskatchewan, resigned to make way for Mackenzie King, and on February 15 King won a by-election, allowing him once again to take up his place on the floor of the House of Commons. The Liberals had managed to hold power, and King had managed to retain his position as prime minister. The position, as King soon discovered, however, was far from secure. Adjourning until March 15, the House left the customs scandal to the appointed commission.[15]

Over the next four months the parliamentary committee conducted its investigation. Made up of nine members, the committee was divided among four Liberals, four Conservatives, and one Progressive. The committee's report, when Parliament convened on June 18, more than substantiated the charges Stevens had made in February.[16] A few of the findings suggested that the problems were systemic. The commissioner of the Royal Canadian Mounted Police, for example, testified that much of the smuggling problem was due to the locations of the customshouses. Being so few and so easily avoided, they were not effective deterrents to smuggling. They were, he noted, "reported to by the honest, [and] avoided by the dishonest at will," and perennial underfunding only exacerbated the problem.[17] The committee's report also recommended that the department prosecute some twenty-five firms, mostly garment manufacturers that habitually used fictitious invoices to undervalue the products they imported. It also recommended that all distilleries be audited.[18]

To the *Toronto Mail and Empire*, the committee's most significant findings dealt "with the most shocking state of affairs ever exposed in a Dominion Government Department." The report, the daily continued, "gave a staggering account of rascalities committed by smugglers, of unfaithful service on the part of government employees. It was a tale of fortune-making by contraband traders on a grand scale."[19] Before the

House, Stevens outlined a scandalous system of bribes, kickbacks, and cover-ups or simple dereliction that went from the lowest of customs inspectors all the way up to the minister of customs:

> The evidence further discloses that ministerial action has been influenced by the improper pressure of political associates and friends of the minister, or acting minister, administering the department, resulting in the suspension and in some instances the abandonment of prosecutions against those charged with violation of the statutes, and in the loss of revenue to the country. Moreover, successful appeals have been made to the minister and acting minister administering the department to improperly interfere with the course of justice between the conviction of the offenders and the execution of judgment thereon. The Prime Minster and the government had knowledge for some considerable time of the rapid degeneration of the Department of Customs and Excise, and their failure to take prompt and effective remedial action is wholly indefensible.[20]

Whereas Sparks and the CPA had confined their investigation to goods smuggled north and had excluded liquor, the parliamentary committee made no such distinction. Indeed, some of the most startling findings concerned not goods smuggled northward but liquor smuggled south. "In my opinion," Stevens reported, "the administration—and in this I include the officers of the department as well as the heads—are either too simple to hold office or else they are deliberately conniving at this traffic, which is contraband so far as our friendly neighbor to the south is concerned. And it is beneath the honour and dignity of this country to be engaged in, or to connive with others who are engaged in, such pursuits." Concluding, he proclaimed it "high time for this unholy partnership between the government of Canada and a gang of bootleggers to be dissolved."[21]

Whatever their validity, the attacks on King were credible enough for the Conservatives to move for a vote of censure, confident that they would gain Progressive support. Hoping that a new election might rid his party of the Customs albatross, King raced to the governor general to request that Parliament be dissolved. The governor general promptly refused, and so King, facing likely censure, resigned on June 28. Lord Byng then invited the Conservative Arthur Meighen to form a government. After receiving assurances of support from a number of Progressives, Meighen accepted.[22]

With only a precarious coalition to support it, Conservative rule was short-lived. On July 1 Liberals defeated the Meighen government with a vote of no confidence. This time it was Meighen asking the governor general for a dissolution of Parliament, and this time the governor general agreed, calling for general election to be held in late September. Before its defeat, the Conservative government succeeded in passing an amendment to the commission's report requiring a full-scale, independent investigation be made. The Royal Commission on Customs and Excise was born.[23]

THE ROYAL COMMISSION IN VICTORIA AND VANCOUVER

Given the findings of the parliamentary commission the previous June, expectations for the royal commission proceedings—slated to open in Victoria and Vancouver in mid-November 1926—were understandably high. The open hearings attracted, in the words of the American consul, all classes of residents, "from water rat to plutocrat, of both sexes."[24] The *Vancouver Province* articulated the expectations of many when it warned, "If, as a result of the thorough ventilation that is promised, we do not succeed in evolving some scheme which will enable us to protect our people and our revenues and cooperate with the American authorities, as we have promised to do, we shall have to admit that the best brains of the country are on the side of the law-breakers and that our capacity for self-government is by no means as high as we had believed it to be."[25] Of course, as the American consul in Halifax, Nova Scotia, observed, Canadians in other parts of the Dominion listened with equal attentiveness, assured that recitals given in British Columbia would offer a preview of coming attractions in their provinces.[26]

That the proceedings began in British Columbia had significant implications for the course they would take throughout Canada. The royal commission's mandate went far beyond an investigation of the liquor traffic to the United States. To have introduced the investigation in such a way would have resulted in its rejection by Parliament. In general, most Canadians continued to hold that it was not Canada's responsibility to investigate a traffic that, in the main, broke only American law. Of greater concern to most members of Parliament remained the allegations concerning commercial smuggling north. Crimes associated with rum-running south would, most assumed, play a role in the commission's investigation, but they would not be its central focus.

Nonetheless, each of the first witnesses called before the commission at Victoria and Vancouver stated unequivocally that it was not commercial but liquor smuggling that posed the greatest threat in the Northwest. Even the local boards of trade had no particular concerns about commercial smuggling in the region, since what contraband traffic existed remained more complementary than competitive, just as it had been for most of the previous century. Consequently, the commission focused almost exclusively on rum-running for the remainder of its two months in British Columbia.[27]

Doing so was not a decision that sat well with those unsympathetic to the prohibition cause, nor with those concerned that the commission's findings would adversely affect political fortunes. Some critics pointed to the "over-zealousness" of Newton Rowell, the commission's chair, known to be an ardent prohibitionist. They questioned whether an inquiry into what everyone agreed was a legal traffic should cost $10,000 per day. It was outrageous that an industry that contributed millions to the provincial and Dominion economies should be the subject of an inquisition, especially when it helped no one but Americans. One British Columbian complained that from the hearings American enforcement officials learned all the routes used by exporters. "It is a fine thing for the U.S. government," he wrote, "[but] will they pay the expenses and salaries of the commission?" Another letter got to the point even quicker: "Uncle Sam, with his usual greed, having bitten off more than he can chew with his Eighteenth Amendment, is ... getting his dirty work done at our expense."[28] For the *Western Tribune*, a local Labour paper, Canada had more important issues to consider than the liquor traffic: how to get more pulp and paper mills, how to manufacture more finished lumber products in British Columbia, and how to reduce taxation.[29]

Because the Liberal provincial government had been in power for a decade, most assumed that revelations of a connection between liquor and politics would hurt Liberals more than Conservatives. Thus some Liberals, including British Columbia's premier, John Oliver, were concerned that Rowell would spill too many "Liberal beans." Neither did Liberals in Ottawa appreciate Rowell's efforts. One warned that the royal commission chairmanship "would be the last job that gentleman will get from his friends [here]."[30]

Despite the criticisms, the commission plunged headlong into the complex world of rum-running on the Pacific coast. One of the greatest challenges the commission faced was in determining whom to call before the committee and how to compel their testimony. First, it was particularly difficult to pin down those involved in the West Coast liquor traffic. Rum-running concerns operated under a myriad of holding companies and fronts, often under assumed names, and it was not uncommon for shares in liquor concerns to be held in trust for persons whose names remained confidential. Second, once identified, it was often difficult to get those persons in front of the commission. James Ball, owner of the British Columbia Vinegar Company—a concern that sold more liquor than vinegar—fled to Seattle just before the commission's arrival, taking the company's records with him. Also, many witnesses called by the commission were Americans who were naturally reluctant to testify, concerned that testimony they gave would be used against them in the United States. Occasionally it was.[31]

Accessing business account books, many of which had been conveniently "misplaced" or destroyed, proved particularly frustrating. In one of its interim reports, the commission reported the difficulty it encountered securing records from the Pacific coast's largest liquor concern, Consolidated Exporters. "It appears to have been a deliberate policy on the part of the company to destroy the books and records," the report noted. "The alleged reason for this procedure," it continued, "was to prevent the United States Government from obtaining information as to the income tax that might possibly be payable by this company in connection with the business transacted by it in the United States."[32] This was certainly true. At the same time, it was true (though not yet in evidence) that Consolidated and other liquor concerns also hoped to hide their books from the prying eyes of Canadian revenue authorities.

The most obstructive behavior came not from Consolidated but from Joseph Kennedy Ltd., one of the other two major liquor export companies operating from British Columbia. The Kennedy company and its subsidiaries were operated by Henry Reifel Sr., British Columbia's leading brewer and distiller, and his two sons, Henry Reifel Jr. and George C. Reifel. The elder Reifel was a German brewmaster who had immigrated to the province in 1888. He purchased the small British Columbia Distillery and soon began to compete quite successfully against the eastern distillers who then controlled a significant portion of the West Coast trade. By 1926 Reifel and his sons had assumed operation of the Joseph Kennedy Export House and British Columbia Distillers and were the main partners in Vancouver Breweries. Not coincidentally, they were a major source of liquor for Roy Olmstead's Puget Sound organization before Olmstead's conviction. Already well known, Reifel became a real celebrity—and a threat to the provincial government—when he testified before the royal commission.[33]

Getting the Reifels in front of the commission proved a chore in itself. The family doctor claimed that ill health made it unwise for Henry Reifel Sr. to appear before the commission, though he was forced to testify later the next week. Henry Reifel Jr., also excused temporarily on account of illness, did not even appear at the first session of the commission before it adjourned for Christmas break. When it reconvened in January, the committee was outraged to discover that he had sailed to London by way of Asia. Apparently his doctor had "ordered" him abroad for "recuperation." Rowell wryly commented, certainly with some irritation, "That's a long way to get to London."[34] Even when the Reifels did appear, their testimony evaded the truth as zealously as their bootleggers evaded American authorities. The commission later reprimanded the

Reifels for their reticence, their obfuscations and outright perjury, and eventually, their admitted guilt in the violation of numerous customs and excise laws.[35]

Despite the best efforts of the liquor industry to thwart the commission, the truth about rum-running on the Pacific coast soon made itself apparent. The revelations centered around four major issues: false declarations given by exporters concerning the destination of their shipments; liquor from export houses being sold illegally in British Columbia; forged liquor labels and revenue stamps; and illegal contributions made by the liquor exporters to political campaigns, provincial newspapers, and government officials.

First, the royal commission confirmed what bootleggers already knew, that the primary purpose of the federally protected liquor export warehouses located throughout British Columbia was to ship liquor to places where it was prohibited. In the main, this meant the United States. The commission demonstrated that liquor exporters routinely filed fraudulent clearance papers suggesting that the liquor was bound not for the United States but for another foreign country, such as Guatemala or Mexico. They did so, naturally, to avoid the twenty-dollars-per-case tax that the Dominion had levied specifically on liquor exports to the United States. In some cases the fraud was quite blatant.

The well-known rumrunner the *Chris Moeller* had the misfortune of being "Exhibit A" for the commission. The steamship had cleared the port of Vancouver ostensibly for San Blas, Mexico, with a 17,779-case load just as the royal commission convened. When it later arrived in Victoria to load an additional 3,700 cases, port authorities revoked the clearance to San Blas pending the royal commission's investigation. After the testimony of officials familiar with San Blas, the commission learned that San Blas did not have a harbor sufficient to handle a vessel the size of the *Chris Moeller*. Moreover, the village did not have "enough thirsty people . . . to consume 20,000 cases of liquor" nor the rail facilities necessary for its shipment to the rest of Mexico. Making the *Chris Moeller*'s shipment even less plausible was the contention that the liquor it shipped was British and that it had arrived at Vancouver through the

Panama Canal. Surely, reasoned the commission, were its final destination truly San Blas, the vessel would have delivered the liquor as it passed Mexico on the way north. The net result was that shipments such as the *Chris Moeller*'s defrauded the Dominion of considerable excise revenue.[36]

The second major discovery made by the royal commission was a process commonly known as "short-circuiting." Evidence disclosed that not all liquor bound for the American or other foreign markets even left British Columbia waters. By law, export companies could not legally sell liquor in British Columbia except to the Liquor Control Board for retail through government vendor stores. However, with high prices resulting from a government monopoly, many exporters and bootleggers found it almost as profitable to undersell the provincial market as it was to export to the American. Indeed, the liquor warehouses abused provincial law almost as much as they did American law. When the commission discovered sales records of the British Columbia Distillery that showed deliveries to Vancouver residents, the distillery explained that they were legal because they were "delivered by American car." When the commission questioned an "exceptionally large" discrepancy between how much liquor the United Distillers of Vancouver produced and how much liquor it reported as exports, the company dubiously replied that the difference was "due to defective plates in the distilling column causing leakage."[37]

Third, liquor exported to the United States was not all its labels indicated it to be. One of the major arguments many Canadians had used to rationalize the liquor traffic was that the Dominion provided pure, unadulterated alcohol to Americans who would otherwise be drinking "rot-gut," or other questionable forms of liquor. One British Columbian had commented, "It is up to us to take all the money we can get from the U.S. by selling her our good whiskey."[38] The royal commission disputed the contention that all liquor exported by Canada during American prohibition contained what its labels indicated. Much of the so-called Kentucky bourbon that Americans imported from Canada—bourbon supposedly exported to Canada by American distilleries before the Eighteenth Amendment took effect—was found to be not American liquor at all but products of British Columbia distilleries packaged with forged U.S. Internal Revenue stamps and false labels. Both Joseph Kennedy's George Reifel and Robert Swanson, one of Consolidated Exporter's managers, admitted that their respective concerns labeled Canadian whisky as "Hill and Hill," "Grand Dad," or "Old Hermitage" (all well-known American brands) with forged labels and revenue stamps. Moreover, to keep up with the insatiable demand, the distillers routinely shortened the aging time required by Dominion law, hastily concocting products that were neither American liquor nor pure, unadulterated Canadian liquor. As one British Columbian exclaimed after hearing the commission's findings, "Why, Sir, since the Volstead Act we have exported more vile fluid, falsely labeled 'Good Scotch Whiskey,' than would float the Ark."[39]

Each of these first three findings—that exporters routinely filed false destinations in clearance papers, that liquor supposedly bound for the United States was instead short-circuited into competition with provincial liquor, and that brewers and distillers used fraudulent labels and revenue stamps—proved to those not already convinced that Canadian exporters violated Canadian law. While many Canadians maintained that it was none of the Dominion's business whether exporters violated American law, it could no longer be said that liquor exports did nothing to hurt Canada. The revenue Canadians thought they were receiving from the liquor traffic was instead diverted to the pockets of bootleggers and rumrunners—hardly the beneficiaries most Canadians envisaged when they argued against cooperation with the United States.

Beyond these discoveries, one revelation made by the commission proved even more unsettling. The socialist J. S. Woodsworth had once wondered before the House of Commons whether Canada's staunch attitude against cooperation with the United States might not have been the result of illegal campaign donations. Just before Christmas recess, the royal commission discovered buried deep in the account books of Reifel's Vancouver Brewing Company a secret account labeled "Assurance and Protection." It documented unspecified expenditures of some $150,000 over a two-year period. When questioned, Henry Reifel proved, as usual, an uncooperative witness. He was unwilling to discuss the assurance and protection accounts, arguing that they were none of the royal commission's business. Many Conservatives assumed this account to be for contributions to the Liberal government in British Columbia—the so-called Liberal beans about which Premier John Oliver had earlier expressed concern.[40] As the committee later discovered, however, the Liberal party was not the only recipient of questionable contributions.

Compelled to divulge which political parties he had contributed to, Reifel finally responded, "Both, I have friends in both parties." Rowell asked Reifel, "But why do you find it necessary to contribute to political campaign funds?" Reifel's answer: "That's what I would like to know myself. I have been paying campaign funds in British Columbia for thirty-five years and I never got any return for my money. I wish, my lords, that you would recommend that a law be passed prohibiting contributions to campaign funds."[41] Digging deeper, the commission discovered that another $24,000 in unvouchered accounts had gone to the Liberal *Vancouver World* and to the Moderation League for antiprohibitionist propaganda. Reifel admitted that $200,000 went to political campaign funds and that he had paid $39,000 directly to one official.[42]

Of course, the Joseph Kennedy company was not the only exporter to contribute to political campaign funds. Russell Whitelaw, a directing officer of Consolidated Exporters, disclosed that Consolidated had, during the previous four years, paid at least $100,000 to the Conservative and Liberal Parties and $17,000 to the *Vancouver World*.[43] Though he claimed that they were outright gifts, with nothing owed in return, Rowell found that hard to believe. He asked, "Do you make gifts of money to everyone who appeals to you?" Whitelaw responded, "I don't recall that the Consolidated has ever turned down an appeal for money." To this another commissioner questioned sarcastically, "And you are still in business?"[44]

Although Whitelaw and Reifel pleaded ignorance, a number of their payments were, indeed, indictable offenses under the Dominion Elections Act. More blatant, Joseph Kennedy books showed that government liquor stores in Vancouver received kickbacks in proportion to the quantity of goods they purchased from Kennedy stocks. Equally disconcerting, a disgruntled beer dispenser disclosed that the local political boss had, after receiving money from Joseph Kennedy Ltd., made it a practice to dictate who would receive vendor licenses from the provincial government.[45]

Revelations of political contributions and payoffs changed public perceptions regarding the nature of the liquor traffic in British Columbia. The Independent-Liberal *Morning Star* of Vancouver pointed out,

> It is not merely that this port has been made a base for the operations of men who openly confess that they are engaged in breaking the laws of friendly neighbor—Vancouver has long been aware of what was going on of that nature and had regarded it as something extraneous, something that did not touch the life of the city. What has shocked the public mind is the disclosure that very large sums have been paid to provincial and federal party men for purposes which could not be openly avowed and the discovery of indications of apparently extensive bribery of public officials.[46]

Other dailies essentially echoed the *Star*'s concerns. The *Vancouver Province* concluded, "Before we had only conjecture. We know that the corruption of good government in British Columbia by the liquor interests has not so much been the corruption of government departments and government officials as it has been a general corruption of our public life. It has been corruptive of our political parties. It has been corruption—what other name will you give it?—of the very Legislature itself."[47]

In early February the royal commission moved on to the Prairie provinces, where it uncovered many of same irregularities. Before it departed, however, the commission left an indelible mark on British Columbian attitudes regarding Canada's role in the liquor traffic. If it accomplished nothing else, the royal commission at least helped to crystallize sentiment against the liquor traffic from British Columbia. Indeed, the American consul in Vancouver, Harold Tewell, believed the royal commission hearings to be the turning point in British Columbian opinion. Like the *Beryl G* incident, many British Columbians began to consider that bootlegging to the United States was inimical to the best interests of the province. The border was not the cultural barrier many thought it to be; its porosity had begun to undermine not only British Columbian society but also the neighborly spirit that the border had long symbolized, especially in the Northwest. "It is an unfriendly act," the *Province* commented, "to defy a neighbor's laws, and the height of business folly to court a neighbor's ill will and to build up among her people a reputation for laxness and indifference."[48] One resident summed it up even more succinctly: "We don't want such prosperity at the price of our national self-respect."[49]

In February 1927 Tewell was finally able to report what his superiors in Washington had long hoped to hear: "A general war on bootlegging is being urged in British Columbia. . . . It has taken five years to fully convince decent Canadians that the bootlegging of liquor into the United States is not good business for either country."[50] It still remained for that sentiment to alter opinions throughout the Dominion. Ottawa would not move to ban liquor exports to the United States until that happened.

1. Canadian and American members of the Kiwanis Club, including its international president, gather for the dedication of the Peace Arch at Blaine, Washington, and Surrey, British Columbia, in September 1921. Also in the background, to the left of the arch and just a few feet north of the border, is the St. Leonard Hotel, which Sen. Wesley Jones argued was nothing more than a "grog shop" intended to attract American tourists during prohibition. Image AM1535-: CVA 99-3438, courtesy City of Vancouver Archives.

2. The interior of the First Methodist Church in Victoria decorated for the 1883 visit of Frances E. Willard, leader of the American Woman's Christian Temperance Union and founder of the British Columbia chapter of the WCTU. Image C-06485, courtesy of Royal BC Museum, BC Archives.

3. Imperial Liquor Company, Seattle, and the start of prohibition in Washington, ca. 1916. Image 1983.10.12280, courtesy PEMCO Webster and Stevens Collection, Museum of History & Industry.

4. Liquor stills captured by the Vancouver Police Department during prohibition in British Columbia, ca. 1917. Image VPD-S214-: CVA 480-215, courtesy City of Vancouver Archives.

5. Two views of the Pacific Highway, British Columbia, ca. 1912 and 1924. First opened as a gravel road sometime between 1910 and 1914, the Pacific Highway reopened as a paved route in 1923, greatly facilitating the movement of Canadians and Americans across the border. Images AM54-S4-: Out P206 and AMAM54-S4-: Out N299, courtesy City of Vancouver Archives.

The Lure
of the
Great Pacific Northwest

Oregon
Washington &
British Columbia

The open road calls you; the majestic scenery of the Pacific Northwest will appeal to you; its trout streams to be found every few miles along the road; the thirty-eight golf courses; sea beaches; national parks and forest reserves lure you to

Enjoy Your Favorite Sport in the
**Finest Summer Climate
on the Continent**

Bright, cool days with sound, restful sleep every night, in the

Great International Pacific Northwest
Oregon, Washington and British Columbia

Take advantage of special reduced fares to the Switzerland of America— a land of enchantment, of opportunity, of family happiness and contentment. There are excellent hotels at very reasonable rates, the same in the tourist season as at any other time, and camping grounds everywhere.

Write for a general booklet on the Pacific Northwest or a booklet on fishing, golfing, automobiling, mountaineering or yachting, to The Pacific Northwest Tourist Association, Herbert Cuthbert Executive Secretary, L. C. Smith Building, Seattle, Washington.

OUR
INTERNATIONAL
PLAYGROUND

One of the advertisements inserted in 55 newspapers throughout the United

6. Pacific Northwest Tourist Association advertisement, ca. 1922. So closely linked were American and British Columbian efforts to promote tourism that, early in the decade, chambers of commerce in Washington and Oregon united with their counterparts in British Columbia to form the Pacific Northwest Tourist Association. Lee Drake Papers, Ax 27, box 1, folder 1, Special Collections and University Archives, University of Oregon Libraries, Eugene.

7. Pacific Highway in 1931, one hundred feet from customs. In addition to indicating speed limits for highways and cities, welcome billboards at border crossings routinely advertised to Americans the ready availability of liquor, in this case B.C. Rye and Old Colonel Bourbon. Image AM54-S4-I-: CVA 20-2, courtesy City of Vancouver Archives.

THAT LEAKY APARTMENT ABOVE

—Morris for the George Matthew Adams Service.

8. "That Leaky Apartment Above," *Literary Digest*, October 6, 1923, p. 20. It was not long after prohibition began in the United States that the consequences of living adjacent to a wet neighbor became obvious.

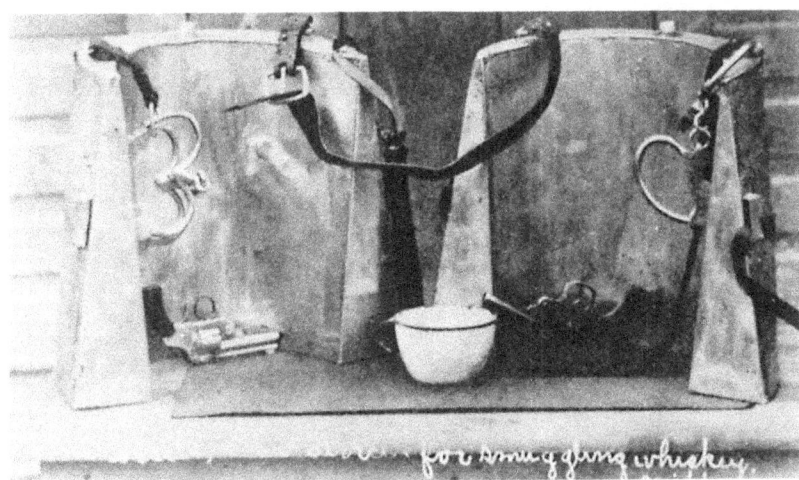

9. (*top*) The *Chief Skugaid*. Generally regarded as the longest serving of rumrunners, the seventy-seven-foot *Chief Skugaid* carried liquor in the Pacific Northwest from 1922 until prohibition ended in 1933. Courtesy Vancouver Maritime Museum.

10. (*bottom*) Tin corsets used for smuggling whiskey. Image B-01366, courtesy of Royal BC Museum, BC Archives.

11. Elise and Roy Olmstead, Seattle, 1925. Image 1986.5G.2261.1, courtesy *Post-Intelligencer* Collection, Museum of History & Industry.

12. Roy Olmstead and his wife, Elise, established the American Radio Telephone Company, which they operated from their home in Seattle's Mount Baker neighborhood. Used to broadcast children's stories read by Mrs. Olmstead, it was generally believed, but never proved, that the radio station was also used to send coded messages instructing rumrunners where to deliver liquor. Image 1986.5G.2263, courtesy *Post-Intelligencer* Collection, Museum of History & Industry.

13. Radio station KFQX in the Olmstead home, Seattle, 1924. Image 1987.30.1, courtesy Museum of History & Industry.

14. Consolidated Exporters warehouse, Vancouver. In 1922 sixteen of the largest liquor wholesalers in British Columbia amalgamated under the name Consolidated. Created specifically to serve the illicit American market, Consolidated established export warehouses not only in Vancouver and Victoria but also well inland in border towns like Greenwood, Grand Forks, Creston, Cranbrook, and Fernie. Image AM1535-: CVA 99-3487, courtesy City of Vancouver Archives.

S.S. Stadacona, (1920) Victoria, B.C.

15. The HMCS *Stadacona*, later the rumrunner *Kuyakuzmt*. In one of the ironies of prohibition, former naval or Coast Guard vessels often became rumrunners and, conversely, captured rumrunners were often pressed into service as enforcement vessels. Before being purchased and renamed *Kuyakuzmt* by Consolidated Exporters for use as a "mother" ship in the Pacific liquor traffic, the *Stadacona* had been the flagship of the New York Yacht Club and, before that, a vessel of the Royal Canadian Navy. Image E-00659, courtesy of Royal BC Museum, BC Archives.

16. U.S. Coast Guard cutter *Arcata*. Until 1925 the U.S. Coast Guard patrolled the waters of the Puget Sound with only two vessels, one of which was the *Arcata*. Barely able to make twelve knots, these vessels compared quite unfavorably with the much speedier and more numerous rumrunners. Courtesy U.S. Coast Guard Historian's Office.

17. (*above*) The rumrunner *Beryl G.* The brutal hijacking of the *Beryl G* quickly turned into one of the most sensational murder cases in the history of British Columbia. The events played a central role in convincing British Columbians that assisting the United States in the enforcement of prohibition was in Canada's best interest. Image B-06106, courtesy of Royal BC Museum, BC Archives.

18. (*right*) Wanted poster circulated by the Province of British Columbia for Owen Benjamin "Cannonball" Baker and Harry F. Sowash, the suspected hijackers of the *Beryl G.* Department of Justice fonds, volume 988, file 1926-1728/1873, courtesy Library and Archives Canada.

THE GOVERNMENT OF
THE PROVINCE OF BRITISH COLUMBIA

WANTED FOR MURDER

$4,000 REWARD

The Government of the Province of British Columbia hereby offers a reward of $2,000 for information leading to the arrest and conviction of OWEN BENJAMIN BAKER, and a reward of $2,000 for similar information in regard to HARRY F. SOWASH, who are charged with the murder of William J. Gillis and his son, William, on the 15th day of September, 1924, at or near Sidney Island, British Columbia.

A Warrant is held by me for the arrest of these two men and their photographs and descriptions are given hereunder :

Name : OWEN BENJAMIN BAKER.

Occupation : Engineer. Age : 36. Height : 5 ft. 10½ in. Weight : 171 lb. Stocky build. Complexion : Dark. Eyes : Blue. Hair : Brown. Fingerprint classification :

$$\frac{5 \quad U \quad I\,O \quad 18}{17 \quad R \quad I\,O \quad 13}$$

McNeil Island, No. 3334 ; Portland, Ore., No. 3115 ; Tacoma, Wash., No. 3559. Released from McNeil Island, June 20th, 1924.

Name : HARRY F. SOWASH.

Nativity: U.S. Age: 25. Height: 5 ft. 9 in. Weight : 164½ lb. Complexion : Dark. Eyes : Brown. Hair : Dark Brown. Fingerprint classification .

$$\frac{9 \quad U \quad O \quad O \quad 16}{2 \quad U \quad O \quad O \quad 15}$$

Teeth : Upper right first bicuspid missing. McNeil Island, No. 3888. Released, August 12th, 1924.

Please wire me, collect, any information you may be able to obtain in regard to either or both of these men, and, if located, arrest and hold.

J. H. McMULLIN,
Superintendent, British Columbia Police.

Victoria, B.C.,
December 1st, 1924.

1M-1224-8339

19. (*above*) Finally arrested in New York after a lengthy manhunt, hijack suspect Owen "Cannonball" Baker is handcuffed to an official and escorted to a waiting vehicle before being extradited to Canada. Image 1986.5G.43, courtesy *Post-Intelligencer* Collection, Museum of History & Industry.

20. (*right*) Henry Herbert Stevens. A Conservative member of Parliament from Vancouver Centre, Stevens led the parliamentary commission that brought to full public view the growing customs scandal of 1926. The findings of this commission were instrumental in temporarily bringing down the government of William Lyon Mackenzie King and in shifting Canadian attitudes in favor of assisting American enforcement against the liquor traffic. Courtesy City of Vancouver Archives.

21. Joseph Kennedy Ltd. building, Vancouver. Though bearing the name of the wealthy American industrialist (and father of a future American president), Joseph Kennedy Ltd. was actually owned by Henry Reifel Sr., who also owned British Columbia Distillers. The Royal Commission on Customs and Excise investigation uncovered evidence that the sole business of Joseph Kennedy Ltd. was shipping liquor illegally to the United States. Image AM54-S4-: Port P937, courtesy City of Vancouver Archives.

22. Two portraits of Henry Reifel Sr. of Vancouver and Nanaimo. Reifel founded and controlled Joseph Kennedy Ltd. and British Columbia Distillers. Image AM54-S4-: Port N56, courtesy City of Vancouver Archives.

In Danger of Drowning

23. "In Danger of Drowning," *Outlook and Independent*, January 16, 1929, p. 94. By late in the decade, both Canadians and Americans began to recognize the danger the liquor traffic posed to a harmonious Canadian-American relationship.

U. S.: "I hope you have good luck, neighbor."

—Morris for the George Matthew Adams Service.

24. "I Hope You Have Good Luck, Neighbor," *Literary Digest*, May 7, 1927, p. 11. As Americans began looking for alternatives to prohibition, Canada, and especially British Columbia, provided a possible model.

25. (*top*) The Cloverdale, British Columbia, government liquor store in 1925. Government control of liquor in British Columbia was a model followed by the state of Washington once national prohibition ended in the United States in 1933. City of Surrey Archives, c-00296.

26. (*bottom*) Roy Olmstead arrives in Seattle, probably upon his release from McNeil Island Penitentiary in 1931. Image 1986.5G.2269, courtesy *Post-Intelligencer* Collection, Museum of History & Industry.

CHAPTER EIGHT

Neighbors and Neighbours

Many meanings of the border serve to define the ways in which Canadians and Americans differ. When one thinks of border, it is the idea of division that most quickly comes to mind. Borders divide states, peoples, and identities. But borders also serve as margins. As citizens of a border nation, Canadians have often felt as though they were *on* the margin of something else—merely a delightful northern playground for their more numerous neighbors to the south. At other times, to be Canadian means to actually *be* the margin—merely a second-tier power serving as interlocutor, interpreter, or linchpin between two greater powers. Used in these contexts, being on the margin means to be marginal or marginalized. By occasionally defining themselves as "not American," Canadians have had to deal with these mostly negative connotations of margin. More positively, however, margin implies a zone of transition, where interests on one side blend ever gradually with those on the other. Even the physical border itself is not a line but a sixty-foot swath whose meaning, according to popular opinion, was more a "neutral" than a "non-transgression" strip.[1] The border as margin implies that Canadians and Americans share something positive in common, perhaps a "special" or at least a unique relationship, and that the border need not be considered entirely perilous. As we have seen, that is not to say that Canadians do not defend against American economic, political, or cultural intrusion. However, while myriad "pinpricks" occasionally disrupt the sense of neighborliness, the reality of the border is that it is physically undefended, more a porous fence than a brick wall.

By the middle of the 1920s reports of border clashes between rum-runners and enforcement officials, hijackings in coastal waters and on backcountry roads, and reports of wholesale corruption had become so widespread that those north of the border quickly recognized that they were not immune to the deleterious effects of ineffective enforcement south of the border. Instead of facilitating the traditional neighborly relationship that had existed between Canadians and Americans in the Northwest, the border had begun to undermine that relationship. For the next five years, convinced that something needed to be done, the province did what it could to limit the illicit traffic of liquor across the border. However, until there was in central and eastern Canada the same consensus for neighborhood cooperation that existed in British Columbia, there was little the province could do.

FINDING REGIONAL CONSENSUS

Throughout the 1920s, Canadian public opinion on the matter of coop-eration with the United States remained divided. Many Canadians maintained that the liquor traffic was entirely legal so far as Canada was concerned. Others had doubts about whether the traffic, whatever its legality, was in the Dominion's best interests. Yet this divide does not appear to have been the result of partisan politics. While Conservatives were generally more inclined to resist American appeals for cooperation and Liberals less so, there were notable exceptions. The *Liberal Presse* in Montreal, for example, agitated against cooperation with the United States, while the Conservative *Ottawa Journal*, as well as the even more Conservative *Montreal Star*, usually endorsed it.[2] In the British Columbia press, however, there was no division at all. Each of the province's major dailies had, by the mid-1920s, become an advocate for greater coopera-tion and that opinion remained unchanged throughout the decade. The British Columbia press was, according to the American consul in Victoria in October 1925, "championing less and less the liquor interests" and "becoming more outspoken for law enforcement."[3]

Sectional factors, then, may offer a better explanation for the variations in sentiment than does political ideology. Despite the general support for cooperation in British Columbia, there were still sizable segments of the population throughout the Dominion—particularly in Quebec, Ontario, and the Maritimes—that refused to recognize Canadian responsibility in the matter. Certainly, Quebec was unlikely to support cooperation with the United States. French-Canadian members of Parliament were notoriously unsympathetic to prohibition, and since Quebec had been the first Canadian province to abolish prohibition, it was unlikely to favor drastic legislation supporting American prohibition. Similarly, Americans could expect little support from Ontario. There the United Empire Loyalist tradition, the province's nationalist outlook, and the powerful liquor lobby militated against cooperating with American overtures. Votes in Ontario as late as 1929 continued to reflect little support for legislation that would prohibit liquor clearances. Finally, recent American tariff restrictions, along with a nationalist outlook similar to that of Ontario, help explain the Maritimes' reluctance to support American requests for enforcement assistance.[4]

On the other hand, the American case received its strongest support in the Far West, where, Richard Kottman argues, "north-south cooperation and orientation overshadowed the imperial overtones of its population."[5] The sectional argument merits consideration, for even before the *Beryl G* incident and the royal commission's appearance in British Columbia, various facets of the historical British Columbia identity seem to have supported cooperation with the United States.

The long, close relationship that existed between Canada and the United States west of the Rocky Mountains undoubtedly contributed to British Columbia's early interest in assisting the United States in enforcement of the Eighteenth Amendment. Like many Canadians, British Columbians remained particularly sensitive about maintaining their sovereignty vis-à-vis the United States. The *Daily Province* had noted in 1924, "We are jealous of our sovereignty. We insist that what we do within our borders is the business of nobody but ourselves, and we should resist any attempt on the part of an outside nation to interfere with our decisions." Yet almost in the same breath, the paper went on to express the opinion, shared by many British Columbians, that Canada should at least be neutral. In affording facilities such as export houses, the paper argued that Canada was providing shelter "to guerrilla bands . . . levying war on a friendly power."[6] While the paper later conceded that it was not Canada's duty to enforce an American law, "it is just as true that it is our duty as a friendly neighbor, not to give aid, comfort, or asylum to those who are defying American laws."[7] Other papers agreed. "It would be," pleaded the *Vancouver Sun*, "a very great pity if the good feeling between these two great sister nations should be destroyed over such a back-alley, disreputable thing as the rumrunning business."[8] Even the *New York Times* recognized the special relationship in the Far West when it added, "At this [western] end of Canada, social, economic and industrial relations with United States individuals and companies are too close to be thus disturbed, and this community is too tolerant to blame the American public for acts of the American Government or acts prompted by the negotiations of the American Government."[9] The spirit of international comity was far more important than the letter of international law.

Yet another factor that contributed to British Columbia's early interest in cooperation was the province's ethnic makeup. Even into the late 1920s, British Columbia remained a decidedly British place. Over one-third of the province's population had been born in some part of the British Empire, and many of these were recent emigrants from the British Isles themselves.[10] To these "British" Columbians, the Dominion played an important role as the "linchpin" in the relationship between the United States and Great Britain. During a banquet held by the Victoria chapter of the Kiwanis Club in 1921, Dr. Herbert Coleman, dean of the British Columbia University Faculty of Arts, articulated this sentiment: "It would seem that Canada, because of her history and her ancestry, should be qualified in a special measure to act as interpreter between America and England. The Canadians are just as American as the Americans—of course, in a special sense. If all Americans knew the Mother Country as Canadians knew her, they would not love her, perhaps, as Canadians love her, but there would be no cause for hate or indifference."[11] At the Vancouver Canadian Club, Conservative leader Arthur Meighen later pointed out that Canada "remains, in very large degree, the interpreter of Britain to the United States and of the United States to Great Britain. As such … it behooves us to be careful of our conduct."[12] Certainly, since Great Britain had already refused clearances of liquor to the United States, it followed that it was Canada's responsibility not to undermine that Anglo-American accord.[13] Some historians have argued convincingly that Canada never really was the linchpin in Anglo-American relations. Whatever the merits of their arguments, the belief in Canada as linchpin was pervasive among Canadian citizens and certainly many British Columbians viewed themselves as such.[14]

Federal-provincial jurisdictional conflicts also contributed to British Columbia's cooperative spirit. As mentioned earlier, an amendment to the Canadian Temperance Act had given to those provinces that adopted prohibition the right to prohibit the private importation of liquor. Provinces that adopted government control, on the other hand—including British Columbia and Quebec—had no such option. In these provinces, private export warehouses remained protected by federal charter. So long as this situation existed, rumrunners naturally gravitated toward the Pacific Northwest, assured that their operations would continue unhindered.[15]

Had the liquor warehouses confined their activities to importing liquor for export to the United States, British Columbians might not have expressed much concern. However, what had been only suspicion before the royal commission proceedings was established fact afterward. There were, reasoned British Columbians, only two markets for the liquor imported by these private export warehouses, both of which were illegal under either provincial or American law. Either the liquor went to the United States in defiance of American laws or it remained in British Columbia to compete with provincial liquor stores.[16] One leading British Columbian prohibitionist, Reverend W. W. Peck, flayed the Dominion law that allowed these conditions to exist. They were, he exclaimed of the export houses, "along with our brewers, the biggest bootleggers we have in our Province."[17] Another found the exporters "immoral and a disgrace to a country claiming to be Christian."[18] They were of so little value to the province economically, most reasoned, that there was no good reason they should continue to operate in British Columbia.

Because British Columbia and the United States shared mutual concerns about liquor export houses, provincial authorities often cooperated with their American counterparts, regardless of the lack of formal agreement between Washington and Ottawa. As early as 1923, Roy Lyle was able to report to his superior in Washington DC that "helpful cooperation given by Canadian officials in British Columbia is doing much to stop liquor smuggling in the Northwest. . . . Officials north of the border are furnishing confidential information of great value."[19] Five years later, the American consul in Victoria reported that "friendly cooperation" continued to characterize the relationship between the Provincial Liquor Control Board, the provincial legislature, and American prohibition officials.[20]

Yet no matter how much British Columbian officials cooperated with their American counterparts, the federally protected liquor export houses remained the primary obstacle to effective enforcement. As long as Dominion law permitted the importation of liquor into British Columbia by private companies, the province could do little to enforce its laws, let alone those of the United States. Consequently, the provincial government agitated throughout the decade for the authority to force out of existence the nine private liquor warehouses operated in British Columbia by Consolidated Exporters and Joseph Kennedy Ltd. Between 1923 and 1928 two attorneys general of the province, one Liberal and one Conservative, made it their primary goal to persuade the Dominion government to cancel the warehouse licenses.

The first, British Columbia attorney general Arthur Manson, regularly faced criticism by H. H. Stevens. Stevens blamed Manson for complicity in the traffic, arguing that the attorney general was more interested in the political patronage that resulted from government control than he was in limiting the abuses of it. To be sure, Manson relished the patronage aspect of his job. Still, the criticisms leveled at him by Stevens and others seem to have been motivated more by politics than by any evidence of wrongdoing. Since as early as 1923, Manson had remained one of the chief advocates of amending the Canadian Temperance Act. Throughout his tenure, he repeatedly agitated against the Dominion government for its policy regarding the liquor warehouses. Eliminating the federal protection exporters enjoyed would, Manson reasoned, "strike a deadly blow at the bootlegging industry on the Puget Sound."[21] During the royal commission hearings of 1926 and 1927, it was Manson who would, on behalf of the attorneys general of Alberta, Saskatchewan, and Manitoba, continue to argue for limits on the export houses.[22]

On three occasions during the 1920s, the Dominion Parliament considered such an amendment to the Canadian Temperance Act. Widespread publicity given to the issue in both British Columbian and American newspapers convinced Manson that there was sufficient public support for the needed amendment. Should the amendment fail, Manson argued that "the responsibility for the lack of enforcement ... [would] rest on the shoulders of those who in the face of the facts ... opposed the measure."[23] On the first two occasions, the House passed the measure overwhelmingly, only to have it fail in the Senate: the first time by six votes, the second time by four. Key among those opposed were two Conservative senators from British Columbia who, conventional wisdom agreed, voted against it because they hoped to undermine the Liberal government's administration of government control.[24] When the same measure failed for the third time in 1926, Manson became so frustrated that he allegedly accused the same senators of being complicit in the murders of the *Beryl G*'s crew. Not until 1928—after most of the other provinces had followed British Columbia's lead in adopting government control—would the Dominion Parliament finally pass the Importation of Intoxicating Liquors Act, giving British Columbia the authority to regulate virtually all the liquor imported into the province.[25]

It was the new attorney general who enjoyed the fruits of Manson's labor. The American consul in Vancouver reported on the energy R. H. Pooley brought to the office. He seemed, according to the consul, "inclined to adopt a different attitude and make certain sweeping changes."[26] The difference the consul noted was probably more a reflection of the times than a substantive difference in the attitudes of both attorneys general. The royal commission's conclusions almost certainly provided Pooley with a powerful mandate that his predecessor did not enjoy. As he took office, Pooley was quick to point out the lessons learned: "We have not forgotten, and we hope our fellow citizens will not forget in an hurry, what the customs inquiry told us of the workings of the bootlegging and rum-running business for the 'protection and assurance' of partisan politics and party politicians."[27]

Bolstered by this mandate, Pooley promptly rejected applications from distillers who hoped to establish new distilleries in the province, and he pointedly charged the Dominion government with facilitating the traffic to the United States. The public response to Pooley's aggressiveness was prompt and emphatically supportive, with the *Daily Province* commenting, "Mr. Pooley has said that he will have no politics in the administration of his office . . . and no nonsense about the liquor laws; and already he has done enough to convince the liquor interests, at any rate, that very likely he means business. What the attorney general has done is to serve notice upon the liquor ring of this province, and also upon the government of Mackenzie King, that there is going to be a new deal about liquor administration in British Columbia."[28] Although the province still had little control over the already established distillers, no longer could the liquor interests import additional liquor to undermine government control in British Columbia or the Eighteenth Amendment in the United States.

TOWARD A NATIONAL CONSENSUS

Ever since the antismuggling treaty of 1924, the addition of a Canadian ban on liquor exports to the United States had remained the chief objective of American diplomats. Not surprisingly, it was also one of the chief recommendations made by the royal commission after it finished its hearings in the other provinces. The 1924 treaty had proved largely ineffective. The only effect of refusing clearance to small liquor vessels was that doing so helped consolidate the traffic for the larger concerns.[29]

The provision requiring Canadian authorities to notify their American counterparts whenever a liquor shipment was cleared for American ports was equally impotent. As Prohibition Commissioner James Doran complained in 1928, by the time American officers received information about the clearances, the shipment had already landed. The biggest problem with the treaty remained the border itself. "There are," the commissioner explained, "a thousand miles of coast along the North Pacific and the shipment is landed somewhere. The treaty as it stands is no good for our purpose."[30] Thus the American position remained that nothing short of eliminating liquor clearances entirely would be of "material assistance."[31]

Mackenzie King, hopeful for closer relations with the United States, seems to have grown more sympathetic to the American plea toward the latter part of the decade. Still, adopting such a policy remained beyond the power of the prime minister. Prohibiting clearances required an amendment to Canadian export law, and such amendments remained the jurisdiction of Parliament. In late 1929, despite considerable opposition in his own party, most notably from the minister of national revenue, W. D. Euler, King expressed assurances to the American consul in Ottawa that Parliament would take up the issue. He pointed out that it was necessary to move slowly on the matter, since Conservatives would seek as much political capital as possible from the cabinet split. In fact, Ottawa had on numerous occasions used precisely this rationale to justify its unwillingness to cooperate.[32]

It was, understandably then, a hard sell. Public opinion outside British Columbia remained adamantly opposed to cooperation. The most often expressed opinions continued to be the old arguments: that the liquor trade was a legitimate enterprise in Canada, that Canadian liquor constituted only a portion of the liquor illegally obtained by Americans, that virtually all the persons engaged in rum-running were American, that enforcement in Canada would only contribute to driving the traffic underground, and that enforcement in the United States remained less than diligent.[33]

Added to these arguments, the excesses of American enforcement were no more welcome in central and eastern Canada than they had been in British Columbia. Probably the most notorious example was the sinking of the *I'm Alone* in March 1929. Pursued nearly two hundred miles off the Gulf coast and inadvertently sunk by the U.S. Coast Guard, the Canadian-registered schooner was indeed a well-known rumrunner. Were it not for the death of the ship's captain, it is unlikely that the event would have raised such a diplomatic ruckus. The issue of search and seizure beyond international waters had been confronted much earlier on the Pacific coast in the *Quadra* and *Pescawha* incidents, as well as in other incidents in the Atlantic.[34] While western newspapers like the *Vancouver Sun* and the *Calgary Herald* recognized the hypocrisy in the United States—the great protagonist of freedom of the seas—sinking foreign vessels, they also recognized the complicity of Canadian rumrunners. On the other hand, it was for eastern Canada a question of whether "as the imperial ties slowly dissolved, [Canada] would be able to stand alone against the encroachments of a powerful neighbor."[35] The conduct of American efforts to enforce prohibition was, according to the *Montreal Gazette*, much too high-handed to suit the majority of Canadians.[36]

The same month, Mackenzie King offered the United States a counterproposal: the Canadian government was prepared to allow the United States to station American officers on the Canadian side of the border. This would, King reasoned, allow U.S. officials to transmit immediately to their colleagues south of the border that information deemed most helpful. King's gesture seems to have been an attempt to placate those Canadians for whom economics remained the most compelling reason not to cooperate. Under such a plan, the lucrative trade and Dominion revenue would have remained intact. Moreover, the economic burden of enforcement would have remained on American, not Canadian, shoulders. On the advice of the Treasury Department, concerned that a partial victory would undermine its efforts for a broader agreement, the United States refused and continued to hold out for the export ban.[37]

While Canadian nationalists and economic interests continued to militate against cooperation, there seems to have been a gradual shift in eastern public opinion so that it began to mirror more closely the sentiments prevalent in the Far West. Prohibition organizations and dry newspapers throughout Canada began to petition Ottawa to cooperate with the United States with a vigor equal to that expended on the much earlier campaign for prohibition.[38] Many in Ottawa at first discounted these petitions, for prohibitionists were not the majority in Canada. Yet with prohibitionists came a large segment of the population who agreed that, wet or dry, it was neither decent nor neighborly for Canada to undermine American public policy.[39] Soon these groups had attracted the support of Conservatives who saw in agitating for cooperation with the United States a moral high ground from which they could attack the slow-moving Liberals. "The condition had existed for several years," R. B. Bennett argued, "and ought to have been dealt with long ago."[40] Coming shortly before a Dominion general election, it proved to be a compelling argument. It is certain that King felt these pressures by late 1929 and began to look more energetically for a way to cooperate with the United States.[41]

Canada's yearning for an independent role in world affairs also seems to have encouraged the shift in public opinion. While always concerned about standing up to the United States, Canada was equally interested in its standing around the world. The *Ottawa Citizen* compared the present liquor question to Britain's role during the American Civil War. It likened Canada offering haven to rumrunners who broke American law to Great Britain allowing the Confederacy to build its ships in British yards during the war. "Canada," wrote the paper, "perhaps is just as liable to be assessed damages in the present war which is between the United States forces of law on the one hand and the criminal agents of the liquor trade on the other."[42] Soon other papers were touting the importance of Canada being a good neighbor. To refuse American requests to ban liquor exports—requests to which countries like Great Britain and Norway had already agreed—only imperiled Canada's good name. Moreover, diplomats in Ottawa thought that a positive gesture in the cause of American prohibition would prove beneficial on other pending diplomatic concerns, most notably the ever-thorny tariff issue and the St. Lawrence waterway project.[43]

The final impetus for a ban on liquor exports to the United States came in January 1930 when President Herbert Hoover proposed stationing ten thousand agents along the Canadian-American border. The proposal was a mixed blessing for Canadians. Many were glad to see the United States finally taking responsibility for its problems. Others were more concerned. The *Chronicle Telegraph* of Quebec worried, "Experience has shown that the type of man employed as a prohibition agent is not conspicuous for his judgment or responsibility and even with the greatest care in selection, there are bound to be a number . . . who are not fit to be trusted with firearms."[44] The *Ottawa Journal* elaborated, commenting that ten thousand rifles could do a lot of damage anywhere, but "when they are in the hands of . . . Volstead enforcement officers, notoriously without discrimination in fingering a trigger, anybody's liable to be shot at any time, whether he is a smuggler, or a bootlegger, or an evangelist." While some Canadians found the whole proposal mildly amusing, pleading only "please don't shoot Canadians," in the opinion of the *Journal* it was "no matter to laugh at."[45]

As might be expected, Hoover's proposed border patrol received an equally mixed, though different, reception in British Columbia. Most British Columbians seem not to have shared the concern of their countrymen about the potential for stray bullets or border conflicts between Canadians and Americans. The *Daily Province* understood exactly why the United States proposed such a plan. "Canada, while she may demur, can scarcely object," the paper wrote, "because she has really put it up to the United States to enforce her own prohibition law."[46] Instead, the primary concern reflected in the British Columbia press was the damage a standing patrol would do to that most enduring symbol of the Canadian-American relationship: the long, undefended border. A border patrol, noted the *Province*, "cannot fail to emphasize everything which divides Canada and the United States. It will give to our border an aspect which it has never had in a hundred years and more — the aspect of an armed frontier, where soldiers patrol the highways of international communication, where guns guard the line which, gunless and peaceful, has been the honorable boast of our friendship."[47] The proposed border force also concerned a number of representatives in the American Congress, especially those from border states. They wailed in protest that guarding the Canadian border would hinder legitimate business, pleasure trips, and tourism. The only answer to the problem was, according to the *Province*, for Canada to assist "her neighbor to the extent of keeping Canadian liquor at home." "She is under no obligation to do this, as it is not her law that is being violated," it noted, "but she would be acting the part of a good neighbor if she could see her way clear to follow such a course."[48]

By March 1930 enough Canadians believed the same that Mackenzie King felt confident enough to introduce a bill in the House of Commons prohibiting the export of liquor to the United States. To placate those still opposed, especially those within his party, King couched the ban as a law wholly for the domestic affairs of Canada. Even the name of the bill itself failed to include "United States." While R. B. Bennett and other Conservatives criticized King for not introducing the bill sooner, King replied with the realistic statement that he had had to wait for Canadian public opinion to catch up.[49] Despite expected opposition in the Senate, after the measure passed overwhelmingly in the House of Commons, most senators were reluctant to flout Canadian public opinion. On May 30, 1930, Canada amended its export act, prohibiting the export of liquor to the United States.[50]

RUMRUNNERS ON THE RUN

Throughout the 1920s, the most oft-repeated complaint from those charged with enforcement of the Eighteenth Amendment was the lack of manpower and equipment. Indeed, the problem with the "Hoover broom"—as many called American enforcement, usually derisively—was that it lacked sufficient bristles. Rumrunners were well aware of this deficiency and were only too eager to use numerical superiority to their advantage. While law enforcement agencies remained perennially underfunded throughout the prohibition era, by mid-decade most had come to terms with their handicap. They became increasingly pragmatic in their approach to stamping out the illicit traffic.[51]

Bolstered by recent Supreme Court decisions that upheld the earlier seizures of the *Quadra* and *Pescawha*, the Pacific fleet of the Coast Guard found that the most successful way to keep rum ships off the high seas was to enmesh them in red tape. The case of the *Federalship* offers an example. In late February 1927 the 205-foot steamship owned by Consolidated Exporters sailed from Vancouver flying the Panamanian flag. The vessel's crew probably thought that its Panamanian registry would protect it from seizure by the United States while on the high seas. Unfortunately, just two months earlier—apparently after some prodding by the State Department—Panama had enacted Law 54, which revoked Panamanian nationality from any vessel devoted to smuggling. Trailing the *Federalship* some 275 miles off the California coast, the Coast Guard eventually seized the rumrunner with 12,500 cases of liquor. The Coast Guard defended the seizure on the grounds that since the *Federalship* was involved in smuggling and had no bona fide nationality, it was therefore subject to seizure under piracy laws. Nevertheless, in federal court, Judge George Borquin dismissed the piracy argument and ruled the seizure illegal.[52]

That the court eventually released the *Federalship* was of little concern to the Coast Guard. As long as seized vessels remained tied up in the courts, they could not run liquor. Many Americans supported the actions, illegal or not, praising the Coast Guard's refusal to be intimidated by foreign rumrunners.[53] So successful was the Coast Guard that the American consul in Vancouver later enumerated a number of the vessels along the coast tied up in red tape: the *Federalship* and *Principio* lay waterlogged in Mexican ports and the *Quadra*, *Pescawha*, and *Chris Moeller* had been captured and were out of service. Likewise, so many idle vessels littered Vancouver's Burrard Inlet that the consul dubbed it the new "Rum Row."[54]

In March 1925 Congress authorized those charged with enforcing prohibition to use any vessel or vehicle seized for smuggling violations. The passage of this act served a double purpose. It ended the "revolving door" through which vessels seized for smuggling were auctioned back to the illegitimate trade. It also provided the government with additional equipment to patrol the border. Soon the Coast Guard was patrolling the Puget Sound with more than a few vessels with a colorful past.

When, in 1924, Congress grudgingly approved $13 million for the Coast Guard, a portion found its way to the Pacific. By 1925 the Coast Guard had twenty-two vessels engaged in operations against rumrunners on the Puget Sound, where, earlier in the decade, there had been only two. Many of these vessels were former rumrunners or surplus navy vessels that were less than ideal for law enforcement. Nonetheless, they were important in countering the numerical superiority enjoyed by the rumrunners. Toward the end of the decade the Coast Guard was able to cover the southern shore of the Juan de Fuca Strait and the Strait of Georgia, making it more effective in deterring water landings in the Puget Sound.[55]

Every announcement of a seizure or new vessel added to the Coast Guard fleet resulted in prompt predictions that the Puget Sound was "drying up." Evidence suggests that the Coast Guard was at least effective enough to raise the market price of bootlegged liquor. At the royal commission hearings, Consolidated Exporter's Robert Swanson had remarked that the use of boats in rum-running had indeed diminished due to greater vigilance on the part of the Coast Guard.[56]

Yet evidence also suggests that rum-running's demise was greatly, and prematurely, exaggerated. When one Canadian official offered his opinion that now the U.S. Coast Guard could, with relative ease, keep under surveillance every vessel that left a British Columbia port, the American consul at Victoria commented more realistically, "We who are engaged in prohibition enforcement understand, of course, the difficulties and limitations under which this task is carried out, but this is not realized by the outsider."[57] Ironically, having seized many of the larger vessels that made up Rum Row, the Coast Guard had increased its workload. In place of large vessels concentrated in groups just off the coast, the rum-running traffic began to be conducted by more numerous and widely dispersed smaller vessels. For the Coast Guard, this required extensive scouting operations over a wider geographic area. The Coast Guard continued to suffer a need for additional patrol vessels until prohibition's repeal in 1932. Moreover, while rum-running by ship seems to have diminished somewhat, the use of automobiles had increased dramatically, with no corresponding increase in resources allotted to defend the land border.[58]

Despite claims that the United States showed little initiative in enforcing prohibition, there were notable exceptions, particularly in terms of institutional reform. In 1925, after recognizing the difficulty inherent in coordinating the actions of myriad agencies, all agencies charged with enforcing Volstead were brought under the control of one assistant secretary of the treasury. The number of federal prohibition directors was reduced to from forty-eight to twenty-two, and the number of border patrolmen increased by Congressional authorization. In 1927 these agencies were further consolidated in the Bureau of Prohibition. In the same year, responding to the criticism that most prohibition agents were unqualified for their jobs, all were required to be certified under the provisions of the Civil Service Commission. Finally, in 1930 the Bureau of Prohibition moved to the Department of Justice, where, many hoped, the attorney general would be better able to enforce the penal provisions of the law.[59]

A reorganization of prohibition forces also occurred in the Northwest. In early 1926 General Lincoln Andrews, head of prohibition enforcement, sent Alf Oftedahl, a special agent in the Intelligence Unit of the Internal Revenue Bureau, to serve as "prohibition czar" on the Pacific coast. When Andrews ordered Roy Lyle, the federal prohibition director for the region, to subordinate his Seattle office to Oftedahl's investigators, Lyle's patron, Senator Wesley Jones, exploded in irritation.[60] Nevertheless, given full authority to represent the Treasury Department with officials of the Canadian government, Oftedahl's impact was almost immediate. His office became the clearinghouse for information and evidence concerning the illicit traffic gathered by all enforcement agencies. Oftedahl included in his web the American consuls, who turned out to be valuable eyes and ears in British Columbia. Rather than send information to the State Department, where it usually languished until no longer of use to other agencies, the consuls sent it directly to Oftedahl, who in turn forwarded it directly to enforcement officers. The enforcement cooperation that developed in the Northwest proved to be a model for the rest of the border. In late 1928 Assistant Attorney General Mabel Walker Willebrandt complimented the coordination in the Seattle office and requested that the American consul in Vancouver travel to the Detroit-Windsor region to facilitate the same type of coordination there.[61]

Coming as late as it did, it is difficult to assess the export ban's impact on American efforts to seal the border. In reality, it only removed the official sanction given the smuggling traffic by Ottawa. It did nothing to prevent rumrunners from continuing their practice of declaring their cargo bound for some point outside the United States and then, once out of Canadian territory, diverting it to the liquor's true destination. Being the great entrepreneurs they were, rumrunners were prepared to continue smuggling liquor to the United States until there was no demand for it. It is likely that the deepening economic depression and prohibition's ultimate repeal played greater roles in reducing the demand than did the export ban. Nonetheless, the struggle to achieve the ban is instructive. Although complicated by Dominion-provincial jurisdictional conflicts, resolution of the prohibition problem demonstrated just how important the concept of "neighbors" was to those who lived along the border, especially in the Far West. By the late 1920s, the desire for a peaceful, undefended border was something about which both Canadians and Americans could agree.

CHAPTER NINE

British Columbia and the Origins of American Repeal

A border divides, but it is also a place where diverse things interact. It is where politically independent peoples, ideas, and systems meet with, act on, and communicate with each other. Along an especially porous border, those who inhabit one side cannot help but be influenced, for good or ill, by those on the other. Stephen Leacock had alluded to this interaction (and to his own wet leanings) in 1920, during the drive for national prohibition, when he warned his British brethren about American temperance workers: "If they come among you, pick them up and throw them into the sea, and throw them good and far."[1] While Canadians with drier sympathies might have commented differently, Leacock's admonition touched upon one of the central realities of both the prohibition and antiprohibition causes. They were movements that paid little attention to borders.

Most Canadians and Americans had welcomed the arrival of prohibition during the First World War. Many more rejoiced at the saloon's demise, and certainly all rejoiced that the sober forces of democracy had triumphed. However, the end of the war diminished in both Canadians and Americans the intensities of their moral ideologies. Absolute prohibition was, according to the *Vancouver Sun*, a "wartime ideal beyond the present and normal abilities of the Canadian people."[2] The same held true, though to a lesser degree, in the United States. It was only natural that the sacrificial fervor that bolstered prohibition during the war would run headlong into the relaxed rhythms of everyday life after the war ended. Despite the lag in time between repeal in Canada and repeal in the United States, there remained a close connection between the two. Just as the border had earlier served as a sort of interface for the prohibition movement, it also served as an interface for those who opposed it. Thus it is to the experience of British Columbia that we look for the origins of American repeal.

LESSONS FROM BRITISH COLUMBIA

Even those willing to concede the benefits of prohibition were quick to realize that the different course taken by Canada might provide useful lessons for the United States. Cornelius Vanderbilt Jr. adopted this theme in a *Seattle Post-Intelligencer* feature when he wrote, "Prohibition has been to the United States, as a whole, a tremendous success. Except in cases of those who could afford bootleg or those who would take a chance, it has proven an excellent thing for the working classes and the great industrial centers." He went on to comment, though, that no matter how successful prohibition had been in the United States, "the example set by our neighbor in the Northwest is one that can well be studied and maybe someday put in effect as a solution towards making of us less the spirit of the bootlegger and more the spirit of the worthy American citizen who stands by, upholds and believes in his constitution."[3]

As we have seen, the success or failure of prohibition in the United States was so closely affected by the liquor situation in Canada that it was impossible for Americans to leave their northern neighbor out of any discussion of the topic.[4] As Americans considered ways of modifying or repealing American prohibition, it was natural that they should look to Canada. Of course, both advocates of repeal and advocates of continued prohibition considered the experiences of many countries that, like Canada, had abandoned national prohibition in favor of some form of government control.[5] Still, it was to Canada that the American eye first turned. Beyond geographic propinquity, many Americans considered Canada the ideal proving ground for an alternative to prohibition; most importantly, according to one American observer, this was because

Canadians were "so very much like ourselves. They and we speak the same tongue, think much the same thoughts, obey or disobey much the same laws, and have an outlook on life that is almost identical."[6] In fact, liquor control was not the only Canadian social policy to which Americans had paid close attention. For example, only a year or two earlier, Americans had been especially interested in the operation of the Canadian sales tax. Unsatisfied with the income tax in the United States, one New York congressman declared that "our opinion as to the applicability of the Sales Tax to the United States must necessarily rest in a large measure upon the verdict of the business men of Canada, familiar with its physical operation."[7] With this history in mind, the value to be had in observing Canada's experiment with liquor was obvious.

If it was natural for Americans to look to Canada, it was even more natural that they should look specifically at British Columbia. As the first English-speaking province to abandon prohibition in favor of government control, British Columbia became the vanguard for a new North American system. Though Quebec instituted a similar policy at about the same time, it was easier for Americans to dismiss its adoption of government sale as "just another example of French Canada's distinctiveness."[8] By early 1923, four members of Congress and one cabinet officer had made extensive investigations of the liquor situation in British Columbia in hopes that it might provide lessons for the United States.[9] Likewise, American consular officers in British Columbia kept close tabs on the province's liquor system. They were acutely aware that it had important implications not only for the ability of the United States to enforce its prohibition laws but also because it had the potential to be a future alternative to the American system. Of course, no less interested in British Columbia's experience were the other Canadian provinces, which, over the course of the decade, followed the path taken by the Pacific province. That provincial liquor control resulted in more actual temperance than did prohibition was an impression soon shared by many throughout the Dominion.[10]

Many Americans, particularly moderates among both wets and drys, admired the statutory manner in which Canada sought temperance as opposed to the constitutional approach taken by the United States. This gave the Dominion the opportunity to test a variety of plans, leaving itself free, according to the *New York Times*, "to walk in the path of expediency . . . [while] Americans improvidently put fetters on their legs."[11] If arrangements made by the various provinces failed, each was free to change its laws accordingly. "It seems so easy for Canadians to change their minds," opined the *Boston Globe*. "We might be trying similar experiments if Prohibition were not a part of the Federal Constitution."[12] For others, the Canadian method provided Americans "the benefit of the Canadian experiment without the cost."[13] Thus, for moderates on the liquor question, British Columbia offered a useful "middle way," in which government control achieved the ends complete prohibition never would.

Of course, the conclusions Americans drew from the Canadian experiment in government control depended largely on whether one was wet or dry. For drys, the verdict on the British Columbia liquor system was never in question. It had failed. It had failed to eradicate the bootlegger, and it had failed to improve the character of the people. Spokane's fanatically dry *Spokesman Review* found "lively proof of the abounding presence in British Columbia of bootleggers, 'blind pigs,'" and all the other evils normally associated with the liquor traffic.[14] The *Spokane Daily Chronicle*, equally dry, called Vancouver a "Bootlegger's Heaven," where bootleggers were so confident, so bold, that they would openly carry liquor across the street in broad daylight while the police looked the other way. To critics of government control, the prevalence of the bootlegger in British Columbia refuted the theory that it would destroy, or even minimize, the liquor traffic. The *Review* asked, "What greater proof could there be that government dispensary does not stop bootlegging?"[15]

It appears that dry advocates like the *Review* and *Daily Chronicle* very selectively gathered their evidence. To be sure, bootleggers remained active in British Columbia even after the adoption of government control. Yet they existed there for different reasons than they did in the United States. In British Columbia bootleggers existed not because they were the only, or the primary, source of liquor to a population that would otherwise be dry. Instead, bootlegging continued because the provincial liquor control board had not yet settled on a price low enough to undermine the bootlegger's profits. It needed to set prices high enough to discourage excess consumption without setting them so high that they encouraged bootlegging. Whenever British Columbian dailies reported on the presence of bootleggers in their own pages, dry papers in the United States were quick to cite them as evidence that government control itself was a failure. Few were willing to acknowledge that the provincial system remained a work in progress.[16]

Even drys who conceded that government control at least minimized bootlegging refused to concede that it eliminated drunkenness. "More drunk men may be seen on the streets of Vancouver, B.C. in one day," commented the *Daily Chronicle*, "than on the streets of all the combined cities of Washington in a month." When advocates of government control released figures showing fewer arrests for drunkenness in Canadian cities compared to cities in the United States, the *Chronicle* admitted that the figures might be true but dismissed them anyway, noting, "The figures do not mean there is less drunkenness . . . [only that] drunkenness without disorder is not a reason for arrest in Canadian cities." Even as late as 1929 the *Chronicle* remained unwilling to consider the merits of the Canadian system. "Let no one in the United States be deluded by the irresponsible assertion that abandonment of prohibition and adoption of the Canadian system would settle the liquor issue," it wrote. "If it can't be settled by prohibition, it can't be settled at all—and it is being settled by prohibition."[17]

Whatever the legitimacy of its arguments, the dry lobby remained as undeterred by the border in guarding prohibition as it had been in establishing prohibition years earlier. The American Woman's Christian Temperance Union went on record as rejecting the Canadian system of government control. Mary Harris Armor of Atlanta, known in convention circles as "The Georgia Cyclone," argued, "Under the Canadian plan as applied to this country, they would take a bartender and put him in the uniform of the United States Government."[18] The evidence American chapters used was more than happily provided by their Canadian counterparts, eager to play a role in keeping the Eighteenth Amendment in the American constitution. In a speech before the Washington WCTU in Seattle, the vice president of the Canadian WCTU termed government control "the biggest curse that ever came to Canada," agreeing with many of her colleagues who "would rather have had the old rotten saloon with its dirty men behind the counter and its dirty people in front of the bar" than to allow government liquor into the home.[19] No more deterred were American prohibitionists who hoped that Canada would admit the failure of government control and return to the prohibition fold. In late August 1927, at the invitation of the Provincial Prohibition Association, the well-known American prohibitionist William "Pussyfoot" Johnson lectured at the Capitol Theatre in Vancouver. Ever aware of Canadian sensitivities, Johnson assured the crowd that he had come "not to interfere or influence in any way the local laws of the land or to tell the people of British Columbia how to conduct their business, but to explain the working of the prohibition laws in the United States."[20]

Many British Columbians continued to find the American experiment with prohibition at least mildly amusing. But Canadians' sense of humor diminished when American drys attacked the Canadian system. When Senator William Borah of Idaho accused the British Columbian government of making "revenue the chief purpose" of the law, many took issue with the senator's "political pabulum." "The liquor law in Vancouver is being reasonably well observed," the *Vancouver Sun* noted. "The city is reasonably temperate. There are fewer drunks on the streets today than there were during strict prohibition." Though the *Sun* admitted that the liquor law in British Columbia was not perfect, it did argue that British Columbians believed it "miles ahead of the hypocritical farce that is being enacted in the United States."[21] One British Columbian obviously concurred when he wrote to the *Victoria Daily Colonist*, "According to the American Bar Association, Cook's County, Illinois has more criminals in her penitentiary than we have in all the penitentiaries of the Dominion of Canada. If this is the record of dry Chicago, let us thank God we live in wet British Columbia, where we do not, like the U.S.A., have to build armored cars to transfer a little money or merchandise from one place to another."[22] Not to be outdone, Senator G. H. Barnard of British Columbia agreed, commenting four years later, "Never has crime been so rife, never were the gaols and penitentiaries of the United States so crowded, as since the passing of the Eighteenth Amendment."[23] In short, a persistent belief shared by many British Columbians was that they were glad prohibition did not extend to their own particular domicile. Further, American criticism only served to remind Canadians of the more unattractive aspects of American society and of why they were Canadian and not American.[24]

Thus, while drys were prone to see the Canadian system as a failure, wets were likely to see it as enlightened policy. That virtually all the Canadian provinces had followed British Columbia's and Quebec's example remained a compelling indication that something was right with government control. Even for those not yet convinced about the moral, economic, and social results of the Canadian experiment, only those Canadians who were irreconcilable prohibitionists denied the failure of prohibition.[25]

For most wets, the evidence was that under government control, bootleggers were "a vanishing race," put out of business by competition.[26] Cornelius Vanderbilt Jr. found little of the bootlegging in British Columbia that the dry Spokane newspapers had so excoriated. Other wets pointed out that even if government control had not eliminated the bootlegger entirely, he was not the same gun-toting peddler of poisoned liquor that he was under American prohibition. Government control had turned the bootlegger into a "one-and-two-bottle man," who was unlikely to debauch seriously the public order.[27] The Canadian example should be a lesson to those in the United States concerned about bootleggers, argued the *New York Times*. "How long could the bootleggers last in this country," it wrote, "if liquor drinkers knew that they could buy at a Government store honest whisky . . . at no fantastic price?"[28] Speakeasies and blind pigs in the United States remained a persuasive argument—especially to moderate wets who remained sympathetic to temperance—that the Canadian system of government control resulted in more actual temperance, without increasing crime or debauching public morals in the process.[29]

Of the lessons learned from government control in Canada, perhaps the most salient and powerful was the economic. That Quebec and British Columbia drew substantial revenue from the sale of liquor in government stores certainly had its influence on public opinion in Alberta and the other provinces as they considered adopting government control. By 1925 all four of the western provinces had abandoned prohibition, attracted by the prospect of increasing provincial revenues at the expense of the bootlegger.[30] But the economics of government control in British Columbia also had an effect on public opinion in the United States. A widely circulated report of the American Association against the Prohibition Amendment lauded the British Columbian system for its efforts in diverting bootlegger profits to provincial social programs, education, hospitals, and road construction. As Vanderbilt pointed out in 1923, after only two years of government control, "The hospitals, insane asylums and orphans' homes have been liberally supported by the provincial government and the treasury of British Columbia resembles King Tut's tomb."[31]

Vanderbilt's conclusion was only barely an exaggeration. During the first five years of government control in British Columbia, the provincial treasury swelled by some $14.7 million. By 1927 annual profits soared to $1.9 million and by 1929 to an even more astounding $4.2 million.[32] Two things must be said about these profits. The first is that they were not enjoyed only by British Columbia. Each of the provinces that adopted government control realized similar profits, usually corresponding to the size of its population. For example, the more populated Quebec's net profit for the year 1928 totaled $6.2 million.[33] Second, the provinces derived these profits not only from Canadian citizens but also from American tourists. In 1925 the American Association against the Prohibition Amendment estimated that American vacationers opposed to prohibition spent over $100 million abroad.[34] Many wets concluded that it would be better for the American economy if Americans stayed home and spent their money on American rather than Canadian liquor. The argument acquired added significance when the effects of the Depression began to be felt in late 1929 and early 1930.

By the late 1920s the success of government control in Canada had attracted the attention of American authorities charged with enforcing the Volstead Act, even those still sympathetic to the prohibition ideal. Admiral Hugh Rodman, who had commanded a battleship fleet in the North Sea during the First World War, advocated adopting the Canadian system when he commented, "In theory, I believe in prohibition, and if it could be enforced I would back it to the utmost. Practically, it is a conspicuous failure. . . . Several of the Canadian [provinces] tried prohibition and abandoned it as being impractical, and now dispense alcoholic beverages under Government supervision, and profit by it morally and financially. I firmly believe that the same policy should be adopted by our Government."[35] Congress also considered asking the Wickersham Commission on Law Enforcement and Observance to study the Canadian system and "to ascertain whether any such method could be used as a substitute for prohibition in the United States." As Wickersham himself remained firmly opposed to its repeal, however, only passing mention of the Canadian system appears in the commission's final report.[36]

Did British Columbia's system of government control of liquor actually decrease drunkenness? While statistical evidence is elusive, anecdotal evidence suggests that it did. Even those who would otherwise be strong advocates of prohibition believed that in British Columbia government control had led to more temperance than had the province's previous experience with prohibition. Reverend Lewis Hooper, the chairman of the Missions to Seamen organization in Vancouver, certainly thought so. In 1926, after working eight years among the notoriously inebriate mariners of the city's wharves and shipyards, Hooper commented,

> I have therefore observed that fewer seamen during the past year have been arrested on charges of drunkenness, and that I am seldom now called to the Police Court to speak for men so charged. . . . I have myself visited some half dozen of the beer parlors at various

times in the day, and I am obliged to confess with gratification, that I saw no signs of intoxication or disorder, that the places were clean and well kept, and that the service was admirable. . . . I am now of the opinion that no better plan than the present one in B.C. has yet been conceived.

Although Hooper admitted that there were occasional problems, success or failure was a relative judgment. Overall he remained "confident that Vancouver will compare most favorably with our neighboring cities in the republic, Seattle and Portland, in regard to convictions resulting from drunkenness while they have the advantage of a Prohibitory Act."[37]

Regardless of government control's actual effects, many Americans remained convinced that it did reduce drunkenness in ways that national prohibition in the United States had not. The conclusion among most Americans dissatisfied with the Eighteenth Amendment was, as a Massachusetts resident reflected, that "any sane man who has witnessed the workings of Volsteadism is this country and the Government-controlled systems . . . will vote for the Canadian system every time."[38]

LESSONS LEARNED

Throughout the 1920s prohibition in the American Northwest gradually but irreversibly lost the support necessary for its continuation. Even groups like organized labor were quick to favor repeal, since the return of beer and liquor would create jobs. By 1930 the State Federation of Labor in Washington—once so outspoken about the place of labor in a sober society but now in the throes of the Depression—had grown "silent as a stone."[39] Equally concerned were American hotel proprietors, who watched helplessly as American tourists filled British Columbian hotels to capacity, while American rooms lay as empty as they were dry. James Crawford Marmaduke, a wealthy Seattle hotel promoter and the president of the Washington State Repeal Association, along with the American Hotel Association, printed leaflets and newspaper ads reminding Americans that prohibition cost the taxpayer over $1 billion per year in lost tourist receipts. Like many in the state's capital,

Governor Clarence Martin saw government control as a possible answer to Washington's problems. It worked well enough in British Columbia, Martin reasoned, and it would certainly contribute nicely to desperately needed state revenues.[40]

Even into the early 1930s, Washingtonians responded to prohibition more than to almost any other political issue. While only 614,000 voted in the presidential election of 1932, some 698,000 turned out to vote for repeal-convention delegates just one year later. Although the state legislature had ratified the Eighteenth Amendment without a dissenting vote in 1919, Washington's voters had become overwhelmingly wet in the ensuing decade. It seems that administrative scandals, wiretapping by federal agents against popular figures like Roy Olmstead, and congested court dockets—all with no apparent decline in drunkenness—had taken their toll. They convinced many Americans in the Pacific Northwest sufficiently that polls taken in the spring of 1930 showed a substantial majority for repeal.[41] Even Senator Wesley Jones, the state's senior U.S. senator and author of many of the most important punitive laws against the liquor traffic, recognized that that the tide was beginning to turn. Responding to the polls, Jones conceded that although he remained a committed dry, if his state asked Congress to submit a referendum to the people, he would not stand in the way. In 1933 Washingtonians voted for repeal by a margin greater than two to one.[42]

Ratification of the Twenty-First Amendment gave each state the right to regulate the liquor traffic in much the same way as the Canadian provinces. The result in Washington was the Steele Act. Among other things, the act established a Liquor Control Board and gave to the state the right to regulate the manufacture, distribution, and sale of all alcoholic beverages.[43] Not surprisingly, its authors modeled the Steele Act on the British Columbia system. Over the next few years, both Washington and British Columbian officials regularly met to compare notes on their respective systems. The head of the Washington Liquor Control Board commented that his counterpart in British Columbia had given "invaluable information based upon ten years' experience in practical Government liquor control."[44]

Much as Governor Martin had hoped, government control in Washington lived up to expectations. With the state having the lowest prices on bottled liquor in the nation, bootleggers were almost nonexistent and revenues well beyond expectations. In 1936 the Washington Liquor Control Board was able to report an enviable $8.6 million in revenue from government sales.[45]

Many Canadians viewed American repeal as a complete validation of the Canadian approach to liquor control. It reconfirmed their belief that the Canadian political system was far more responsive "to the ebb and flow of public thought" than was that of its neighbor to the south.[46] Nonetheless, Washington's adoption of government control in 1933 had significant economic implications, not only for British Columbian brewers, distillers, and bootleggers but for the province's Liquor Control Board as well.

Nationally, Canadian distillers and brewers had prepared for American repeal by storing under government seal some forty-five million gallons of scotch and rye whiskey. To put the figure in perspective, this amount would have been sufficient to meet the Dominion's domestic needs for some twenty years. As the *New York Times* commented in early 1933, "Canada, like a good neighbor, will go to great lengths to render service.... When the United States wants liquor, this country will supply it, even if every distillery and brewery and winery in the Dominion has to work overtime."[47]

For the British Columbia Liquor Control Board and BC hoteliers, the outlook was not so good. Thirsty Americans no longer needed to make the short trek to British Columbia for their liquor. Even more distressing, board officials worried that Washington's inexpensive liquor would favorably compete with British Columbia's, cause the bootleg flow to reverse directions and flood the provincial market with cheap American liquor. To forestall this, the provincial government promptly reduced the price of its liquor permits from two dollars to twenty-five cents. Nonetheless, with the continuing effects of the Depression and bootlegging from Washington, British Columbia's profits did not return to their prerepeal levels until the Second World War.[48]

Repeal of the Eighteenth Amendment almost certainly induced sighs of relief along the international boundary. The preprohibition attitude that Americans could do without liquor so long as they did not know it existed was certainly shared by many. Unfortunately, the proximity of a wet neighbor to the north guaranteed that liquor could not remain so conveniently out of mind. Canadians had, for more than a decade, provided to thirsty Americans more than inexpensive, sometimes-unadulterated whiskey. They also provided a model. The perceived successes of government control in Canada united wets in the United States to those drys who had voted for prohibition with the idea that it would at least promote temperance. When it failed to do so, the British Columbian model became an increasingly attractive alternative. While Canadians more often paid attention to matters south of the border than Americans did to matters north, prohibition's repeal offered one compelling example of the latter. The border was, as it had always been, an interface between the social policies of both countries.

Epilogue

PARADOX REVISITED

By the summer of 1933 prohibition was but a memory along the North Pacific borderlands. American brewers and distillers had, in the months since repeal, finally caught up to the American demand and obviated the need for the services of the rumrunner. On August 24 Fraser Miles called it quits. Rum-running had treated him well, as it had many of his counterparts, Canadian and American. Yet the British Columbian had not yet finished crossing the border. In September, with a bulging money belt around his waist, Miles did what many Canadians had done before. He headed south of the border to attend college. There was a certain logical irony in his doing so, since it was American money, spent by Americans for Canadian whisky, that allowed him to go to college at all.[1]

Miles's American colleague, Johnny Schnarr, found crossing the border again equally irresistible. Schnarr made the last of his four hundred liquor runs across the border on April 2, carrying 250 cases to Seattle. Averaging 150 cases per trip, Schnarr calculated that he had smuggled over 60,000 cases between 1920 and 1933. In doing so, he had contributed some $4 million to the Canadian economy, a staggering amount that he was reluctant to abandon. He eventually settled north of the border at Telegraph Bay. As far as those who did not know better were concerned, Schnarr was an American who had made his fortune in a land deal in the States and had come to Canada to retire. At least that was the story he gave when the income tax people came.[2]

Other rumrunners did not cross the border as often once prohibition ended. Robert Pamphlet, captain of the *Pescawha* and heroic savior of the *Caoba*, would cross the border only once more. After serving a two-year sentence at McNeil Island Penitentiary, he returned home to Vancouver, where he soon died of tuberculosis. The disease was a souvenir of sorts, some said, from his time at McNeil.[3] Likewise, after his release in May 1931, Roy Olmstead spent more time crossing the Puget Sound to do Christian Science missionary work among the prisoners of McNeil Island than he did crossing the border to run liquor. When later asked by interested reporters, inmates, or grateful former patrons if he was Roy Olmstead, the king of rumrunners, Olmstead would reply, "No, not any more. The old Roy Olmstead is dead."[4]

For his part, Henry Reifel, head of the liquor export company Joseph Kennedy Ltd., found crossing the border in the years after prohibition still problematic. On July 6, 1934, Henry and his son, George, were arrested by American authorities in Seattle on charges of violating U.S. tariff laws stemming from their role in the liquor traffic. After posting bonds of $100,000 each, both Reifels promptly returned to Vancouver, having learned a valuable lesson about the border, the danger it presented, and the refuge it might offer. As they had during the royal commission proceedings, the senior Reifel's physicians asserted that he was too ill to return to Seattle. Though granted a one-month reprieve, when the Reifels again failed to appear on August 20, the court took only two minutes to order the bond forfeited and the defendants rearrested. Unable to force the Canadians to return to the United States on the criminal matter, U.S. attorneys continued instead with a civil suit for $17,250,000. In July 1935 the Reifels agreed to settle the suit for $500,000 and—it was strongly hinted—dismissal of the criminal charges. They were free to cross the border once more.[5]

Many of the boats that made up the rum-running fleet returned to their former roles as fishing or cargo vessels, never again to be quite as profitable. In 1929 the ill-fated *Beryl G*, now the *Manzette*, came to an inglorious end on the rocks of Valdez Island. Used to tow logs in the Strait of Georgia, the former rumrunner apparently never was able to escape its haunted past.[6] In February 1933 Pamphlet's *Pescawha*, on its first legitimate voyage after being released by the Coast Guard, met a similar fate at the mouth of the Columbia River. In sad irony, it was the same location at which the *Pescawha* had rescued the crew of the *Caoba* some eight years earlier.[7]

With wets firmly in control in both Canada and the United States, the British Columbia Prohibition Association reluctantly recognized the futility of pushing for world prohibition. At an executive meeting held in November 1933, the association adopted a resolution changing its name to the British Columbia Temperance League.[8] Though one would think that the cause of prohibition was dead, it was not. Five months later, William D. Upshaw, a former Georgia congressman and one-time dry candidate for president of the United States, visited Victoria's Metropolitan Church to participate in a prohibition rally. "This is our day of renaissance," Upshaw optimistically proclaimed. "British Columbia is waking up, we've started on the way back to national prohibition. We do not intend to surrender one inch."[9]

As they had during prohibition, tourists continued to flood across the line as well. In the postprohibition case, however, the flow reversed. To the chagrin of provincial hotel proprietors and restaurateurs, British Columbians headed south for Washington's lower liquor prices and liberal Sunday drinking laws.[10] Not surprisingly, the reception they received in the United States closely mirrored the reception Americans had received during prohibition. While American business establishments welcomed the economic windfall, Canadian "rowdyism and strenuous celebration" led local residents to question tourism's value. Stumped as to how to preserve the peace, officials at Boundary Bay, Washington, eventually canceled beer licenses in that community altogether.[11]

Of course, Americans continued to travel north of the border, though—given repeal and economic depression—in decreasing numbers. Instead of liquor, it was the "certain quiet charm that we do not get in our busy everyday life in the States" that attracted Americans to British Columbia.[12] While one tourist found the attitude of a local restaurant cashier "snippish" about accepting American money, most Americans continued to find Canadians very hospitable. In turn, British Columbians remained generally happy to see American tourists, though a gentleman who complained that it was now "inconvenient to get beer, ale, and liquor" was probably an exception.[13]

So it was that life in the Pacific Northwest borderlands returned to its normal, somewhat ambivalent self. Had the noble experiment not come when it did, it is unlikely that liquor would have been anything other than one of the myriad "pinpricks" that had always plagued bilateral relations at this distant edge of the continent. Coming as it did, however, at the height of Canada's effort to assert an independent foreign policy and at a time of rapid growth of cross-border tourism and economic interaction, the prohibition issue assumed significance disproportionate to its intrinsic value.

In more harmonious times Canadians and Americans cross the border almost as if it does not exist, or at least with little thought about what it represents, figuratively or literally. It is only during periods of tension or conflict that one might expect to see the border's full character and meaning become more apparent, making visible and more seemingly important what is usually latent and hidden. Prohibition was one of those periods.

In some ways—as interface, as opportunity, as refuge, as margin—the prohibition-era border tied together Canadians and Americans who shared common interests and common needs. It provided a market for the liquor industry, tax revenue for the Dominion and its provinces, and employment for the bootlegger and rumrunner during the early years of the Depression. It provided respite for American tourists, a delightfully wet oasis in which they could take refuge from a legislated social morality with which they disagreed. Always, it served to divide two peoples who were different, but not too different.

In other overlapping ways—as interface, as refuge, as symbol of sovereignty, and as peril—the border served as a metaphor for everything that was significantly different about Canadians and Americans, their values, and their institutions. In this sense, it helped shape or reinforce the Canadian identity. The border juxtaposed radically different approaches to the temperance problem, approaches rooted in fundamentally different outlooks and beliefs. No less important, for a nation bent on demonstrating its newly gained sovereignty, the very existence of a border seemed to require conflict rather than conciliation.

Indeed, it is precisely because the border meant so many different things to so many different people and interests on both sides that there could be no clear consensus about what the Canadian role should be. To some degree this was true across the entirety of the Canadian-American border. Yet, as many scholars have shown, the Canadian-American relationship is not homogenous but varies according to regional peculiarities. Geography often plays an important role in defining the relations between nations, and so it follows that where that geography varies, there will be unique variations in those relations as well. Thus historians looking for evidence of a "good neighbor" relationship or its opposites, Canadian nationalism and anti-Americanism, must do so with these regional differences in mind.

The central paradox of prohibition in the Pacific Northwest is that it was the very heritage that had enabled the smuggling traffic before prohibition that led British Columbians to advocate cooperation against the liquor traffic ahead of the more eastern provinces. Throughout the nineteenth and early twentieth centuries, economic, social, and cultural ties made necessary by a geography that ran north-south more than east-west, as well as a shared sense of marginalization from the countries of which they were a part, led many Canadians and Americans in the Northwest to relate more to each other than to their respective sovereignties. As a consequence, regional interests that British Columbians and Americans shared in the Northwest did not always coincide with national interests espoused by Ottawa and Washington DC or by Canadians and Americans elsewhere along the border. While British Columbians were initially reluctant to cooperate with the United States for the same reasons that animated Canadians generally, they were clearly more concerned, and more concerned at an earlier stage, about the overall tenor of the Canadian-American relationship. When incidents like the *Beryl G* and revelations of corruption became so commonplace that they threatened the fabric of the previously close borderlands relationship, British Columbia became the vanguard for ending rum-running, regardless of the economic cost. It had become apparent that prohibition undermined everything that was "special" and "neighborly" about the "undefended" border in this distant part of the continent. Although the border remained a symbol of separate sovereign loyalties, during prohibition it magnified regional loyalties even more. Future decades would increasingly direct the Pacific province's outlook more and more toward Canada but, in the meantime, British Columbians and Americans remained *neighbours* first and nationalists a distant second.

Notes

ABBREVIATIONS USED IN THE NOTES

BCA British Columbia Archives, Victoria

CAR *Canadian Annual Review of Public Affairs*

DCER Canada, Department of External Affairs, *Documents on Canadian External Relations*

FRUS U.S. Department of States, *Foreign Relations of the United States*

LAC Library and Archives Canada, Ottawa

"Morrison Court Book Notes" "Notes from the Court Book of The Honourable Mr. Justice Morrison, Trial Judge," RG 13, vol. 1536, file 1–4, LAC

NARA National Archives and Records Administration, College Park, MD

NAS National Archives and Records Administration, Seattle

RCCE Royal Commission on Customs and Excise evidence, RG 33/88, LAC

PREFACE

1. Deutsch, "Contemporary Report on the 49° Boundary Survey," 30–31.
2. McDougall, *On Western Trails*, 70.
3. To date, the surprisingly few historians who have approached prohibition as a foreign relations issue have done so primarily from the diplomatic perspective. The standard, and most comprehensive, study is Kottman, "Volstead Violated." For a study written just as prohibition ended, see R. Jones, *Eighteenth Amendment*. Other studies include Holsinger, "The *I'm Alone* Controversy"; and William H. Siener, "Barricade of Ships, Guns, Airplanes and Men."
4. James Skitt Matthews, "Canadian and American Boy Scouts at Peace Arch Dedication," AM54-S4-:ArchP49, September 6, 1921, and Stuart Thomson, "Kiwanis Club Meeting—International President at Boundary," (group photograph), AM1535-:CVA99–3438, City of Vancouver Archives.

5. Keenleyside quoted in McKinsey and Konrad, *Borderlands Reflections*, 30.
6. McKinsey and Konrad, *Borderlands Reflections*, iii. While the historiography for the U.S.-Mexican borderlands is well established, that of the Canadian-American borderlands is in its nascent, though maturing, stage. For early examples, see Lecker, *Borderlands*; Konrad, "Borderlands of the United States and Canada"; and New, *Borderlands*. An important, and more recent, work that explores the bilateral relationship from borderlands and transnational perspectives is Stuart, *Dispersed Relations*. For more on the theoretical underpinnings of this framework in the Canadian-American context, see Randy William Widdis, "Migration, Borderlands, and National Identity," in Bukowczyk et al., *Permeable Border*, 152–74. An excellent anthology that compares both the northern and southern borderlands is Johnson and Graybill, *Bridging National Borders*.
7. Kottman makes this argument in passing in "Volstead Violated," 112.
8. Even more staggering, three-fourths of all Canadians live south of the northernmost point of the forty-eight contiguous states and over 90 percent live within two hundred miles of the border. By comparison, only 12 percent of Americans live within one hundred miles of the boundary. See W. Thompson, *Canada 2001*, 14.
9. Lipset, *Continental Divide*, xvii.
10. Stephen Leacock, *My Discovery of the West: A Discussion of East and West in Canada* (Toronto, 1937), 163, quoted in Russell Brown, "The Written Line," in Lecker, *Borderlands*, 1.
11. For examples of historians who have crossed borders in the Pacific Northwest, see Schwantes, *Radical Heritage*; Evans, *Borderlands of the American and Canadian Wests*; Findlay and Coates, *Parallel Destinies*; Wadewitz, *Nature of Borders*; Robbins and Barber, *Nature's Northwest*; J. Fahey, *Inland Empire: D.C. Corbin and Spokane*; J. Fahey, *Inland Empire: Unfolding Years*; MacDonald, *Distant Neighbors*; Morrissey, *Mental Territories*; and Ficken, *Unsettled Boundaries*. A number of important studies cover the West east of the Rockies. See, e.g., Bennett and Kohl, *Settling the Canadian American West*; Sharp, *Whoop-Up Country*; LaDow, *Medicine Line*; Graybill, *Policing the Great Plains*; McCrady, *Living with Strangers*; as well as McManus, *Line Which Separates*. For the transnational West in general, one might examine Shah, *Stranger Intimacy*.
12. Stuart, "Continentalism Revisited," 408.
13. Lipset, *Continental Divide*, xvii; and Winks, *Relevance of Canadian History*, xiii–xiv.
14. As Lipset has pointed out, Americans can learn more about their own country because "Canada is close enough to provide a frame of reference yet different enough to search for different explanations." Lipset quoted in McKinsey and Konrad, *Borderlands Reflections*, 2.
15. Hansen and Brebner, *Mingling of the Canadian and American Peoples*. More recent explorations of migration across the Canada-U.S. border during the first part of

the twentieth century can be found in Ramirez, *Crossing the 49th Parallel*; Widdis, *With Scarcely a Ripple*; E. Lee, "Enforcing the Borders"; Geiger, *Subverting Exclusion*; Chang, *Pacific Connections*; and Bukowczyk et al., *Permeable Border*.

16. Paul Rutherford, "Made in America: The Problem of Mass Culture in Canada," in Flaherty and Manning, *Beaver Bites Back?*, 265.

17. Russell Brown has examined border meanings found in Canadian and American literature. For a few examined in this study, his insights have been invaluable. See Russell Brown, "The Written Line," in Lecker, *Borderlands*, 1–27.

18. For his study, Schwantes defined the region variously as the "Pacific Northwest" and the "North Pacific Industrial Frontier," while Joel Garreau, in *The Nine Nations of North America*, labeled the region stretching from Northern California to Alaska "Ecotopia." Not surprisingly, five of the nine distinct regions into which Garreau divides North America encompass parts of both Canada and the United States. For a contrary view that argues that the border provides too much of a political discontinuity to consider British Columbia part of any transnational region, see Gastil, "Pacific Northwest as a Cultural Region."

19. *Maclean's Magazine*, April 1, 1926, 30; Geddes, *Skookum Wawa*.

I. CREATING A SMUGGLER'S PARADISE

1. Kipling, *Letters of Travel*, 210; Talbot, *New Garden of Canada*, vix–vii; Leacock quoted in Geddes, *Skookum Wawa*, 46.

2. Holbrook, *Far Corner*, 4.

3. Kipling, *Letters of Travel*, 204–5, 210; Talbot, *New Garden of Canada*, vix.

4. British Columbia, Bureau of Provincial Information, *Handbook of British Columbia*, 69. The land area of British Columbia covers 370,000 square miles. By comparison, the states of Washington, Idaho, Montana, and Oregon collectively encompass 390,892 square miles.

5. Harrington, "Kootenay Area of British Columbia," 193; Laurie Ricou, "Crossing the Borders in the Literature of the Pacific Northwest," in Lecker, *Borderlands*, 292.

6. Bennett and Kohl, *Settling the Canadian American West*, 13. See also Morrissey, *Mental Territories*, 1–20.

7. As Donald Warner points out, this north-south geographical alignment also applies to most of the Canadian-American border: "Since the grain of the continent runs generally north and south, each section of Canada was linked to the neighboring section of the United States rather than to the nearest part of Canada." Warner, *Idea of Continental Union*, 61.

8. McDonald, "Victoria, Vancouver, and the Economic Development of British Columbia," 370; Schwantes, *Pacific Northwest*, 139; and Seager, "Resource Economy," 212.

9. CAR, 1921, 136.

10. Angus, Howay, and Sage, *British Columbia and the United States*, 406; *CAR*, 1926–27, 624; *Maclean's Magazine*, April 1, 1926, 31.

11. Knight and Knight, *Very Ordinary Life*, 143. Richmond Hobson, in his own travels, commented that what British Columbians called a "highway" was actually no more than a "bush road." *Grass beyond the Mountains*, 18. Not much had changed even forty years later. The *Seattle Times* commented that BC's roads, "excluding those in and around Vancouver and Victoria, are basic Wagon Trail Modern: one lane each way, few guard rails, scarred and buckled by tough winters. Vast areas have either dirt roads or no roads at all." April 10, 1983, 1.

12. Warner, *Idea of Continental Union*, 127; Hansen and Brebner, *Mingling of the Canadian and American Peoples*, 155; Sage, "British Columbia Becomes Canadian," 173; Barman, *West beyond the West*, 123, 213; Schwantes, *Radical Heritage*, 4, 70, 122.

13. Quoted in B. Palmer, *Working-Class Experience*, 169.

14. McDonald, "Victoria, Vancouver, and the Economic Development of British Columbia," 386–87.

15. Sage, "British Columbia Becomes Canadian," 171.

16. John A. Schultz, "Whose News"; Ronyk, "United States in the Twenties," 12–28.

17. Barman, *West beyond the West*, 244; Schwantes, *Radical Heritage*, 37.

18. Barman, *West beyond the West*, 345.

19. Stevenson, "Sectional Factors in Canadian Foreign Policy," 677. See also census statistics in Barman, *West beyond the West*, 379–82.

20. McDonald, "Victoria, Vancouver, and the Economic Development of British Columbia," 388; Schwantes, *Radical Heritage*, 13–14.

21. Freeman interview and Georgeson interview, British Columbia Aural History Programme Collection, BCA; Victoria & Island Development Association, *Tourists' Map and Guide to Victoria*; Union Pacific Railroad Company, *Pacific Northwest and Alaska*.

22. Kipling, *Letters of Travel*, 204; Schwantes, *Radical Heritage*, 13–14.

23. Holbrook, *Far Corner*, 47; Barman, *West beyond the West*, 243.

24. Ronyk, "United States in the Twenties," 39–40. For similar evidence of this tendency for comparison, see Angus, *Canada and Her Great Neighbor*, 430–31.

25. See *Maclean's Magazine*, April 1, 1926, 30.

26. Angus, *Canada and Her Great Neighbor*, 443.

27. Holbrook, *Far Corner*, 30.

28. Angus, *Canada and Her Great Neighbor*, 443; Angus, Howay, and Sage, *British Columbia and the United States*, 386; Granatstein, *Yankee Go Home?*, 73.

29. Schwantes, *Radical Heritage*, 9.

30. Harrington, "Kootenay Area of British Columbia," 199.

31. British Columbia, Bureau of Provincial Information, *Handbook of British Columbia*, 71.

32. Brebner, *North Atlantic Triangle*, 295; Schwantes, *Radical Heritage*, 68.

33. Coates, "Controlling the Periphery," 147.

34. Schwantes, *Pacific Northwest*, 47–68.

35. Robbins, *Colony and Empire*, 44, 53.

36. As Norbert MacDonald points out, "Although original settlement was similar and private initiative was dominant, public authority played a much bigger role in the Canadian setting than in the American one. . . . The American settlers had a freer hand to choose as they saw fit; their counterparts in Canada faced partial, but nonetheless significant restrictions." *Distant Neighbors*, 19–20, 42–43, quote on pp. 19–20.

37. *Guide to the Province of British Columbia for 1877–78*, 46.

38. McDougall, *On Western Trails*, 144.

39. Ireland, "First Impressions," 100. Even the *California Bulletin* later shared this view: see *Guide to the Province of British Columbia for 1877–78*, 38. See also Ficken, *Unsettled Boundaries*, 54.

40. For a statistical study of these attitudes, with a breakdown by province, see Angus, *Canada and Her Great Neighbor*, 431–47. For a careful exploration of these views of Canada as a place of peace and the United States as a place of violence, see See, "Nineteenth-Century Collective Violence."

41. Findlay and Coates, *Parallel Destinies*, xii.

42. Sage, "British Columbia Becomes Canadian," 181; Brebner, *North Atlantic Triangle*, 296–300; Hansen and Brebner, *Mingling of the Canadian and American Peoples*, 203. As others have noted, the settlement of Canada and the United States can properly be told only in North American (not simply national) terms. See, e.g., Meinig, "Continental America, 1800–1915," 200.

43. Kipling, *Letters of Travel*, 205; Talbot, *New Garden of Canada*, 2.

44. For recent studies that explore Asian migration to the Pacific West and the racial tensions it created, see E. Lee, "Enforcing the Borders"; Annis, "'Chinese Question' and the Canada-US Border"; P. Roy, *White Man's Province*; Chang, *Pacific Connections*; and Geiger, *Subverting Exclusion*, particularly 99–123.

45. Holbrook, *Far Corner*, 32–37; Angus, *Canada and Her Great Neighbor*, 57. Even much later, the *Seattle Times* commented that although British Columbia is officially bilingual—English and French—like all of Canada, "across the province one can hear almost every tongue in the world including a lot of Russian in the Grand Forks and Castelgar areas along the border." French, it noted, "is rarely spoken." *Seattle Times*, April 10, 1983, 1.

46. Bennett and Kohl, *Settling the Canadian-American West*, 36–37.

47. Diary entry of October 6, 1911, in Craig, *But This Is Our War*, 14–15.

48. D. Smith, *Reminiscences of Doctor John Sebastian Helmcken*, 172.

49. Warner, *Idea of Continental Union*, vi, 137; J. Thompson and Randall, *Canada and the United States*, 300.

50. *London Times* quoted in Warner, *Idea of Continental Union*, 137. See also Fedorak, "U.S. Consul in Victoria."
51. *Chicago Tribune*, December 2, 1867, cited in Allan, *Bomb Canada*, 8.
52. D. Smith, *Reminiscences of Doctor John Sebastian Helmcken*, 247–48.
53. Henrickson, *Journals of the Colonial Legislatures*, 5:467.
54. D. Smith, *Reminiscences of Doctor John Sebastian Helmcken*, 247.
55. *Victoria Daily Times* quoted in Sage, "British Columbia Becomes Canadian," 170.
56. Berton, *Impossible Railway*, 8–9.
57. D. Smith, *Reminiscences of Doctor John Sebastian Helmcken*, xxiii.
58. Cody, "Evolution of Federal-Provincial Relations," 57.
59. See R. Roy, "Early Defense and Militia of the Okanagan Valley."
60. This saying is variously attributed to Vancouver's mayor in the 1930s, Gerry McGeer, and to W. A. C. Bennett. See Barman, *West beyond the West*, 347.
61. "The Spirit of the Northwest," *Outlook*, September 30, 1925, 149; Sage, "British Columbia Becomes Canadian," 169; Angus, *Canada and Her Great Neighbor*, 442; A. Scott, "Notes on a Western Viewpoint," 8.
62. Schonberger, *Transportation to the Seaboard*, 38; Cody, "Evolution of Federal-Provincial Relations," 55–65; Seager, "Resource Economy," 208–9. The initial and major proponents of confederation argued that a strong central government, along with a railway to the West, would open up the region's fur, mineral, oil, timber, and grain potential. This in turn would spur Ontario's industrial development. See Robbins, *Colony and Empire*, 55.
63. Pollard, "Pacific Northwest," 190.
64. Schonberger, *Transportation to the Seaboard*, xii.
65. Schwantes, *Pacific Northwest*, 266–78; "Election of 1892," in John Wooley and Gerhard Peters, *The American Presidency Project*, last modified 2013, http://www.presidency.ucsb.edu/showelection.php?year=1892.
66. Hitchman, *Maritime History of the Pacific Coast*, 50.
67. McIntosh, *Collectors*, 97–99, 230. In contrast to the rampant commercial smuggling along the more eastern border between Canada and the United States, most customs districts in the Pacific Northwest later reported much petty, but little commercial, smuggling. See RCCE, Victoria Evidence, 1677; Vancouver Evidence, 1813–25, 1947, 2086.
68. McCurdy, "Criss-cross over the Boundary," 182–84. Though most smuggled goods were complementary, one contested commodity was fish, particularly salmon. Consequently, residents on both sides of the border were quick to seek assistance of authorities whenever smugglers sought to undermine the legitimate market. See Wadewitz, *Nature of Borders*, particularly 144–67.
69. *Seattle Post-Intelligencer*, July 24, 1904, 8; McCurdy, *By Juan de Fuca's Strait*, 66.
70. *Washington Standard*, June 17, 1871, 2–3; RCCE, Vancouver Evidence, 1630; *Seattle Post-Intelligencer*, May 29, 1902, 5.

71. Richardson, *Pig War Islands*, 256.

72. Klug, "Immigration and Naturalization Service," 397.

73. *Seattle Post-Intelligencer*, June 18, 1922, 6R; *Literary Digest*, August 29, 1925, 43–44; McCurdy, *By Juan de Fuca's Strait*, 209; and McCurdy, "Criss-cross over the Boundary," 191–92.

74. As a future prime minister would report in 1907, "The amount consumed in Canada, if known, would probably appal [*sic*] the ordinary citizen who is inclined to believe that the habit is confined to the Chinese." See, "Report by W. L. Mackenzie King on the Need for the Suppression of the Opium Traffic in Canada," *Sessional Papers, Canada*, 1907–8, no. 36b, cited in S. Clark, *Social Development of Canada*, 439.

75. McIntosh, *Collectors*, 250; Splitstone, *Orcas*, 54.

76. *Seattle Post-Intelligencer*, June 18, 1922, 6R; Georgeson interview, British Columbia Aural History Programme Collection, BCA; RCCE, Vancouver Evidence, 1946–67.

77. William Ross to Deputy Collector—Sumas, Washington, May 31, 1907, RG 36, box 39, file 1907, NAS.

78. *Seattle Post-Intelligencer*, April 21, 1903.

79. *Victoria Chronicle*, August 1865, cited in Ramsay, *Ghost Towns of British Columbia*, 147.

80. Quoted in McCurdy, "Criss-cross over the Boundary," 182.

81. U.S. Department of the Treasury, *Annual Report*, 1915, 169.

82. *Literary Digest*, August 29, 1925, 43–44.

83. J. H. McLeod to Commissioner of Customs, May 19, 1914, RG 16, vol. 790, file 1058, LAC.

84. *Seattle Post-Intelligencer*, July 24, 1904, 8; McCurdy, "Criss-cross over the Boundary," 184.

85. McCurdy, *By Juan de Fuca's Strait*, 66.

86. W. Carmichael to Commissioner of Customs, September 9, 1914, RG 16, vol. 790, file 1058, LAC.

87. Commissioner of Customs to W. Carmichael, September 22, 1914, RG 16, vol. 790, file 1058, LAC.

88. Browne, *Crusoe's Island*, 254–55.

89. RCCE, Calgary Evidence, 8026.

90. De Lorme, "United States Bureau of Customs and Smuggling," 80. De Lorme's work remains the best introduction to smuggling in the Pacific Northwest. See also De Lorme, "Liquor Smuggling in Alaska."

91. *Seattle Post-Intelligencer*, April 21, 1903; D. Smith, *Reminiscences of Doctor John Sebastian Helmcken*, 208.

92. McCurdy, *By Juan de Fuca's Strait*, 59–60.

1. *Vancouver Daily News-Advertiser*, August 11, 1916, 1–2; *Vancouver Daily Province*, August 11, 1916, 4; *Vancouver World*, August 10, 1916, 2; August 11, 1916, 8.

2. W. F. Tolmie to H. M. Ball, October 16, 1866, GR 332, vol. 6, 150, BCA; Irving, *Astoria*, 337.

3. Cox, *Columbia River*, 173.

4. Merk, *Fur Trade and Empire*, 109; McLoughlin to Governor, October 20, 1831, in Barker, *Letters of Dr. John McLoughlin*, 215. For an overview of the Indian liquor traffic, see B. Gough, "Send a Gunboat!," 151–68; as well as N. Clark, *Dry Years*, 3–20.

5. Merk, *Fur Trade and Empire*, 182–83.

6. Merk, *Fur Trade and Empire*, 110; Governor Kennedy to Mr. Cardwell, Victoria, September 3, 1866, GR 332, vol. 6, 128, BCA. One historian, while affirming the Hudson's Bay Company's occasional use of liquor as a trade commodity, attributes this charge more to personal animosity between Beaver and the chief factor, John McLoughlin. See Galbraith, "Hudson's Bay Company under Fire," 324.

7. Rich, *Samuel Black's Rocky Mountain Journal*, xxv; Merk, *Fur Trade and Empire*, 110; McLoughlin to Governor of the Russian Fur Company, March 20, 1829, in Barker, *Letters of Dr. John McLoughlin*, 16–17.

8. McLoughlin to Peter Skene Ogden, December 15, 1831, in Barker, *Letters of Dr. John McLoughlin*, 237; William Smith to William B. Astor, March 3, 1830, in Merk, *Fur Trade and Empire*, 320–21.

9. Victor, *River of the West*, 303; Merk, *Fur Trade and Empire*, 110n; McLoughlin to Governor, Deputy Governor, and Committee, October 20, 1831, and McLoughlin to Governor, October 31, 1842, in Rich, *McLoughlin's Fort Vancouver Letters*, 2:71–72, 215; McLoughlin to Manson, October 5, 1829, McLoughlin to Sinclair, December 21, 1831, and McLoughlin to Ogden, January 31, 1832, in Barker, *Letters of Dr. John McLoughlin*, 59, 239, 252.

10. Rich, *McLoughlin's Fort Vancouver Letters*, 1:lxxxviii; Simpson to J. H. Pelly, February 1, 1837, in Merk, *Fur Trade and Empire*, 335.

11. "Diary of Robert Melrose," 199.

12. Soden, "Woman's Christian Temperance Union," 105.

13. N. Clark, *Dry Years*, 59–60.

14. Although it is difficult to substantiate the claim of the *Victoria Colonist* (October 9, 1877) that British Columbians consumed twenty-seven gallons of liquor per capita, it is well documented that liquor consumption in the province was at least one and a half times higher than in other provinces per capita. Per capita figures for annual liquor consumption in 1892 for the various provinces were: Prince Edward Island, 0.20; Nova Scotia, 0.41; New Brunswick, 0.49; Ontario, 0.81; Quebec, 0.90; Manitoba, 0.95; and British Columbia, 1.51. See Popham and

Schmidt, *Statistics of Alcohol Use*, 15–23. Another source corroborates the trend of these figures by calculating the average per capita annual liquor consumption for the three years ending in 1893 (in gallons): Prince Edward Island remained the lowest at 0.15, followed by Nova Scotia, 0.31; New Brunswick, 0.36; Ontario, 0.65; Quebec, 0.67; Manitoba, 0.67, and British Columbia, 1.26, twice the Dominion average of 0.60. See F. Spence, *Facts of the Case*, 20–21.

15. *Victoria Colonist*, September 15, 1881, cited in H. Allen, *Forty Years' Journey*, 81–82.

16. Gowan, *Church Work in British Columbia*, 45.

17. Synod report quoted in Soden, "Woman's Christian Temperance Union," 105.

18. Governor Kennedy to Cardwell, September 3, 1866, GR 332, vol. 6, 132, BCA.

19. Carr, *Book of Small*, 86.

20. Soden, "Woman's Christian Temperance Union," 105; N. Clark, "Hell-Soaked Institution," 4.

21. R. Smith, "Bibles and Booze," 2; Schwantes, *Radical Heritage*, 127; *Spokane Review*, January 8, 1894, 3; Fish, *Law Enforcement in Washington State*, 34–35. For more on the role of saloons in American society, see Powers, *Faces along the Bar*; Duis, *Saloon*; and T. Noel, *City and the Saloon*.

22. McDougall, *On Western Trails*, 11.

23. D. Lee and Frost, *Ten Years in Oregon*, 140.

24. Crosby, *Among the An-ko-me-nums*, 132.

25. Cronin, *Cross in the Wilderness*, 52–54, 90.

26. R. Smith, "Bibles and Booze," 2.

27. *Spokane Spokesman-Review*, November 12, 1901, 6; *Spokane Falls Morning Review*, October 4, 1888, 3.

28. N. Clark, *Dry Years*, 62, 76.

29. R. Campbell, *Demon Rum or Easy Money*, 15 and Barman, *West beyond the West*, 218–19. To a degree, this seems to have been true in the United States, where the eleven states that adopted female suffrage prior to passage of the Nineteenth Amendment in 1917 were all in the West. Seven of these were prohibition states while the other four had substantial areas under local option. See Sinclair, *Prohibition*, 95. This belief proved unfounded in the British Columbia context, however. For a recent study that explores prohibition in British Columbia, see Hamilton, *Sobering Dilemma*. See also Mattingly, *Well-Tempered Women*; and DuBois, *Feminism and Suffrage*. For more on the temperance movement and the social history of alcohol in Canada, one should consult Heron, *Booze*.

30. CAR, 1923, 506.

31. *Washington Standard*, June 20, 1879, 1.

32. CAR, 1922, 133–34; Dashaway Association, No. 15, *Constitution and By-Laws*; Warsh, *Drink in Canada*, 21, 94. See Barron, "American Origins of the Temperance Movement."

33. See *Journal of Proceedings: Grand Lodge of Washington Territory and British Columbia*, third annual session, 1872, and seventh annual session, 1876, University of Washington Special Collections.

34. Nancy M. Sheehan, "Temperance, the WCTU and Education in Alberta," 60–61; *Spokane Spokesman-Review*, January 17, 1920, 6; *New York Times*, November 14, 1922, 21, January 27, 1922, 17.

35. Willard, *Woman and Temperance*, 603; *Canadian Woman's Journal*, January 1891, 3, February 1891, 8, and March 1891, 5, cited in Tyrrell, *Woman's World/Woman's Empire*, 77; CAR, 1922, 386–88.

36. Tyrrell, *Woman's World/Woman's Empire*, 77; Willard, *Woman and Temperance*, 602–3.

37. Lydia MacPherson, "Historical Sketch of the Woman's Christian Temperance Union of British Columbia," 3, manuscript in BCA; Sheehan, "Temperance, the WCTU and Education in Alberta," 70–71; Barnes, *Centennial Mosaic*, 39, 43; R. Smith, "Bibles and Booze," 3; MS 0017, British Columbia Alcohol Research and Education Council Originals, vol. 2, file 18, BCA.

38. H. Allen, *Forty Years' Journey*, 30, 36, 37.

39. Holbrook, *Far Corner*, 10.

40. *Vancouver Daily News-Advertiser*, August 11, 1916, 1; *Vancouver B.C. Federationist*, August 18, 1916; *Vancouver Daily Province*, August 9, 1916, 4, 13.

41. *Vancouver B.C. Federationist*, August 18, 1916; *Vancouver World*, August 10, 1916, 2; *Vancouver Daily News-Advertiser*, August 11, 1916, 2; *Vancouver Daily Province*, August 9, 1916, 13, and August 10, 1916, 5.

42. *Electoral History of British Columbia*, 530; *Nation*, April 1925, 460–62; CAR, 1922, 133–34; and Barman, *West beyond the West*, 211.

43. Canada, Commission to Inquire into the Working of the Prohibitory Liquor Law in the United States, *Report of Commissioners*; G. Smith, "Prohibitionism in Canada and the United States"; F. Spence, *Facts of the Case*, 92.

44. Hamilton, *Sobering Dilemma*, 77–79.

45. *Victoria Daily Times*, April 3, 1924, 1; F. Spence, *Facts of the Case*, 13, 117; Royal Commission on the Liquor Traffic, *Minutes of Evidence: California*, December 2–3, 1892, in Canada, *Sessional Papers*, vol. 27, no. 14, pp. 2–4, 9, 13.

46. *Victoria Colonist*, May 10, 1874, November 12, 1887, May 5, 1888, and September 25, 1898, cited in H. Allen, *Forty Years' Journey*, 33, 77, 87, 90.

47. Berner, *Seattle, 1910–1920*, 190–93.

48. *Literary Digest*, July 12, 1919, 33–34; N. Clark, *Dry Years*, 142.

49. *Vancouver Saturday Sunset*, November 7, 1914, 1.

50. *Victoria Daily Colonist*, December 31, 1915, 4; *Winnipeg Tribune*, cited in Gray, *Booze*, 101.

51. In 1891 over 60 percent of non-native British Columbians lived in the four coastal cities of Vancouver, Victoria, Nanaimo, and New Westminster, while only 29.8

percent of Canadians nationally lived in cities of one thousand or more. By 1931 the figures had converged slightly: British Columbia remained 62.3 percent urban while Canada as a whole climbed to 52.5 percent. Not coincidentally, the Canadian provinces that held onto prohibition the longest were the Maritimes, which remained only 39.7 percent urban. See table 2.2 in Stone, *Urban Development in Canada*, 29; and Barman, *West beyond the West*, 189. In addition, in 1911 a staggering 70 percent of British Columbia's population was male. See Census of Canada statistics in Barman, *West beyond the West*, 385.

52. See *Victoria Daily Times*, August 16, 1917, 3.

53. *Christian Guardian*, September 22, 1915, quoted in Bliss, "Methodist Church and World War I," 225.

54. Barman, *West beyond the West*, 218–19.

55. *New York Times*, December 22, 1919, 1; April 18, 1920, sec. 7, 16; *Literary Digest*, March 12, 1919, 22; CAR, 1919, 686–89.

56. *Literary Digest*, March 8, 1919, 21; *New York Times*, June 6, 1920, 6; October 22, 1920, 13; Hose, *Prohibition or Control?*, 124–27. Although government control varied among the provinces, it can be defined broadly as a system under which the retail sale of liquor is a government monopoly. In the United States, government control was often called the dispensary system. See *Outlook*, May 19, 1926, 98–100.

57. Gray, *Booze*, 2, 59; Rose, "Labbe Affair," 50. Portland was particularly successful with prohibition, partly, Rose argues, because it was unique in that its immigrant and ethnic populations were small. Only 18 percent of whites were foreign-born. In Seattle this share was 23 percent and in San Francisco, 28 percent. In British Columbia this number was over 50 percent in 1921. See Census of Canada, 1941, in Barman, *West beyond the West*, 380. Other contemporaries speculated that the reason Prince Edward Island remained dry for so long was its nearly complete homogeneity in race and customs. See *Literary Digest*, July 26, 1927, 11.

58. Piers, *Sport and Life in British Columbia*, 122; *Literary Digest*, July 12, 1919, 33–34; R. Campbell, "Liquor and Liberals," 34; W. Smith, *Liquor Traffic in British Columbia*, 7.

59. *Victoria Colonist*, July 18, 1877, cited in H. Allen, *Forty Years' Journey*, 36; F. Spence, *Facts of the Case*, 298–303. Elsewhere in Canada, Anglicans accounted for one in five in Ontario and only one in seven in the Maritimes.

60. Quotes in Schwantes, *Radical Heritage*, 41–42.

61. No province is more illustrative of this irony than Ontario. Although the province remained dry itself until 1927, the majority of Canadian brewers and distillers nonetheless operated from Ontario. With creative shipping, it was not difficult for Ontario to become the major source of trouble for other dry provinces and the United States; a pattern British Columbia followed as well, albeit to a lesser degree. See *Literary Digest*, March 2, 1919, 22; Warsh, *Drink in Canada*, 25; R. Campbell, "Liquor and Liberals," 51.

62. R. Campbell, *Demon Rum or Easy Money*, 32; Sinclair, *Prohibition*, III–12.
63. Stretch, "From Prohibition to Government Control," 32–33.
64. *Victoria Daily Times*, February 6, 1920, in *British Columbia Legislative Assembly Sessional Clipping Books: Newspaper Accounts of the Debates, 1890–1972*, BCA; *Seattle Post-Intelligencer*, October 21, 1920, 1; October 22, 1920, 1, 14.
65. CAR, 1922, 141; *New York Times*, June 15, 1921, 17; W. Smith, *Liquor Traffic in British Columbia*, 19–20.
66. Schwantes, *Radical Heritage*, 72.
67. Richard de Brisay, "Our Neighbors to the South," *Canadian Forum*, January 1929, III. For the intriguing argument that Canadian political culture has been much less utopian than its American counterpart, see Hargrove, "On Canadian and American Political Culture."
68. *Le Canada*, February 28, 1922, quoted in Halstead to Secretary of State, March 6, 1922, 842.114/49, RG 59, NARA. See also Franklin, *What Prohibition Has Done to America* (New York, 1922), 7.
69. *Seattle Post-Intelligencer*, December 21, 1920, 6.

3. REFUGEES FROM VOLSTEAD

1. *Victoria Daily Colonist*, August 30, 1925, 14.
2. R., "Neighbors," 417.
3. *Literary Digest*, September 6, 1924, 19.
4. *Literary Digest*, September 6, 1924, 19.
5. Only recently have historians of American foreign relations begun to recognize the value of studying tourism as a transmitter of social and cultural values. Sources for the scholar in the Canadian-American context are surprisingly few. An introduction to the topic can be found in Hart, *Selling of Canada*. For British Columbia specifically, see Dawson, *Selling British Columbia*; and Mattison, *Projected Image*. See also Bregent-Heald, "Tourism of Titillation."
6. *Outlook*, December 16, 1925, 587; Black Ball Ferries, *Olympic Peninsula, Victoria and the San Juan Islands*; "Trails to Two Cities," *Sunset Magazine*, May 1933, 22–24; *Spokane Spokesman Review*, January 4, 1920, sec. 4, 1.
7. W. R. Dobbin to Deputy Collector (Sumas), n.d., file 237–1, box 12, RG 36, NAS.
8. Puget Sounders and British Columbians Associated, *Evergreen Playground*); Victoria & Island Development Association, *Call of Victoria*; Parks, *Tourists' Guide of Vancouver*; Victoria & Island Publicity Bureau, *Vancouver Island and Its Holiday Resorts*.
9. *Portland Oregonian*, August 22, 1922, 11; CAR, 1926/27, 229; Canada, House of Commons, *Debates*, May 18, 1925, 3314; Dawson, *Selling British Columbia*, 44–45.
10. *New York Times*, January 1, 1922, sec. 2, 15; Holbrook, *Far Corner*, 29–30; Piers, *Sport and Life in British Columbia*, 112–13.
11. For works that have explored this democratization of travel brought about by

the automobile, see Belasco, *Americans on the Road*; and Hyde, "From Stagecoach to Packard Twin Six."

12. H. Palmer and T. Palmer, *Alberta*, 224–29; *Spokane Daily Chronicle*, October 27, 1929, 4; CAR, 1925/26, 525; Piers, *Sport and Life in British Columbia*, 116.

13. *Seattle Post-Intelligencer*, August 21, 1924, editorial page; *Vancouver Sun*, July 8, 1925, 1.

14. Victoria & Island Development Association, *Tourists' Map and Guide to Victoria*.

15. Dominion Hotel, Victoria, *Information for Our Guests*.

16. *New York Times*, February 24, 1930, 20.

17. Quoted in Sinclair, *Prohibition*, 335.

18. *Seattle Post-Intelligencer*, December 6, 1920, 6; December 13, 1920, 6.

19. *New York Times*, April 6, 1930, sec. 10, 4, 7; Sinclair, *Prohibition*, 317.

20. Stowe and Stegner quoted in Russell Brown, "The Written Line," in Lecker, *Borderlands*, 8.

21. For those who sought the border as refuge, see also Gerhard J. Ens, "The Border, the Buffalo, and the Métis of Montana," in Evans, *Borderlands of the Canadian and American Wests*, 139–54; McCrady, *Living with Strangers*; LaDow, *Medicine Line*; McManus, *Line Which Separates*; and Graybill, *Policing the Great Plains*.

22. *Literary Digest*, February 15, 1930, 60–61; *New York Times*, February 24, 1930, 20.

23. Brebner, *North Atlantic Triangle*, 294–95.

24. *New York Times*, February 23, 1930; Norman Haynor, "Auto Camps in the Evergreen Playground," *Social Forces* 9 (1930): 256–57, cited in Dawson, *Selling British Columbia*, 43.

25. U.S. Department of the Treasury, *Annual Report*, 1927, 115; 1928, 82.

26. McIntosh, *Collectors*, 338.

27. *Vancouver Sun*, April 4, 1925, 1.

28. Assistant Secretary of the Treasury to Secretary of State, August 4, 1927, 842.114/14, RG 59, NARA.

29. Wesley Jones to Secretary of State, 1 September 1913, 842.114/7, RG 59, NARA.

30. Canada, House of Commons, *Debates*, June 3, 1921, 4495.

31. *Victoria Daily Times*, March 17, 1921, 1, 3; American Consul (Prince Rupert) to Secretary of State, August 26, 1930, 811.114Canada/4349, RG 59, NARA; *New York Times*, July 13, 1928, 2.

32. *Seattle Post-Intelligencer*, October 3, 1920, sec. 5, 1.

33. Canada, House of Commons, *Debates*, May 2, 1923, 2415.

34. *Seattle Post-Intelligencer*, July 15, 1923, sec. D, 1; American Consul (Vancouver) to Secretary of State, September 30, 1927, 842.114/290, RG 59, NARA.

35. *New York Times*, September 9, 1928, sec. 3, 1, 5; March 27, 1931, 24; December 21, 1932, 18; June 24, 1929, 38; Canada, Senate, *Debates*, May 23, 1934, 401; Stokes, "Prohibition's Decline and Fall," 174.

36. *New York Times*, March 15, 1933, 13. For further prohibition-period tourism statistics that corroborate these general trends, see *New York Times*, April 14, 1932, 38; September 23, 1934, sec. 4, 4.

37. *Victoria Daily Times* quoted in Canada, House of Commons, *Debates*, April 16, 1925, 2096.

38. *New York Times*, February 15, 1925, sec. 8, 18.

39. *British Columbia Legislative Assembly Clipping Books*, February 17, 1920, BCA.

40. *Vancouver Daily Province*, December 15, 1928, 1; *Victoria Daily Times*, November 8, 1930, 4.

41. For a full history of licensed beer parlors in British Columbia, see R. Campbell, *Sit Down and Drink Your Beer*.

42. *Vancouver Daily Province*, November 17, 1924, 6.

43. *Literary Digest*, September 23, 1922, 21.

44. H. W. Thornton to Minister of Railways and Canals, January 7, 1929, RG 25, DI, vol. 742, reel T1758, frames 514–16, LAC.

45. Canada, House of Commons, *Debates*, April 16, 1925, 2094.

46. McIntosh, *Collectors*, 336–37.

47. Russell Brown, "The Written Line," in Lecker, *Borderlands*, 9.

48. Frye, *Bush Garden*, 213–51.

49. *New York Times*, June 1, 1930, sec. 3, 2; *Seattle Argus*, August 22, 1931, 2.

50. American Consul (Prince Rupert) to Secretary of State, December 3, 1929, 842.114Liquor/73, RG 59, NARA.

51. Quoted in McIntosh, *Collectors*, 337.

52. Piers, *Sport and Life in British Columbia*, 63–64; *New York Times*, May 23, 1925, 14.

53. American Consul (Prince Rupert) to Secretary of State, August 26, 1930, 811.114Canada/4349, RG 59, NARA.

54. Glynn-Ward, *Glamour of British Columbia*, vii–viii.

55. *Victoria Daily Times*, September 29, 1929.

56. American Consul (Vancouver) to Secretary of State, February 26, 1925, 811.114Canada/181, RG 59, NARA.

57. *Spokane Daily Chronicle*, May 29, 1928, 4.

58. *Vancouver Daily Province*, June 4, 1928, 6.

59. Sinclair, *Prohibition*, 336.

4. THE HALCYON DAYS OF RUM-RUNNING

1. Haynes, *Prohibition Inside Out*, 87.

2. If one were pressed to make a distinction between a bootlegger and a rumrunner, a bootlegger was generally one who smuggled liquor by land while a rumrunner was one who smuggled liquor by water. Colloquially, however, contemporaries used both terms interchangeably. So too does this story.

3. Kramer quoted in Merz, *Dry Decade*, 123.

4. Kottman, "Volstead Violated," 109.

5. Miles, *Slow Boat on Rum Row*, 214.

6. *Vancouver Daily Province*, January 20, 1929, 6; Mendeville, "Sources of the Booze Supply"; Merz, *Dry Decade*, 66–67; Hacker, "Rise and Fall of Prohibition," 667.

7. Merz, *Dry Decade*, 196–97; *Seattle Post-Intelligencer*, November 28, 1921, 6.

8. *New York Times*, March 22, 1926, 1–2.

9. *Maclean's Magazine*, December 1, 1928, 5. One Washington daily unappreciatively called Canada's participation "a national indulgence toward the export trade." See *Spokane Spokesman-Review*, July 30, 1922, 1.

10. Lonsdale, "Rumrunners on Puget Sound," 30; Gray, *Booze*, 131, 189.

11. *Portland Oregonian*, November 11, 1923, 9; Richardson, *Pig War Islands*, 309; R. Campbell, *Demon Rum or Easy Money*, 24.

12. Ernest R. Forbes, "The East-Coast Rum-Running Economy," in Warsh, *Drink in Canada*, 166–67.

13. RCCE, Victoria Evidence, 1205–07; Vancouver Evidence, 6140.

14. Miles, *Slow Boat on Rum Row*, 96.

15. Marinoff testimony, in "Notes from the Court Book of the Honourable Mr. Justice Morrison, Trial Judge," RG 13, vol. 1536, file 1–4, LAC; American Consul (Victoria) to Secretary of State, November 30, 1926, 811.114Chris Moeller/2, RG 59, NARA; RCCE, Victoria Evidence, 1203–06.

16. Miles, *Slow Boat on Rum Row*, 3, 128, 141, 160.

17. Parker and Tyrrell, *Rumrunner*, 66–67.

18. Deputy Collector (Sumas WA) to Deputy Collector in Charge (Puget Sound Collection District), January 4, 1924, RG 36, box 22, file 410, NAS.

19. *Portland Oregonian*, March 10, 1922, 7.

20. Parker and Tyrrell, *Rumrunner*, 218.

21. Bittancourt interview, British Columbia Aural History Programme Collection, BCA; Parker and Tyrrell, *Rumrunner*, 167.

22. Lonsdale, "Rumrunners on Puget Sound," 29.

23. MacGregor, *History of Alberta*, 241; Gary A. Wilson, *Honky- Tonk Town*, 97.

24. The *New York Times* (April 1, 1928, sec. 3, 2) called Olmstead the "King of the Bootleggers in the Pacific Northwest"; the *Vancouver Sun* (January 14, 1926, 1) called him the "reputed King of the Pacific Coast Rumrunners," and the *Seattle Star* (November 18, 1924, 1), "The King of the Bootleggers."

25. For the best analysis of Olmstead's career, see N. Clark, "Roy Olmstead."

26. *Seattle Union Record*, March 22, 1920, 1; *Seattle Daily Times*, March 22, 1920, 1, 5.

27. *Seattle Union Record*, March 22, 1920, 1; *New York Times*, May 26, 1930. Before Olmstead got around the twenty-dollars-per-case duty, the going rate for a quart of whiskey was as high as twenty-four dollars; afterward it dropped to as low as

seven dollars per bottle. The retail price charged by bootleggers did, of course, fluctuate according to supply and demand. As the industry became more and more competitive and more organized, the profit margins decreased. See *Seattle Post-Intelligencer*, April 2, 1924, II; Parker and Tyrrell, *Rumrunner*, 107–8; and Lonsdale, "Rumrunners on Puget Sound," 33.

28. *Seattle Post-Intelligencer*, May 16, 1931, editorial page.
29. Potts, *Seattle Heritage*, 83–84; N. Clark, *Dry Years*, 166.
30. *New York Times*, April 1, 1928, sec. 3, 2; *Seattle Star*, November 18, 1924, 1.
31. *Seattle Daily Times*, November 19, 1924, 1, 4; *New York Times*, April 1, 1928, sec. 3, 2; *Seattle Argus*, February 27, 1926, 1; *Seattle Post-Intelligencer*, January 21, 1925.
32. *Seattle Post-Intelligencer*, November 19, 1924, 1, 6; November 21, 1924, 1, 4; January 21, 1925, 1, 3; *Vancouver Sun*, January 14, 1926, 1. So thoroughly did Willebrandt disapprove of the practice of wiretapping that she had refused to argue the case against Olmstead. The Solicitor General of the Justice Department had to appoint outside counsel to present the United States' case. See Willebrandt, *Inside of Prohibition*, 231–32, 237.
33. *New York Times*, June 5, 1928, 31; *Seattle Daily Times*, December 26, 1932, sec. 2, 18. For a wide variety of opinion on the decision see, "Wiretapping Held Legal," *Literary Digest*, June 16, 1928, 10.
34. Olmstead quoted in N. Clark, "Roy Olmstead," 98.
35. *Seattle Daily Times*, December 26, 1932, sec. 2, 18.
36. *Seattle Argus*, February 27, 1926, 1.
37. Customs Circular, December 29, 1919, RG 36, box 5, file 135, NAS; RCCE, Vancouver Evidence, 7608.
38. Rogers, *Rogers-isms*, 13.
39. *Seattle Daily Times*, March 8, 1926, 4.
40. *New York Times*, June 13, 1920, sec. 7, 1; Cameron interview, British Columbia Aural History Programme Collection, BCA.
41. Reiber, "Old Whiskey Trail"; *New York Times*, January 12, 1922, 19.
42. "Blind pig" was a commonly used synonym for speakeasies, or underground saloons.
43. *Maclean's Magazine*, June 15, 1922, 15; *Spokane Spokesman-Review*, January 14, 1920, II; *Victoria Daily Times*, March 12, 1931, 4.
44. *Literary Digest*, April 4, 1925, 77; *Seattle Argus*, June 27, 1925, 1, 4; *Maclean's Magazine*, November 1, 1929, 6–7.
45. Hargrove to Commissioner of Prohibition, May 1, 1928, RG 56, box 3, file 97s, NAS.
46. *Nation*, May 31, 1922, 637.
47. Rogers, *Rogers-isms*, 14; RCCE, Vancouver Evidence, 2007; Sessional Paper 5d, January 5, 1927, RG 14, D2, vol. 171, LAC; *CAR*, 1924/25, 87.

48. Special Deputy Collector (Seattle) to Deputy Collector (Sumas), December 16, 1920, RG 36, box 5, file 135, NAS.

49. *Literary Digest*, October 22, 1921, 44–45.

50. Gray, *Booze*, 156; Deputy Collector in Charge (Blaine) to Deputy Collector (Sumas), August 2, 1924, RG 36, box 22, file 410, NAS; RCCE, Calgary Evidence, 8204; Vancouver Evidence, 6141, 6150.

51. RCCE, Calgary Evidence, 8101, 8114, 8206–7.

52. Wilson, *Honky-Tonk Town*, 48, 55, 74.

53. *Seattle Post-Intelligencer*, November 29, 1924, 4; *Annual Report of the Liquor Control Board*, in British Columbia, Legislative Assembly, *Sessional Papers*, 1923, B11; RCCE, Victoria Evidence, 1272.

54. Joseph Kennedy Ltd. was owned by Henry Reifel Sr., who also owned British Columbia Distillers. Though popular lore has long associated Joseph Kennedy with bootlegging during prohibition, there is little evidence that such is the case. There is even less evidence that he was at all related to Reifel's Joseph Kennedy Ltd. For the best analysis of the Kennedy myth, see Okrent, *Last Call*, 366–71.

55. Canada, Royal Commission on Customs and Excise, *Final Report*, 23–24; American Consul (Prince Rupert) to Secretary of State, May 4, 1926, 811.114Canada/1670, RG 59, NARA; RCCE, Victoria Evidence, 927, 1273; Vancouver Evidence, 2016; *Annual Report of the Liquor Control Board*, in British Columbia, Legislative Assembly, *Sessional Papers*, 1923, B10; Canada, House of Commons, *Debates*, May 2, 1923, 2405–6.

56. *Ford et al. v. United States*, 273 U.S. 593, 104; *New York Times*, May 16, 1926, 23. Manitoba Refineries also sent land agents to the United States. See RCCE, Victoria Evidence, 1399; Vancouver Evidence, 5032.

57. American Consul (Vancouver) to Secretary of State, September 15, 1927, 811.114Canada/3763, RG 59, NARA.

58. Gray, *Booze*, 153; Parker and Tyrrell, *Rumrunner*, 116, 119, 167–79.

59. Miles, *Slow Boat on Rum Row*, 145.

60. American Consul (Vancouver) to Special Agent Charles Emery (Seattle), July 12, 1928, RG 56, box 1, file 7A, NAS; Miles, *Slow Boat on Rum Row*, 216–17.

61. Lonsdale, "Rumrunners on Puget Sound," 31; Vassilopoulos, "Fast Rumrunner—Albi Wahoo," 33.

62. American Consul (Victoria) to Commander, U.S. Coast Guard (Port Townsend), December 19, 1925, 811.114Canada/1139, RG 59, NARA; Miles, *Slow Boat on Rum Row*, 255–70.

63. Parker and Tyrrell, *Rumrunner*, 129.

64. American Consul (Victoria) to Captain F. G. Dodge (Seattle), February 16, 1925, 811.114Canada/164, RG 59, NARA; *Seattle Post-Intelligencer*, April 2, 1924, 11; Starkins, "Rum Running," 15; Richardson, *Pig War Islands*, 311.

65. *Ford et al. v. United States*, 273 U.S. 593, 624; *Seattle Post-Intelligencer*, November 29, 1924, 4; Miles, *Slow Boat on Rum Row*, 194.

66. Parker and Tyrrell, *Rumrunner*, 66.

67. Roe interview, British Columbia Aural History Programme Collection, BCA.

68. RCCE, Victoria Evidence, 919.

69. Burford to Read, June 6, 1928, and Read to Commissioner of Prohibition, December 11, 1929, RG 56, box 1, file 7A, NAS; *Seattle Post-Intelligencer*, November 29, 1924, 4; Wheeler, "Liquor in International Trade," 149.

70. Deputy Collector (Sumas) to Collector (Seattle), January 15, 1920, RG 36, box 5, file 135, NAS.

71. Harris to Secretary of State, April 23, 1926, 811.114Canada/1600, RG 59, NARA.

72. American Consul (Vancouver) to Secretary of State, September 5, 1928, 811.114Canada/4082, RG 59, NARA; Parker and Tyrrell, *Rumrunner*, 68; *New York Times*, March 22, 1926, 1–2; April 21, 1927, 26; March 30, 1930, sec. 9, 4.

73. *Seattle Post-Intelligencer*, October 22, 1920, 14.

74. *Seattle Post-Intelligencer*, November 18, 1920, 6.

75. Sinclair, *Prohibition*, 163–67, 191–92.

76. *Seattle Post-Intelligencer*, December 8, 1920, 1; June 8, 1922, 1; Parker and Tyrrell, *Rumrunner*, 122; *New York Times*, March 3, 1926, 8.

77. Parker and Tyrrell, *Rumrunner*, 79–80.

78. *New York Times*, December 14, 1923, 23.

79. Cameron interview, British Columbia Aural History Programme Collection, BCA.

80. A. E. McFatridge to Director of Prohibition, August 8, 1931, RG 56, box 19, file 948M, NAS.

81. A. E. McFatridge, Sandpoint Memorandum, June 7, 1931, and Newport Memorandum, May 25, 1931, RG 56, box 19, file 948M, NAS.

82. Merz, *Dry Decade*, 67–68.

83. *New York Times*, March 30, 1930, sec. 9, 4.

84. *Outlook*, July 15, 1925, 400.

85. Vancouver *Daily Province*, January 20, 1929, 6; Merz, *Dry Decade*, 114.

86. *Seattle Argus*, June 27, 1925, 1, 4; *Portland Oregonian*, November 11, 1923, 9.

87. Lyle quoted in N. Clark, *Dry Years*, 153; *Portland Oregonian*, November 11, 1923, 9.

88. W. Baud to Collector of Customs (Port Townsend), n.d., RG 36, box 39, file 1913, NAS.

89. Memorandum by Earle E. Koehler, January 27, 1928, RG 56, box 2, file 48S, NAS; RG 56, box 27, file 1953M, NAS; Harding quoted in N. Clark, *Dry Years*, 183.

90. Lonsdale, "Rumrunners on Puget Sound," 29, 32.

91. Jones quoted in Lonsdale, "Rumrunners on Puget Sound," 70.

92. *Seattle Times*, April 30, 1961, magazine section; *Seattle Post-Intelligencer*, June 13, 1922, 3; June 14, 1922, 2; June 16, 1922, 3.

93. Lonsdale, "Rumrunners on Puget Sound," 31; *Newport Miner*, January 19, 1922, quoted in Bamonte and Bamonte, *History of Pend Oreille County*, 191; Miles, *Slow Boat on Rum Row*, 248.

94. *Spokane Spokesman-Review*, October 3, 1927, 4.

95. American Consul (Vancouver) to Secretary of State, July 25, 1929, 811.114Canada/4221, RG 59, NARA; Willebrandt, *Inside of Prohibition*, 234–35; *Nation*, September 18, 1929, 291.

96. Kennedy to Koehler, November 30, 1928, RG 56, box 3, file 132S, NAS.

97. *Seattle Post-Intelligencer*, December 21, 1920, 6.

98. *Seattle Post-Intelligencer*, November 8, 1921, sec. 2, 20.

5. SYMBOL OF SOVEREIGNTY

1. Clark and Illinois congressman George Prince quoted in Granatstein, *Yankee Go Home?*, 61–62.

2. Bemis, *American Secretaries of State*, 10:293.

3. Inglis, "'W.H. Eastwood' Affair," 55. For an analysis of Anglo-American diplomacy during this period, see Spinelli, *Dry Diplomacy*.

4. J. Thompson and Randall, *Canada and the United States*, 104; Inglis, "'W.H. Eastwood' Affair," 55.

5. *Aide-Mémoire*, Department of State to the British Embassy, June 27, 1922, FRUS, 1922, 563.

6. Secretary of State to Ambassador Geddes, June 26, 1922, DCER, 3:946–48; Ambassador Geddes to Secretary of State, October 13, 1922, and December 6, 1922, FRUS, 1922, 578–81, 589–90.

7. Senator Thomas Sterling to Secretary of State, July 28, 1922; Secretary of State to Sterling, August 16, 1922, FRUS, 1922, 564–74.

8. Mackenzie King, Address to Imperial Conference, October 8, 1923, DCER, 3:236.

9. *Aide-Mémoire*, Colonial Secretary to Governor General, September 6, 1923, DCER, 3:962.

10. Secretary of State to Ambassador Geddes, March 7, 1923, FRUS, 1923, 228–29.

11. Chilton (for Ambassador Geddes) to Secretary of State, June 19, 1923, DCER, 3:958.

12. CAR, 1922, 141.

13. Chilton to Secretary of State, July 16, 1923, DCER, 3:958–59; Secretary of State to Chilton, July 19, 1923, FRUS, 1923, 231.

14. Secretary of State to the Assistant Secretary of the Treasury, November 24, 1923, FRUS, 1923, 233–39.

15. Chilton to Acting Foreign Secretary, June 30, 1922, DCER, 3:945–46; Chilton to Governor General, September 19, 1923, DCER, 3:984–86.

16. Chilton to Secretary of State, August 9, 1923, DCER, 3:960–61; George Black to Prime Minister, July 7, 1922, Mackenzie King Papers, vol. 70, reel C-2242, LAC.

17. Acting Secretary of State to Chilton, September 13, 1923, *FRUS*, 1923, 232–33. For *Cunard v. Mellon*, see 262 U.S. 100.
18. Secretary of State to the Assistant Secretary of the Treasury, November 24, 1923, *FRUS*, 1923, 233–39.
19. Chilton to Governor General, June 29, 1922, *DCER*, 3:943.
20. Assistant Secretary of the Treasury to Secretary of State, December 29, 1923, *FRUS*, 1923, 240–50.
21. Bemis, *American Secretaries of State*, 10:296. In practice, however, many rumrunners and enforcement officers understood the rule to mean twelve miles—an imprecision that would later create new diplomatic controversies of its own.
22. Convention between the United States of America and Great Britain, signed at Washington, January 23, 1924, *FRUS*, 1924, 158–61.
23. Memorandum, "The Dominion Government and the Control of the Liquor Traffic," n.d., reel T1758, frames 465–72, RG 25, D1, vol. 742, file 149, part 1–4, LAC; *New York Times*, June 7, 1924, 15.
24. Headline quoted in Parker and Tyrrell, *Rumrunner*, 75.
25. Parker and Tyrrell, *Rumrunner*, 74–75.
26. *Maclean's Magazine*, December 1, 1928, 4.
27. Convention between the United States of America and Great Britain in Respect of Canada, signed at Washington, June 6, 1924, *FRUS*, 1924, 189–92; *New York Times*, November 30, 1923, 7.
28. *Financial Post*, July 20, 1923, cited in *CAR*, 1923, 61.
29. *Annual Report of the Department of Trade and Commerce*, in Canada, *Sessional Papers*, 1922–23, 1925; *New York Times*, March 30, 1930, sec. 9, 4.
30. Richard de Brisay, "Canada Turns against Prohibition," *Nation*, April 1925, 461.
31. Dominion Brewers' Association, *Facts on the Brewing Industry*, 31, 61; Canada, Department of Trade and Commerce, Dominion Bureau of Statistics, *Control and Sale of Liquor*, table 3, p. 15; table 11, p. 21; *Vancouver Daily Province*, March 11, 1930, 1.
32. Dominion Brewers' Association, *Facts on the Brewing Industry*, 43–44; Richardson, *Pig War Islands*, 311.
33. Quoted in American Consul (Vancouver) to Secretary of State, February 8, 1927, 811.114Canada/339, RG 59, NARA.
34. Canada, Department of Trade and Commerce, Dominion Bureau of Statistics, *Control and Sale of Liquor in Canada*, table 2, p. 14. Total federal revenue for 1929 was $378 million. See Urquhart, *Historical Statistics of Canada*, series G1–25, 197.
35. Commissioner of Excise to O. D. Skelton, February 27, 1930, reel T1758, frame 441, RG 25, D1, vol. 742, file 149, part 1–4, LAC; Dominion Brewers' Association, *Facts on the Brewing Industry*, 74; McIntosh, *Collectors*, 11, 15.
36. Ernest R. Forbes, "The East-Coast Rum-Running Economy," in Warsh, *Drink in Canada*, 170.

37. *Victoria Daily Colonist*, May 10, 1922, 9; American Consul (Vancouver) to Secretary of State, September 1928, 811.114Canada/4098, RG 59, NARA.

38. *New York Times*, March 24, 1922, 17; American Consul (Vancouver) to Secretary of State, February 8, 1927, 811.114Canada/339, RG 59, NARA.

39. American Consul (Ottawa) to Secretary of State, January 1930, 842.114Liquor/74, RG 59, NARA; *Victoria Daily Colonist*, August 5, 1922, 5.

40. American Consul (Montreal) to American Consul (Vancouver), October 25, 1927, and American Consul (Vancouver) to Secretary of State, November 2, 1927, 811.114Canada/3819, RG 59, NARA.

41. R. Allen, *Ordeal by Fire*, 290–91; CAR, 1924/25, 88.

42. Memorandum, "The Dominion Government and the Control of the Liquor Traffic," n.d., reel T1758, frames 465–72, RG 25, D1, vol. 742, file 149, part 1–4, LAC.

43. R. Campbell, *Demon Rum or Easy Money*, 25, 46–47.

44. Ernest R. Forbes, "The East-Coast Rum-Running Economy," in Warsh, *Drink in Canada*, 170–72.

45. *Victoria Daily Colonist*, November 18, 1927, 4. See also *Toronto Saturday Night*, quoted in Vancouver *Daily Province*, January 20, 1929, 6.

46. American Consul (Vancouver) to Secretary of State, February 8, 1927, 811.114Canada/3392, RG 59, NARA; *Vancouver Sun* quoted in *Literary Digest*, October 6, 1923, 84.

47. Richard de Brisay, "Our Neighbors to the South," *Canadian Forum*, January 1929, 111.

48. *New York Times*, February 26, 1933, sec. 4, 7.

49. *New York Times*, April 14, 1929, sec. 3, 2.

50. *Toronto Saturday Night* quoted in *Vancouver Daily Province*, January 20, 1929, 6.

51. *Vancouver Sun*, April 23, 1926, cited in American Consul (Vancouver) to Secretary of State, April 23, 1926, 811.114Canada/1600, RG 59, NARA.

52. American Consul (Victoria) to Secretary of State, February 27, 1926, 811.114Canada/1385, RG 59, NARA; Kottman, "Volstead Violated," 115; CAR, 1922, 140. Similar sentiments were expressed in *Literary Digest*, October 6, 1923, 21;

53. *Ottawa Journal*, January 10, 1930, quoted in American Consul (Ottawa) to Secretary of State, 842.114Liquor/74, RG 59, NARA.

54. *Ottawa Journal* quoted in Kottman, "Volstead Violated," 115.

55. *Literary Digest*, October 6, 1923, 21.

56. Kottman, "Volstead Violated," 114.

57. Letter to editor quoted in American Consul (Vancouver) to Secretary of State, February 8, 1927, 811.114Canada/3392, RG 59, NARA.

58. *Canadian Forum*, January 1929, 112.

59. See American Consul (Vancouver) to Secretary of State, April 23, 1926, 811.114Canada/1600, RG 59, NARA. *New York Times*, January 13, 1929, 6; R. Allen, *Ordeal by Fire*, 289.

60. Letter to the editor quoted in American Consul (Vancouver) to Secretary of State, February 8, 1927, 811.114Canada/3392, RG 59, NARA.

61. *CAR*, 1923, 61; letter to the editor quoted in American Consul (Vancouver) to Secretary of State, February 8, 1927, 811.114Canada/3392, RG 59, NARA.

62. *Literary Digest*, October 6, 1923, 20.

63. *Toronto Mail and Empire* quoted in *Literary Digest*, October 6, 1923, 81.

64. *Nation*, September 4, 1929, 243.

65. *New York Times*, May 1, 1925, 18.

66. *New York Times*, March 7, 1923, 14, quoted in J. Thompson and Randall, *Canada and the United States*, 124.

67. *Nation*, September 4, 1929, 243; LaGuardia quoted in R. Allen, *Ordeal by Fire*, 290–91.

68. *Seattle Post-Intelligencer*, November 21, 1924, 4; Memorandum, "Decision of the Supreme Court of the United States regarding *Quadra*," n.d., reel T1758, frames 107–9, RG 25, DI, vol. 743, file 155, LAC.

69. Starkins, "Rum Running," 14; Newsome, *Pass the Bottle*, 90; *B.C. Magazine*, September 17, 1955. The Supreme Court later affirmed the conviction. See *Ford et al. v. United States*, 273 U.S. 593.

70. *Victoria Daily Colonist*, December 4, 1924; *Seattle Post-Intelligencer*, November 16, 1924, 1, 2; November 19, 1924, 1; November 30, 1924, 1; December 2, 1924, 2.

71. U.S. Attorney (District of Oregon) to Attorney General, January 9, 1928, 811.114Pescawha/23, RG 59, NARA.

72. Memorandum, "Pescawha," n.d., reel T1758, frame 110, RG 25, DI, vol. 743, file 155, LAC; American Consul (Vancouver) to Secretary of State, March 7, 1925, 811.114Pescawha/2, RG 59, NARA.

73. Assistant Attorney General to Secretary of State, May 13, 1926, 811.114Pescawha/14, RG 59, NARA.

74. U.S. Attorney (District of Oregon) to Attorney General, January 9, 1928, 811.114Pescawha/23, RG 59, NARA.

75. *Vancouver Daily Province*, May 1, 1929, quoted in William Phillips to Secretary of State, May 23, 1929, 811.114Pescawha/55, RG 59, NARA.

76. P. E. Bisland to State Department, September 9, 1931, 811.114Pescawha/68, RG 59, NARA.

77. *Prince Rupert News*, November 25, 1927, in American Consul (Prince Rupert) to Secretary of State, November 28, 1927, 811.114Pescawha/19, RG 59, NARA.

78. Newsome, *Pass the Bottle*, 66, 71.

79. Assistant Secretary of State, "Memorandum of Conversation with the Canadian Minister," March 8, 1928, 811.114Pescawha/28, RG 59, NARA; *Vancouver Daily Province*, May 1, 1929, copy in American Legation (Ottawa) to Secretary of State, May 23, 1929, 811.114Pescawha/55, RG 59, NARA.

80. Solicitor (Department of State) to Hackworth, October 3, 1928, 811.114Pescawha/44, RG 59, NARA; American Legation (Ottawa) to Secretary of State, May 23, 1929, 811.114Pescawha/55, RG 59, NARA; *Victoria Daily Colonist*, April 28, 1929; Canadian Legation (Washington) to Secretary of State, August 17, 1929, 811.114Pescawha/60, RG 59, NARA; Attorney General to Secretary of State, August 29, 1929, 811.114Pescawha/63, RG 59, NARA.

6. THE *BERYL G*

1. Waters testimony and Kier testimony, in "Morrison Court Book Notes"; *Victoria Daily Times*, 26 March 1925, 16; Newsome, *Case of the* Beryl G, 24.

2. The *Victoria Daily Times* (September 4, 1925) proclaimed the *Beryl G* case "The Most Sensational Trial in History of British Columbia," while the *Vancouver Sun* (January 24, 1926) found the *Beryl G* slaying a "unique crime in Canadian annals." Indeed, throughout the investigation and trial, the *Beryl G* received front-page attention, not only in each of the British Columbia dailies but in those of other provinces and in Seattle and Spokane as well. Even the *New York Times* ran regular updates as the case progressed.

3. Deputy Collector (Sumas) to Collector (Seattle), May 8, 1924, RG 36, box 22, file 410, NAS.

4. Cameron interview, British Columbia Aural History Programme Collection, BCA.

5. *Literary Digest*, August 4, 1923, 52; Rogers interview, British Columbia Aural History Programme Collection, BCA.

6. Richardson, *Pig War Islands*, 314.

7. *Seattle Post-Intelligencer*, November 26, 1924, 3; November 29, 1924, 1.

8. American Consul (Victoria) to Secretary of State, March 5, 1925, 811.114Canada/218, RG 59, NARA; *Seattle Post-Intelligencer*, November 26, 1924, 1, 3; November 27, 1924, 1, 2.

9. Extradition deposition of Elmer Anderson, December 17, 1924, in *Rex v. H. Fred Myers, alias Harry F. Sowash*, 211.42M991/1, RG 59, NARA; *Victoria Daily Times*, March 25, 1925, 2; July 10, 1925, 2.

10. Extradition deposition of Albert Clausen, December 17, 1924, in *Rex v. H. Fred Myers*, 211.42M991/1, RG 59, NARA; *Victoria Daily Times*, March 26, 1925, 16.

11. *Victoria Daily Times*, June 17, 1925, 1, 2; *Seattle Post-Intelligencer*, November 27, 1924, 1, 2; December 2, 1924, 1; December 15, 1924, 4.

12. Extradition deposition of Paul Strompkins, December 24, 1924, in *Rex v. H. Fred Myers*, 211.42M991/1, RG 59, NARA; *Seattle Post-Intelligencer*, November 26, 1924, 1, 3; November 27, 1924, 1, 3.

13. Attorney General to Deputy Minister of Justice (Ottawa), December 12, 1924, RG 13, vol. 998, file 1926 1728/1873, LAC; *Seattle Post-Intelligencer*, November 27, 1924,

1; November 28, 1924, 1, 3; November 29, 1924, 4; *New York Times*, November 28, 1924, 1.

14. RCMP Criminal Record of Charles Morris, February 15, 1937, RG 13, vol. 1536, file 3–2, LAC.

15. *Seattle Post-Intelligencer*, November 27, 1924, 1, 2; RCMP to Justice Department, August 27, 1925, RG 13, vol. 1536, file 2–1, LAC. Unfortunately for the real "Cannonball" Baker, an internationally known motorcycle racer after whom Owen Baker had named himself, Owen Baker was often described in early accounts of the *Beryl G* case as the "motorcycle racer, ex-convict, Puget Sound rum smuggler and hijacker." See *Seattle Post-Intelligencer*, December 28, 1924, 1; December 29, 1924, 1.

16. Extradition deposition of Walter James Hanniger, January 21, 1925, in *Rex v. H. Fred Myers*, 211.42M991/1, RG 59, NARA.

17. *Seattle Post-Intelligencer*, December 28, 1924, 1; December 29, 1924, 1; *New York Times*, January 20, 1925, 6.

18. Attorney General of British Columbia to Thomas Parsons, January 19, 1925, 211.42M991, RG 59, NARA.

19. British Embassy to Secretary of State, December 24, 1924, 211.42M831/-, RG 59, NARA; Report of the Commissioner in the Matter of the Application for the Extradition of Owen Benjamin Baker, January 28, 1925, 211.42B17/1, RG 59, NARA; Assistant Attorney General to Secretary of State, March 2, 1925, 211.42M991/3, RG 59, NARA; *Seattle Post-Intelligencer*, December 29, 1924, 1; *Victoria Daily Times*, March 2, 1925, 1.

20. Assistant Attorney General to Secretary of State, December 16, 1925, 211.42B17/3, RG 59, NARA; Assistant Attorney General to Secretary of State, December 11, 1926, and Under Secretary of State to Attorney General, December 16, 1926, 211.42M991/5, RG 59, NARA.

21. Attorney General to Cruickshank, December 16, 1924, and Attorney General to Ross, December 16, 1924, 211.42M831/2, RG 59, NARA; *New York Times*, November 28, 1924, 1.

22. Motion for Dismissal in the Matter of the Extradition of Charles Morris, January 12, 1925, and Commitment to Extradition, January 12, 1925, 211.42M831/2, RG 59, NARA; John J. Sullivan to Secretary of State, February 11, 1925, 211.42M831/4, RG 59, NARA.

23. British Ambassador to Secretary of State, May 15, 1925, 211.42M831/7, RG 59, NARA; Secretary of State to British Ambassador, February 20, 1925, 211.42M831/4, RG 59, NARA; *Victoria Daily Times*, May 7, 1925, 1.

24. *Vancouver Sun*, March 29, 1941, magazine sec., 12.

25. *Victoria Daily Times*, June 15, 1925, 1; June 16, 1925, 16; June 18, 1925, 6.

26. *Victoria Daily Times*, January 12, 1925, 1; March 27, 1925, 1, 2; *Seattle Post-Intelligencer*, January 21, 1925, 1; Strompkins testimony and Hatcher testimony, in "Morrison Court Book Notes."

27. Strompkins testimony and Marinoff testimony, in "Morrison Court Book Notes."

28. Strompkins testimony, in "Morrison Court Book Notes"; *Victoria Daily Times*, March 28, 1925, 1, 22; June 18, 1925, 6.

29. *Victoria Daily Times*, June 17, 1925, 1, 2, 16; June 18, 1925, 1, 2; June 19, 1925, 20.

30. *Vancouver Sun*, July 16, 1925, 1; *Victoria Daily Times*, July 16, 1925, 9; June 19, 1925, 1.

31. *Victoria Daily Times*, June 22, 1925, 1; October 21, 1925, 1, 2; October 22, 1925, 1, 2, 18; October 23, 1925, 1, 14, 18.

32. American Consul (Vancouver) to Secretary of State, April 10, 1926, 842.114/203, RG 59, NARA; *Victoria Daily Times*, January 14, 1926, 1; *Victoria Daily Colonist*, March 16, 1926, 1; *Vancouver Sun*, January 14, 1926, 1; *Ottawa Evening Journal*, January 14, 1926; and *Winnipeg Free Press*, January 22, 1926, in RG 13, vol. 1536, file 2–2, LAC.

33. *Victoria Daily Times*, June 17, 1925, 16; *Seattle Post-Intelligencer*, November 28, 1924, 3; *New York Times*, March 22, 1926, 2.

34. *Seattle Post-Intelligencer*, December 5, 1924, 4.

35. *Seattle Post-Intelligencer*, November 29, 1924, 4.

36. *Victoria Daily Times*, March 26, 1925, 16; June 15, 1925, 1; January 14, 1926, 8.

37. Roe interview, Georgeson interview, Richardson interview, and Cameron interview, all in British Columbia Aural History Programme Collection, BCA.

38. *Vancouver Sun*, January 16, 1926, 4.

39. Ronyk, "United States in the Twenties," 31–32.

40. *Seattle Argus*, June 27, 1925, 1; *Seattle Post-Intelligencer*, November 27, 1924, 3.

41. *Calgary Albertan*, January 3, 1929, 4, in Ronyk, "United States in the Twenties," 37.

42. American Consul (Vancouver) to Secretary of State, April 10, 1926, 842.114/203, RG 59, NARA; *Seattle Argus*, June 27, 1925, 1.

43. Quoted in American Consul (Vancouver) to Secretary of State, April 10, 1926, 842.114/203, RG 59, NARA.

44. *Seattle Argus*, June 27, 1925, 1; December 8, 1934, 1.

45. Roe interview and Richardson interview, British Columbia Aural History Programme Collection, BCA.

46. Richardson interview, British Columbia Aural History Programme Collection, BCA.

47. O. S. Moore to Prime Minister, September 5, 1930, R. B. Bennett Papers, vol. 432, reel M-1095, frames 2714138–43, LAC.

7. CUSTOMS SCANDALS

1. *Maclean's Magazine*, March 1, 1926, 24; April 15, 1926, 7–8. Euler quoted in McIntosh, *Collectors*, 254.

2. *Literary Digest*, July 3, 1926, 14; Sessional Paper 5d, January 5, 1927, RG 14, D2, vol. 171, LAC; *CAR*, 1924–25, 86–88.

3. *Maclean's Magazine*, March 1, 1926, 24; April 15, 1926, 7; McIntosh, *Collectors*, 11–12, 144.

4. *Toronto Globe*, August 8, 1924, quoted in CAR, 1924/25, 88; *Literary Digest*, July 3, 1926, 14.
5. *New York Times*, March 21, 1926, sec. 9, 4.
6. Sparks to Mackenzie King, February 26, 1925, and March 20, 1925, quoted in *Maclean's Magazine*, March 1, 1926, 24–25; *New York Times*, March 21, 1926, sec. 9, 4.
7. Customs officers quoted in McIntosh, *Collectors*, 267.
8. Wilbur, *H. H. Stevens*, 3–15.
9. Wilbur, *H. H. Stevens*, 9.
10. Canada, House of Commons, *Debates*, May 2, 1923, 2407–8.
11. Wilbur, *H. H. Stevens*, 16, 90.
12. Neatby, *William Lyon Mackenzie King*, 76, 82.
13. W. L. Morton, *The Progressive Party in Canada* (Toronto, 1950), 241, quoted in Neatby, *William Lyon Mackenzie King*, 115.
14. Neatby, *William Lyon Mackenzie King*, 115.
15. Neatby, *William Lyon Mackenzie King*, 113, 116.
16. *Maclean's Magazine*, March 1, 1926, 24; *New York Times*, March 21, 1926, sec. 9, 4; June 19, 1926, 1, 5.
17. Quoted in McIntosh, *Collectors*, 148.
18. Wilbur, *H. H. Stevens*, 57; *Literary Digest*, July 3, 1926, 15.
19. *Toronto Mail and Empire* quoted in *Literary Digest*, July 3, 1926, 14–15; July 10, 1926, 9.
20. Canada, House of Commons, *Debates*, June 22, 1926, 4818–46, quote on 4832.
21. Canada, House of Commons, *Debates*, June 22, 1926, 4822–23.
22. *New York Times*, June 29, 1926, 1, 3; *Literary Digest*, July 10, 1926, 9; *Nation*, July 14, 1926, 21–22; *New Republic*, July 14, 1926, 223.
23. *New York Times*, June 30, 1926, 3.
24. American Consul (Vancouver) to Secretary of State, February 8, 1926, 811.114Canada/3392, RG 59, NARA.
25. *Vancouver Daily Province*, November 19, 1926, 6.
26. American Consul (Halifax) to Secretary of State, December 11, 1926, 811.114Canada/3316, RG 59, NARA.
27. Sessional Paper 5d, January 5, 1927, RG 14, D2, vol. 171, p. 9, LAC; American Consul (Vancouver) to Secretary of State, December 30, 1926, 811.114Canada/3441, and February 8, 1927, 811.114Canada/3392, RG 59, NARA; *Vancouver Sun*, January 26, 1927. Canada, Royal Commission on Customs and Excise, *Interim Reports*, 7.
28. Letter to editor quoted in American Consul (Vancouver) to Secretary of State, February 8, 1927, 811.114Canada/3392, RG 59, NARA.
29. *Vancouver Western Tribune* quoted in American Consul (Vancouver) to Secretary of State, February 8, 1927, 811.114Canada/3392, RG 59, NARA.
30. American Consul (Vancouver) to Secretary of State, January 17, 1927, 811.114Canada/3442, RG 59, NARA.

31. *Vancouver Daily Province*, November 30, 1926, 1; American Consul (Vancouver) to Secretary of State, September 23, 1924, 811.114Stadacona, RG 59, NARA.

32. Canada, Royal Commission on Customs and Excise, *Interim Reports*, 62.

33. Rannie, "Old Big, Colourful," 26; R. Campbell, "Liquor and Liberals," 48. See also file 48s, box 2, RG 56, NAS.

34. *Vancouver Sun*, December 9, 1926, 1; January 19, 1927, 1, 15; January 25, 1927, 2.

35. *Vancouver Sun*, December 16, 1927, 1, 2; American Consul (Vancouver) to Secretary of State, December 30, 1926, 811.114Canada/3441, RG 59, NARA.

36. Canada, Royal Commission on Customs and Excise, *Interim Reports*, 3–6, 63; *Vancouver Sun*, November 29, 1926, 1; November 30, 1926, 1; December 1, 1926, 1; *Vancouver Morning Star*, November 30, 1926, 1; December 1, 1926, 1; *Vancouver Daily Province*, December 2, 1926, 1.

37. *New York Times*, November 28, 1926, sec. 2, 1; American Consul (Vancouver) to Secretary of State, February 8, 1927, 811.114Canada/3392, RG 59, NARA; Canada, Royal Commission on Customs and Excise, *Interim Reports*, 67, 115.

38. Quoted in American Consul (Vancouver) to Secretary of State, February 8, 1927, 811.114Canada/3392, RG 59, NARA.

39. *Vancouver Sun*, December 10, 1926, 1; December 14, 1926, 4; F. J. A. Demers to District Attorney, December 13, 1920, RG 36, box 5, file 135, NAS.

40. R. Allen, *Ordeal by Fire*, 290–91; American Consul (Vancouver) to Secretary of State, February 8, 1927, 811.114Canada/3392, RG 59, NARA; R. Campbell, "Liquor and Liberals," 48.

41. *Vancouver Sun*, December 16, 1926, 4; January 25, 1927, 2; American Consul (Vancouver) to Secretary of State, February 8, 1927, 811.114Canada/3392, RG 59, NARA.

42. RCCE, Vancouver Evidence, 6224–42, 6982–90, 7743–52, 7876–82.

43. *Vancouver Daily Province*, January 24, 1927, 15; *Vancouver Sun*, January 25, 1927, 2.

44. American Consul (Vancouver) to Secretary of State, February 8, 1927, 811.114Canada/3392, RG 59, NARA.

45. *Vancouver Sun*, December 15, 1926, 1; December 20, 1926, 1; American Consul (Vancouver) to Secretary of State, February 8, 1927, 811.114Canada/3392, RG 59, NARA.

46. *Vancouver Morning Star*, December 18, 1926, in American Consul (Vancouver) to Secretary of State, December 30, 1926, 811.114Canada/3441, RG 59, NARA.

47. *Vancouver Daily Province*, n.d., in American Consul (Vancouver) to Secretary of State, February 8, 1927, 811.114Canada/3392, RG 59, NARA.

48. *Vancouver Daily Province*, December 29, 1926, 6.

49. Letter to the editor quoted in American Consul (Vancouver) to Secretary of State, February 8, 1927, 811.114Canada/3392, RG 59, NARA.

50. Letter to the editor quoted in American Consul (Vancouver) to Secretary of State, February 8, 1927, 811.114Canada/3392, RG 59, NARA.

8. NEIGHBORS AND NEIGHBOURS

1. RCCE, Vancouver Evidence, 2020.
2. *Victoria Daily Times*, January 18 1929, 4. See Kottman, "Volstead Violated," 112.
3. American Consul (Victoria) to Secretary of State, October 1, 1925, 811.114Canada/842, RG 59, NARA.
4. *New York Times*, January 13, 1929, sec. 9, 6; *Toronto Mail and Empire*, cited in *Literary Digest*, January 26, 1929, 16–17; American Consul (Ottawa) to Secretary of State, December 1929, 842.114Liquor/74, RG 59, NARA; Kottman, "Volstead Violated," 112.
5. Kottman, "Volstead Violated," 112.
6. *Vancouver Daily Province*, November 17, 1924, 6.
7. *Vancouver Daily Province*, December 29, 1926, 6. For similar sentiments, see *New York Times*, January 13, 1929, sec. 9, 6.
8. *Vancouver Sun*, n.d., in American Consul (Vancouver) to Secretary of State, February 8, 1927, 811.114Canada/3392, RG 59, NARA.
9. *New York Times*, June 1, 1930, sec. 3, 2. See also *Vancouver Morning Star*, April 22, 1926, cited in American Consul (Vancouver) to Secretary of State, April 23, 1926, 811.114Canada/1600, RG 59, NARA; and "Canada Turns Against Prohibition," *Nation*, April 1925, 460.
10. Barman, *West beyond the West*, 380.
11. *CAR*, 1921, 130, 137.
12. *Vancouver Daily Province*, November 17, 1924, 6.
13. *Victoria Daily Times*, January 15, 1929, 4; *Victoria Daily Colonist*, August 21, 1926, 4.
14. For an example of those who argue that Canada never was a "linchpin" in the "fulcrum of Anglo-American relations," see Stuart, review of *Canada and the United States*. On the other hand, Canada clearly saw itself as the "friendly interpreter"—as Mackenzie King liked to phrase it—between Great Britain and the United States, leading the Dominion to consider very carefully how its relationship with the United States might imperil its relationship to the larger British Empire. For this latter interpretation, see McKercher, "Between Two Giants"; see also *New York Times*, April 4, 1926, sec. 2, 8.
15. *Victoria Daily Colonist*, June 6, 1923, 1.
16. *Vancouver Daily Province*, November 17, 1924, 6; February 21, 1925, 6; *Victoria Daily Times*, January 29, 1930, 14.
17. *CAR*, 1923, 765.
18. Letter to editor quoted in American Consul (Vancouver) to Secretary of State, February 8, 1927, 811.114Canada/3392, RG 59, NARA. See also *Vancouver Daily Province*, February 21, 1925, 6.
19. *Seattle Post-Intelligencer*, July 17, 1923, 2.

20. American Consul (Victoria) to Secretary of State, November 10, 1928, 811.114Canada/4119, RG 59, NARA. See also American Consul (Regina) to Secretary of State, February 14, 1921, 842.114/38, RG 59, NARA; and CAR, 1921, 136–37.

21. Canada, House of Commons, *Debates*, May 2, 1923, 2407–11; May 3, 1923, 2419–20; *Vancouver Daily Province*, January 13, 1925, in American Consul (Vancouver) to Secretary of State, January 14, 1925, 811.114Canada/60, RG 59, NARA; *Vancouver Morning Star*, July 9, 1926, in American Consul (Vancouver) to Secretary of State, February 8, 1927, 811.114Canada/3392, RG 59, NARA; *Vancouver Daily Province*, November 19, 1926, 6; *Seattle Post-Intelligencer*, June 5, 1923.

22. *Vancouver Daily Province*, November 26, 1926, 1; RCCE, Victoria Evidence, 890–950.

23. *Victoria Daily Times*, May 28, 1923, 2.

24. *Seattle Post-Intelligencer*, June 5, 1923; American Consul (Victoria) to Secretary of State, February 24, 1925, 811.114Canada/182, RG 59, NARA.

25. Canada, Senate, *Debates*, May 4, 1928, 438–40; Dominion Brewers' Association, *Facts on the Brewing Industry*, 79.

26. American Consul (Vancouver) to Secretary of State, October 25, 1928, 811.114Canada/4114, RG 59, NARA.

27. *Vancouver Daily Province*, October 1, 1928, 6.

28. *Vancouver Daily Province*, October 1, 1928, 6.

29. *Vancouver Daily Province*, November 17, 1924, 6.

30. *New York Times*, January 13, 1929, sec. 9, 6.

31. "Press Release Issued by the Department of State," May 15, 1929, FRUS, 1929, 2:53.

32. *New York Times*, January 13, 1929, sec. 9, 6; October 2, 1929, 1, 9; American Consul (Ottawa) to Secretary of State, October 23, 1929, 842.114Liquor/67, RG 59, NARA.

33. "Memorandum on Liquor Clearances," March 11, 1930, RG 25, D1, vol. 742, file 149, parts 1–4, reel T1758, frames 445–48, 477–79, LAC; see also frames 552–53.

34. *Montreal Gazette*, cited in *Literary Digest*, December 22, 1928, 5; Inglis, "'W.H. Eastwood' Affair," 51; Briggs, *Law of Nations*, 386.

35. *Vancouver Sun*, cited in *Literary Digest*, April 13, 1929, 16; *Calgary Herald* cited in Holsinger, "The *I'm Alone* Controversy," 307. See also Inglis, "'W.H. Eastwood' Affair," 56.

36. *Montreal Gazette* quoted in *Literary Digest*, December 22, 1928, 5.

37. Kottman, "Volstead Violated," 118–19; "Press Release Issued by the Department of State," May 15, 1929, FRUS (1929), 2:55.

38. *Victoria Daily Times*, November 16, 1929; *Vancouver Daily Province*, October 20, 1928, 3; Rev. R. J. McIntyre to Under Secretary of State for External Affairs, January 19, 1929, MS 17, British Columbia Alcohol Research and Education Council Originals, BCA; "Memorandum for the Prime Minister," February 9, 192,9 RG 25, D1, vol. 742, file 149, part 1–4, reel T1757, frames 161–63, LAC; F. E. Runnalls to the Prime Minister, January 22, 1930, vol. 181, reel C2322, frames 154099–101, and

United Church of Canada to the Prime Minister, June 8, 1929, vol. 195, reel C231, frames 139290–92, Mackenzie King Papers, LAC.

39. *New York Times*, April 14, 1929, sec. 3, 2; *Vancouver Daily Province*, March 29, 1930, 6.

40. *Literary Digest*, March 29, 1930, 13, 14.

41. *New York Times*, October 13, 1929, sec. 3, 1; February 16, 1930, 1, 7.

42. *Ottawa Citizen*, September 28, 1928, quoted in American Consul (Ottawa) to Secretary of State, September 28, 1928, 842.114Liquor/5, RG 59, NARA.

43. *Ottawa Citizen, Montreal Daily Star, Toronto Globe*, cited in *Literary Digest*, January 26, 1929, 16–17; *New York Times*, February 16, 1930, 1, 7.

44. *Montreal Chronicle Telegraph* quoted in *New York Times*, January 24, 1930, 22.

45. *Literary Digest*, February 8, 1930, 17–18, cited in Kottman, "Volstead Violated," 121.

46. *Vancouver Daily Province*, January 4, 1930, 6.

47. *Vancouver Daily Province*, March 31, 1930, 6.

48. *New York Times*, January 24, 1930, 22; *Vancouver Daily Province*, January 4, 1930, 6.

49. American Consul (Montreal) to Secretary of State, February 18, 1930, 811.114Canada/4291, RG 59, NARA; *Vancouver Daily Province*, March 17, 1930, 6.

50. U.S. Department of Justice, *Annual Report of the Attorney General*, 1930, 61; *Literary Digest*, March 29, 1930, 13. The vote in the House of Commons was 162 in favor, 11 against. See *New York Times*, March 26, 1930, 20.

51. *Maclean's Magazine*, November 15, 1929, 65.

52. U.S. Department of Justice, *Annual Report of the Attorney General*, 1928, 35; Willoughby, *Rum War at Sea*, 83–85. In one of the unsolved mysteries of the case, the 12,500 cases of liquor were removed for safekeeping by the Coast Guard and placed in storage in San Francisco. They apparently disappeared while in the custody of U.S. Customs.

53. *Literary Digest*, May 11, 1929, 6; *Outlook*, April 10, 1929, 582.

54. *Victoria Daily Colonist*, February 15, 1925, in American Consul (Victoria) to Captain F. G. Dodge (U.S. Coast Guard, Seattle), February 16, 1925, 811.114Canada/164, RG 59, NARA; American Consul (Vancouver) to Secretary of State, July 25, 1929, 811.114Canada/4221, RG 59, NARA.

55. U.S. Department of the Treasury, *Annual Report* , 1924, 324; 1925, 393; Miles, *Slow Boat on Rum Row*, 209; *Seattle Times*, April 30, 1961, magazine section; Willoughby, *Rum War at Sea*, 76.

56. Richardson, *Pig War Islands*, 324. On the San Francisco market, prices apparently increased from $8.00 to $10.20 per bottle. See *Victoria Daily Colonist*, February 15, 1925, in American Consul (Victoria) to Captain F. G. Dodge (U.S. Coast Guard, Seattle), February 16, 1925, 811.114Canada/164, RG 59, NARA; *Vancouver Sun*, December 8, 1926, 12.

57. American Consul (Victoria) to Secretary of State, February 27, 1926, 811.114Canada/1385, RG 59, NARA.

58. U.S. Department of the Treasury, *Annual Report* , 1927, 117, 158; American Consul (Vancouver) to Secretary of State, September 1928, 811.114Canada/4098, RG 59, NARA; *Vancouver Sun*, December 8, 1926, 12.

59. U.S. Department of the Treasury, *Annual Report*, 1925, 84, 383; 1926, 141–42; 1927, 117; 1929, 203; 1930, 228.

60. N. Clark, *Dry Years*, 192.

61. *New York Times*, May 9, 1926, 9; Assistant Secretary of Treasury to Secretary of State, November 16, 1926, 811.114Canada/3256; American Consul (Vancouver) to Secretary of State, June 9, 1926, 811.114Canada/1763; American Consul (Vancouver) to Secretary of State, December 2, 1926, 811.114Canada/3293; Assistant Attorney General to Secretary of State, March 13, 1929, 811.114Canadian Border Conferences/1, all in RG 59, NARA.

9. BRITISH COLUMBIA AND THE ORIGINS OF AMERICAN REPEAL

1. *Victoria Daily Colonist*, May 6, 1920, 21.

2. *Outlook*, September 9, 1925, 49–51; *Vancouver Sun* quoted in *Literary Digest*, December 15, 1923, 20.

3. *Seattle Post-Intelligencer*, June 10, 1923, magazine sec., 6.

4. *Nation*, April 1925, 460–62.

5. These included, for example, Sweden, Finland, Norway, Switzerland, Australia, Poland, Norway, Scotland, and Russia. See *New York Times*, November 8, 1933, 30, as well as *Literary Digest*, July 15, 1922, 17–18; August 15, 1925, 31; October 10, 1925, 19; November 6, 1926, 9; September 29, 1928, 18; May 3, 1930, 13; January 16, 1932, 12, 15. Surprisingly, very few studies of prohibition in the United States acknowledge the impact that the abandonment of prohibition around the world had on repeal in the United States. One exception is Kyvig's *Repealing National Prohibition*. Even Kyvig's study, however, fails to make more than a cursory reference to the topic. This deficiency is especially true regarding Canada's impact on American repeal. While almost all studies of Canadian prohibition acknowledge the influence of the American temperance movement on Canada's short-lived prohibition effort, no American study makes a systematic effort to study how ideas about government control in Canada affected American repeal. There is ample evidence that it did. For example, throughout the 1920s the *New York Times* proved particularly attuned to liquor control in Canada, perhaps reflecting its less-than-dry leanings. See *New York Times*, February 2, 1919, sec. 2, 1; July 19, 1924, 8; April 12, 1926, 20.

6. J. Campbell, "Canada's Retreat from Prohibition," 27; *Victoria Daily Times*, August 20, 1933, 20; *Outlook*, April 22, 1925, 600.

7. *CAR*, 1921, 131, 134.

8. R. Campbell, *Demon Rum or Easy Money*, 68.

9. *Seattle Post-Intelligencer*, June 10, 1923, magazine sec., 6.

10. See, e.g., American Consul (Vancouver) to Secretary of State, April 10, 1926, 842.114/203, RG 59, NARA. For a contemporary discussion on how the other Canadian provinces followed British Columbia's lead on liquor control issues, particularly those in western Canada, see "Another Canadian Drink Vote," *Literary Digest*, November 24, 1923, 20; as well as Richard de Brisay, "Canada Turns against Prohibition," *Nation*, April 1925, 460–62.

11. *New York Times*, April 12, 1926, 20. See also July 19, 1924, 8.

12. *Boston Globe* quoted in *Literary Digest*, December 25, 1926, 9.

13. *New York American* quoted in *Literary Digest*, December 25, 1926, 9.

14. *Spokane Spokesman-Review*, October 6, 1925, 4.

15. *Spokane Daily Chronicle*, November 21, 1927, 4; *Spokane Spokesman-Review*, October 12, 1927, 4.

16. *Yakima Republic* quoted in *Spokane Spokesman-Review*, October 15, 1927, 4.

17. *Spokane Daily Chronicle*, May 29, 1928, 4; October 27, 1929, 4. Equally undeterred in its dry cause was the *Spokane Spokesman-Review*. See November 27, 1927, 4, and December 2, 1927, 4.

18. *New York Times*, August 30, 1927, 6.

19. *New York Times*, July 20, 1928, 4; December 27, 1929, 12; *Victoria Daily Times*, August 16, 1932, 7.

20. American Consul (Vancouver) to Secretary of State, September 30, 1927, 842.114/290, RG 59, NARA.

21. *Vancouver Sun* quoted in American Consul (Vancouver) to Secretary of State, September 18, 1928, 811.114Canada/4098, RG 59, NARA.

22. *Victoria Daily Colonist*, November 18, 1927, 4.

23. Canada, Senate, *Debates*, June 18, 1931, 294.

24. American Consul (Vancouver) to Secretary of State, September 30, 1927, 842.114/290, RG 59, NARA.

25. *New York Times*, April 21, 1927, 26.

26. *Maclean's Magazine*, June 15, 1922, 54.

27. *Seattle Post-Intelligencer*, June 10, 1923, magazine sec., 6; *New York Times*, March 27, 1927, sec. 8, 1.

28. *New York Times*, April 21, 1927, 26.

29. *Literary Digest*, November 24, 1923, 20; *Nation*, April 1925, 461.

30. *Literary Digest*, November 24, 1923, 20; December 15, 1923, 20.

31. CAR, 1922, 137; *Vancouver Daily Province*, November 25, 1929, 2; *Seattle Post-Intelligencer*, June 10, 1923, magazine sec., 6.

32. *New York Times*, December 25, 1926, 3; American Consul (Vancouver) to Secretary of State, September 30, 1927, 842.114/290, RG 59, NARA; *Victoria Daily Times*, January 28, 1930, 1, 3.

33. American Consul (Montreal) to Secretary of State, February 2, 1929, 842.114Liquor/20, RG 59, NARA.

34. *New York Times*, May 31, 1925, 16; *Literary Digest*, November 24, 1923, 20.

35. *New York Times*, June 30, 1927, 35.

36. See *New York Times*, March 29, 1930, 6; United States, Wickersham Commission, *Enforcement of Prohibition Law*.

37. Letter to the editor quoted in American Consul (Vancouver) to Secretary of State, April 23, 1926, 811.114Canada/1600, RG 59, NARA.

38. F. G. R. Gordon to editor, *New York Times*, June 29, 1924, sec. 8, 13.

39. N. Clark, *Dry Years*, 222–23, 242.

40. N. Clark, *Dry Years*, 222–23, 242.

41. Rose, "Labbe Affair," 32–41.

42. *New York Times*, July 1, 1930, 28; N. Clark, *Dry Years*, 237–38.

43. *Seattle Times*, March 29, 1970, magazine sec., 3.

44. Washington State Advisory Liquor Control Commission, *Report*, 4.

45. N. Clark, *Dry Years*, 244.

46. *Vancouver Daily Province*, January 4, 1934, 1, 3; *New York Times*, February 26, 1933, sec. 4, 7.

47. *New York Times*, February 26, 1933, sec. 4, 7.

48. R. Campbell, *Demon Rum or Easy Money*, 80.

EPILOGUE

1. Miles, *Slow Boat on Rum Row*, 227–28.

2. Parker and Tyrrell, *Rumrunner*, 4, 140, 218–19.

3. *Seattle Daily Times*, February 28, 1933, 1, 7.

4. Olmstead quoted in N. Clark, "Roy Olmstead," 103.

5. *Victoria Daily Times*, July 24, 1934, 2; August 1, 1934, 1; August 20, 1934, 11; *Seattle Argus*, September 22, 1934, 2; *Vancouver Daily Province*, July 30, 1935.

6. *Victoria Daily Colonist*, January 22, 1929, 23; *Victoria Daily Times*, January 22, 1929, 18.

7. *Seattle Daily Times*, February 28, 1933, 1, 7.

8. Finding aid, p. 1, MS 17, British Columbia Alcohol Research and Education Council Originals, 1915–1972, BCA.

9. *Victoria Daily Times*, October 13, 1934, 14; April 4, 1935, 11.

10. *Vancouver Daily Province*, January 4, 1934, 1, 3. See also Don Duncan, "British Columbia, a Foreign Yet Familiar Friend," *Seattle Times*, April 10, 1983, 1, 4.

11. *Victoria Daily Times*, July 25, 1934, 12.

12. *Victoria Daily Times*, February 21, 1935, 10.

13. *Victoria Daily Times*, February 21, 1935, 10.

Bibliography

MANUSCRIPT COLLECTIONS

British Columbia Archives, Victoria

British Columbia Aural History Programme Collection

Bittancourt, Len A. Interview by Imbert Orchard. October 1965. In "Saltspring Island Recollections," tape T798-1.

Cameron, Slim. Interview by Bill Ward. 1982. In "A B.C. Game Warden's Recollections," tapes 4029:1-4.

Freeman, J. Interview by Imbert Orchard. October 4, 1965. In "South Pender Island Before 1920," tape T785.

Georgeson, Mr. and Mrs. Peter. Interview by Imbert Orchard. February 1, 1966. In "Gulf Island Region B.C.," tape T805-1.

Gisborne, Robert. Interview by Susan Winifred Mayse. 1984. Tape T4136-1.

Richardson, Dorothy. Interview by Imbert Orchard. January 1966. In "Saturna Island, 1885-1925," tape T806-1.

Roe, Robert. Interview by Imbert Orchard. October 4, 1965. In "Reminiscences of Pender Island, 1896-1930," tape T787.

Rogers, Sheldon. Interview by John Hodgins. 1972. In "Life of an Independent Man," tape T91-2.

Smith, Mrs. Fred. Interview by Imbert Orchard. October 5, 1965. In "Early Agriculture and Settlement on Pender Island, 1885-1925," tape T788-1.

Specht, Allen. British Columbia Game Commission Interviews. 1984. Tapes 4129:1-7.

GR 62, Liquor Control Board Scrapbooks

GR 93, British Columbia Provincial Police Force Prohibition Files

GR 107, Victoria Provincial Police Records

GR 332, Great Britain Colonial Office Correspondence with the Hudson's Bay Company

GR 770, Liquor Control Board Selected Files

MS 17, British Columbia Alcohol Research and Education Council Originals, 1915–72

MS 30, Sidney Hutcheson Papers, 1908–75

MS 566, George Salier Willis Nicholson Papers

MacPherson, Lydia. "Historical Sketch of the Woman's Christian Temperance Union of British Columbia"

Glenbow Archives, Calgary AB

Picariello, Emilio, Fonds, 1904–63

Library and Archives Canada, Ottawa

Bennett, R. B., Papers

King, W. L. Mackenzie, Papers

RG 13, Records of the Department of Justice

RG 14, Records of Parliament

RG 16, Records of the Department of National Revenue

RG 18, Records of the Royal Canadian Mounted Police

RG 25, Records of the Department of External Affairs

RG 33/88, Records of the Royal Commission on Customs and Excise, 1926–27

RG 42, Records of the Marine Branch

The WCTU of British Columbia: Yearbooks and Proceedings, 1920–30

National Archives and Records Administration, College Park MD

RG 59, General Records of the Department of State

National Archives and Records Administration, Seattle

RG 21, Records of the District Courts of the United States, Western District of Washington, Northern Division, 1890–1978

RG 26, Records of the U.S. Coast Guard, Thirteenth Coast Guard District, 1873–1988

RG 36, Records of the U.S. Customs Service, Puget Sound District

RG 56, General Records of the Department of Treasury, Bureau of Prohibition, Seattle, 1924–33

RG 267, Records of the U.S. Court of Appeals

City of Vancouver Archives, Vancouver BC

Pamphlet Collection

Stevens, Henry Herbert, Fonds, 1878–1935

University of Oregon Special Collections, Eugene

Drake Papers

University of Washington Special Collections, Seattle

International Order of Good Templars, Proceedings of the Grand Lodge of Washington Territory and British Columbia

Jones, Wesley, Papers

Poindexter, Miles, Papers

PUBLISHED SOURCES

Ajzenstadt, Mimi. "The Medical-Moral Economy of Regulations: Alcohol Legislation in B.C., 1871–1925." PhD diss., Simon Fraser University, 1992.

Allan, Chantall. *Bomb Canada and Other Unkind Remarks in the American Media.* Edmonton: AU Press, 2009.

Allen, Harold Tuttle. *Forty Years' Journey: The Temperance Movement in British Columbia to 1900.* Victoria: H.T. Allen, 1981.

Allen, Ralph. *Ordeal by Fire: Canada 1910–1945.* Toronto: Doubleday Canada, 1961.

Anderson, Frank W. *The Rum Runners.* Edmonton: Lone Pine, 1968.

Andrews, Lincoln C. "Prohibition Enforcement as a Phase of Federal versus State Jurisdiction in American Life." *Annals of the American Academy of Political and Social Science* 129 (January 1927): 77–87.

Angus, H. F. *Canada and Her Great Neighbor: Sociological Surveys of Opinions and Attitudes in Canada Concerning the United States.* Toronto: Ryerson Press, 1938.

Angus, H. F. F. W. Howay, and W. N. Sage. *British Columbia and the United States: The North Pacific Slope from Fur Trade to Aviation.* Toronto: Ryerson Press for the Carnegie Endowment for International Peace, 1942.

Annis, Matthew. "The 'Chinese Question' and the Canada-US Border, 1885: 'Why Don't Governor Squire Send His Troops to Semiahmoo to Prevent the Twelve or Fifteen Thousand Pagans from Crossing Our Borders from British Columbia?'" *American Review of Canadian Studies* 40, no. 3 (2010): 351–61.

Asbury, Herbert. *The Great Illusion: An Informal History of Prohibition.* New York: Doubleday, 1950.

Baglier, Janet. "The End of America: The Beginning of Canada—A Response." *Canadian Geographer* 34, no. 3 (1990): 270–71.

Bamonte, Tony, and Suzanne Schaeffer Bamonte. *History of Pend Oreille County.* Spokane: Tornado Creek, 1996.

Barker, Burt Brown, ed. *Letters of Dr. John McLoughlin: Written at Fort Vancouver, 1829–1832.* Portland OR: Binfords & Mort, 1948.

Barman, Jean. *The West beyond the West: A History of British Columbia.* Toronto: University of Toronto Press, 1991.

Barman, Jean, and Robert A. J. McDonald, eds. *Readings in the History of British Columbia.* Richmond BC: Open Learning Agency, 1989.

Barnes, Fern L. *Beams from a Lighthouse: Woman's Christian Temperance Union of B.C., 1883–1983.* British Columbia, 1983.

———. *A Centennial Mosaic, 1874–1974.* Toronto: Canadian Women's Christian Temperance Union, 1974.

Barron, F. Laurie. "The American Origins of the Temperance Movement in Ontario, 1828–1850." *Canadian Review of American Studies* II, no. 2 (1980): 131–50.

Belasco, Warren James. *Americans on the Road: From Autocamp to Motel, 1910–1945*. Baltimore: Johns Hopkins University Press, 1997.

Bell, Archie. *Sunset Canada, British Columbia and Beyond*. Boston: Page , 1918.

Bemis, Samuel Flagg, ed. *The American Secretaries of State and Their Diplomacy*. Vol. 10. New York: Pageant, 1958.

Bennett, John W., and Seena B. Kohl. *Settling the Canadian American West, 1890–1915: Pioneer Adaptation and Community Building: An Anthropological History*. Lincoln: University of Nebraska Press, 1995.

Berger, Carl C. "Internationalism, Continentalism, and the Writing of History: Comments on the Carnegie Series on the Relations of Canada and the United States." In *The Influence of the United States on Canadian Development: Eleven Case Studies*, edited by Richard A. Preston, 32–54. Durham NC: Duke University Press, 1972.

Berner, Richard C. *Seattle, 1910–1920: From Boomtown, Urban Turbulence, to Restoration*. Seattle: Charles Press, 1991.

———. *Seattle, 1921–1940: From Boom to Bust*. Seattle: Charles Press, 1992.

Berton, Pierre. *The Impossible Railway: The Building of the Canadian Pacific*. New York: Knopf, 1972.

Bingham, Edwin R., and Glen A. Love, eds. *Northwest Perspectives: Essays on the Culture of the Pacific Northwest*. Seattle: University of Washington Press, 1979.

Black Ball Ferries. *Olympic Peninsula, Victoria and the San Juan Islands*. Seattle: Puget Sound Navigation Company, 1929. Available at British Columbia Archives, Victoria.

Bliss, J. M. "The Methodist Church and World War I." *Canadian Historical Review* 49, no. 3 (1968): 213–33.

Blocker, Jack S. *Retreat from Reform: The Prohibition Movement in the United States, 1890–1913*. Westport CT: Greenwood Press, 1976.

Bordessa, Ronald, and James M. Cameron. "The End of America: The Beginning of Canada—A Commentary." *Canadian Geographer* 34, no. 3 (1990): 264–69.

Bordin, Ruth. *Francis Willard: A Biography*. Chapel Hill: University of North Carolina Press, 1986.

Bothwell, Robert. *Canada and the United States: The Politics of Partnership*. Toronto: University of Toronto Press, 1992.

Boyce, Cyril D. "Prohibition in Canada." *Annals of the American Academy of Political and Social Science* 109 (September 1923): 225–29.

Brebner, John Bartlet. *North Atlantic Triangle*. New Haven CT: Yale University Press for the Carnegie Endowment for International Peace, 1945.

Bregent-Heald, Dominique. "The Tourism of Titillation in Tijuana and Niagara Falls: Cross-Border Tourism and Hollywood Films between 1896 and 1960." *Journal of the Canadian Historical Association* 17, no. 1 (2006): 179–203.

Brewers Association of Canada. *Breweries in Canada*. Montreal: Ronalds-Federated, 1928.

Briggs, Herbert. *The Law of Nations: Cases, Documents, and Notes.* New York: Appleton-Century-Croft, 1952.

British Columbia. Bureau of Provincial Information. *British Columbia, Canada: The Centre of the Empire.* Victoria: Charles F. Banfield, 1925.

——. *Handbook of British Columbia, Canada: History, Topography, Climate, Resources, Development.* 2d ed. Victoria, 1921.

——. *Highways, Motor Camps and Stopping-Places in British Columbia.* Victoria: Charles F. Banfield, 1926.

British Columbia. Legislative Assembly. *Journals of the Legislative Assembly of the Province of British Columbia.* Victoria: Queen's Printer.

——. *Debates of the Legislative Assembly of the Province of British Columbia.* Victoria: Queen's Printer.

——. *Sessional Papers of the Province of British Columbia.* Victoria: Legislative Assembly.

Brown, Richard Maxwell. "The Great Raincoast of North America: Toward a New Regional History of the Pacific Northwest." In *The Changing Pacific Northwest: Interpreting its Past,* edited by David H. Stratton and George A. Frykman, 39–53. Pullman: Washington State University Press, 1988.

Brown, William G. "State Cooperation in Enforcement." *Annals of the American Academy of Political and Social Science* 163 (September 1932): 30–38.

Browne, J. Ross. *Crusoe's Island: A Ramble in the Footsteps of Alexander Selkirk.* New York: Harper & Brothers, 1864.

Bukowczyk, John J., Nora Faires, David R. Smith, and Randy William Widdis, eds. *Permeable Border: The Great Lakes Basin as Transnational Region, 1650–1990.* Pittsburg: University of Pittsburg Press, 2005.

Campbell, J. M. "Canada's Retreat from Prohibition." *Current History* 28 (April 1928): 27–29.

Campbell, Kenneth. "A Tribute to Pioneer Members of British Columbia Hotels' Association." *British Columbia Hotelman,* September—October 1958, 6–13.

Campbell, Robert A. *Demon Rum or Easy Money: Government Control of Liquor in British Columbia from Prohibition to Privatization.* Ottawa: Carleton University Press, 1991.

——. "Liquor and Liberals: Patronage and Government Control in British Columbia, 1920–1928." *BC Studies* 77 (Spring 1988): 30–53.

——. *Sit Down and Drink Your Beer: Regulating Vancouver's Beer Parlours, 1925–1954.* Toronto: University of Toronto Press, 2001.

Canada. *Annual Departmental Reports.* Ottawa: F.A. Acland.

——. *Sessional Papers.*

——. *Statutes of Canada.*

Canada. Commission to Inquire into the Working of the Prohibitory Liquor Law in the United States. *Report of Commissioners.* Ottawa: Maclean Roger & Company, 1875.

Canada. Department of External Affairs. *Documents on Canadian External Relations*. Ottawa: Queen's Printer.

Canada. Department of Trade and Commerce. *Annual Report of the Department of Trade and Commerce*. Ottawa: Printer to the King.

Canada. Department of Trade and Commerce. Dominion Bureau of Statistics. *The Control and Sale of Liquor in Canada*. Ottawa, 1931.

Canada. House of Commons. *Debates*. Ottawa: King's Printer.

Canada. National Parks Branch. *The Kicking Horse Trail: Scenic Highway from Lake Louise, Alberta, to Golden, British Columbia*. Ottawa: Dominion Parks Branch, 1927.

Canada. Royal Commission on Customs and Excise. *Final Report*. Ottawa: King's Printer, 1928.

———. *Interim Reports (Nos. 1 to 10)*. Ottawa: F.A. Acland, 1928.

Canada. Royal Commission on the Liquor Traffic. "Minutes of Evidence, Volume III, Provinces of Manitoba, North-West Territories and British Columbia." In *Sessional Papers of Canada*. Ottawa: S.E. Dawson, 1894.

———. *Report of the Royal Commission on the Liquor Traffic in Canada*. Ottawa: S.E. Dawson, 1895.

Canada. Senate. *Debates*. Ottawa: King's Printer.

Canada. Supreme Court. *Canada Law Reports*. Ottawa: F.A. Acland, 1926.

Canadian Annual Review of Public Affairs. Toronto: Canadian Review Company, 1915–35.

Canadian Pacific Railway. *Across Canada: An Annotated Guide to the Country Served by the Canadian Pacific Railway and Its Allied Interests*. Montreal: Canadian Pacific Railway, 1923.

———. *Resorts in the Canadian Pacific Rockies*. Canada: Canadian Pacific Railway, 1924.

Canney, Donald L. *Rum War: The U.S. Coast Guard and Prohibition*. Washington DC: U.S. Coast Guard, 1989.

Carr, Emily. *The Book of Small*. Toronto: Irwin, 1942.

Caswell, John E. "The Prohibition Movement in Oregon." *Oregon Historical Quarterly* 39 (March–December 1938): 235–61.

Chang, Kornel. *Pacific Connections: The Making of the U.S.-Canadian Borderlands*. Berkeley: University of California Press, 2012.

Chicago, Burlington & Quincy Railroad Company. *The Western Gateway to World Trade: The Pacific Northwest*. Chicago: Chicago Burlington & Quincy Railroad, 1924.

Chicago, Milwaukee, and St. Paul Railway Company. *The Pacific Northwest*. Buffalo: Matthews-Northrup Works, 1911.

Chisholm, Addie. *Why and How: A Hand-Book for the Use of the W.C.T. Unions in Canada*. Montreal: Witness Printing House, 1884.

Chittenden, Hiram M., and Alfred T. Richardson, eds. *Life, Letters, and Travels of Father Pierre-Jean DeSmet*. 4 vols. New York: F.P. Harper, 1904.

Church, Campbell. *Westward*. Seattle, 1929.

Circle Tours. *Pacific Northwest: Seattle-Portland-Banff-Vancouver-Victoria*. Seattle: Mail Advertising, [1924].

Clark, Norman H. "A Booze Baron's Flamboyant Reign." *Seattle Magazine*, August 1964, 14–18.

———. *Deliver Us from Evil: An Interpretation of American Prohibition*. New York: W.W. Norton, 1976.

———. *The Dry Years: Prohibition and Social Change in Washington*. Rev. ed. Seattle: University of Washington Press, 1988.

———. "The Hell-Soaked Institution and the Washington Prohibition Initiative of 1914." *Pacific Northwest Quarterly* 56, no. 1 (1965): 1–16.

———. "Roy Olmstead, A Rumrunning King on Puget Sound." *Pacific Northwest Quarterly* 54, no. 3 (1963): 89–103.

Clark, S. D. *The Social Development of Canada*. Toronto: University of Toronto Press, 1942.

Coates, Ken. "Controlling the Periphery: The Territorial Administration of the Yukon and Alaska, 1867–1959." *Pacific Northwest Quarterly* 78, no. 4 (1987): 145–51.

Cody, Howard. "The Evolution of Federal-Provincial Relations in Canada: Some Reflections." *American Review of Canadian Studies* 7, no. 1 (1977): 55–83.

Coffey, Thomas. *The Long Thirst: Prohibition in America, 1920–1933*. New York: Norton, 1975.

Cohen, Martin Bernard. "The First Legation: Canadian Diplomacy and the Opening of Relations with the United States." PhD diss., George Washington University, 1976.

Cook, Sharon Anne. *Through Sunshine and Shadow: The Woman's Christian Temperance Union, Evangelicalism, and Reform in Ontario, 1874–1930*. Montreal: McGill-Queen's University Press, 1995.

Corbett, David C. "Liquor Control Administration in British Columbia." *Canadian Public Administration* 2 (1959): 19–37.

Cox, Ross. *The Columbia River: Scenes and Adventures during a Residence of Six Years on the Western Side of the Rocky Mountains*. Norman: University of Oklahoma Press, 1957.

Craig, Grace Morris. *But This Is Our War*. Toronto: University of Toronto Press, 1981.

Cronin, Kay. *Cross in the Wilderness*. Vancouver: Mitchell Press, 1960.

Crosby, Thomas. *Among the An-ko-me-nums, or Flathead Tribes of Indians of the Pacific Coast*. Toronto: William Briggs, 1907.

———. *Up and Down the North Pacific Coast by Canoe and Mission Ship*. Toronto: Frederick Clarke Stephenson, 1914.

Dashaway Association, No. 15. *Constitution and By-Laws of the Dashaway Association of Victoria*. Victoria, 1860. Available at British Columbia Archives, Victoria.

Davison, J. F. "The Problem of Liquor Legislation in Canada." *Canadian Bar Review* 4, no. 7 (1926): 468–82.

Dawson, Michael. *Selling British Columbia: Tourism and Consumer Culture 1890–1970*. Vancouver: University of British Columbia Press, 2005.

De Lorme, Roland L. "Liquor Smuggling in Alaska." *Pacific Northwest Quarterly* 66, no. 4 (1975): 145–52.

———. "The United States Bureau of Customs and Smuggling on Puget Sound, 1851 to 1913." *Prologue* 5, no. 2 (1973): 77–88.

Dennison, William C. "The Sinking of the *I'm Alone*." *American Journal of International Law* 23, no. 2 (1929): 351–362.

De Smet, Pierre-Jean. *Oregon Missions and Travels over the Rocky Mountains in 1845–46*. 1847. Repr., Fairfield WA: Ye Galleon Press, 1978.

Deutsch, Herman J. "A Contemporary Report on the 49° Boundary Survey." *Pacific Northwest Quarterly* 53, no. 1 (1962): 17–33.

"Diary of Robert Melrose: Royal Emigrant's Almanack Concerning Five Years Servitude under the Hudson's Bay Company on Vancouver's Island." *British Columbia Historical Quarterly* 7, no. 2 (1943): 119–34; 7, no. 3 (1943): 199–218; 7, no. 4 (1943): 283–95.

Dimmel, Brandon. "Bats along the Border: Sport, Festivals, and Culture in an International Community during the First World War." *American Review of Canadian Studies* 40, no. 3 (2010): 326–37.

Dominion Brewers' Association. *Facts on the Brewing Industry in Canada: A National Industry; A Manual Outlining the Development of the Industry and Its Place in the Canadian Economy*. Ottawa, 1948.

Dominion Hotel, Victoria. *Information for Our Guests*. Victoria: Colonist Presses, 1929. Available at British Columbia Archives, Victoria.

Donnelly, Joseph Peter. "The Liquor Traffic among the Aborigines of the New Northwest, 1800–1860." PhD diss., St. Louis University, 1940.

DuBois, Ellen Carol. *Feminism and Suffrage: The Emergence of an Independent Women's Movement in America, 1848–1869*. Ithaca NY: Cornell University Press, 1999.

Duis, Perry R. *The Saloon: Public Drinking in Chicago and Boston, 1880–1920*. Urbana: University of Illinois Press, 1983.

Eagle, John A. *The Canadian Pacific Railway and the Development of Western Canada, 1896–1914*. Montreal: McGill-Queens University Press, 1989.

Electoral History of British Columbia 1871–1986. Victoria: Elections British Columbia, 1988.

Ellison, Joseph. "Designs for a Pacific Republic." *Oregon Historical Quarterly* 31, no. 4 (1930): 319–42.

Espinola, Judith. *The Prohibition Era in Washington State*. Seattle: Metrocenter YMCA, 1980.

Evans, Sterling, ed. *The Borderlands of the American and Canadian Wests: Essays on Regional History of the Forty-Ninth Parallel*. Lincoln: University of Nebraska Press, 2006.

Fahey, Edmund. *Rum Road to Spokane: A Story of Prohibition*. Missoula: University of Montana Press, 1972.

Fahey, John. *Inland Empire: D.C. Corbin and Spokane*. Seattle: University of Washington Press, 1965.

———. *Inland Empire: Unfolding Years, 1879–1929*. Seattle: University of Washington Press, 1986.

Fairfield, William S., and Charles Clift. "The Wiretappers." *Reporter*, December 23, 1952, 8–22.

Fedorak, Charles John. "The U.S. Consul in Victoria and the Political Destiny of British Columbia, 1862–1870." *B.C. Studies* 79 (Autumn 1988): 8–23.

Feldman, Herman. *Prohibition: Its Economic and Industrial Aspects*. New York: Appleton, 1930.

Ficken, Robert E. *Unsettled Boundaries: Fraser Gold and the British-American Northwest*. Pullman: Washington State University Press, 2003.

Findlay, John M., and Ken S. Coates, eds. *Parallel Destinies: Canadian-American Relations West of the Rockies*. Seattle: University of Washington Press, 2002.

Fish, Harriet U. *Law Enforcement in Washington State: The First 100 Years, 1889–1989*. Olympia: Washington Association of Sheriffs and Police Chiefs, 1989.

Fisher, Robin. *Contact and Conflict: Indian-European Relations in British Columbia, 1774–1890*. Vancouver: University of British Columbia Press, 1977.

———. "Duff and George Go West: A Tale of Two Frontiers." *Canadian Historical Review* 68, no. 4 (1987): 501–28.

Flaherty, David H., and Frank E. Manning, eds. *The Beaver Bites Back? American Popular Culture in Canada*. Montreal: McGill-Queens University Press, 1993.

Francis, Daniel. *Battle for the West: Fur Traders and the Birth of Western Canada*. Edmonton: Hurtig, 1982.

Francis, R. Douglas, and Howard Palmer, eds. *The Prairie West: Historical Readings*. Edmonton: University of Alberta Press, 1985.

Frankfurter, Felix. "A National Policy for Enforcement of Prohibition." *Annals of the American Academy of Political and Social Science* 109 (September 1923): 193–95.

Franklin, Fabian. *What Prohibition Has Done to America*. New York: Harcourt, Brace, 1922.

Frye, Northrop, ed. *The Bush Garden: Essays on the Canadian Imagination*. Toronto: Anansi, 1971.

Galbraith, John S. *The Establishment of Canadian Diplomatic Status at Washington*. Berkeley: University of California Press, 1951.

———. *The Hudson's Bay Company as Imperial Factor, 1821–1869*. Toronto: University of Toronto Press, 1957.

———. "The Hudson's Bay Company under Fire, 1847–62." *Canadian Historical Review* 30, no. 4 (1949): 322–35.

Galloway, C. F. J. *The Call of the West—Letters from British Columbia*. New York: F. A. Stokes, 1916.

Garreau, Joel. *The Nine Nations of North America*. New York: Avon, 1982.

Gastil, Raymond D. *Cultural Regions of the United States*. Seattle: University of Washington Press, 1975.

———. "The Pacific Northwest as a Cultural Region." *Pacific Northwest Quarterly* 64, no. 4 (1973): 147–56.

Geddes, Gary, ed. *Skookum Wawa: Writings of the Canadian Northwest*. Toronto: Oxford University Press, 1975.

Geiger, Andrea. *Subverting Exclusion: Transpacific Encounters with Race, Caste, and Borders, 1885–1928*. New Haven CT: Yale University Press, 2011.

Gibbins, Roger. *Canada as a Borderlands Society*. Orono ME: Borderlands Project, 1989.

Gibbs, James A. *Pacific Graveyard*. Portland OR: Binfords & Mort, 1964.

Glynn-Ward, H. *The Glamour of British Columbia*. New York: Century, 1926.

Gough, Barry M. "Send a Gunboat! Checking Slavery and Controlling Liquor Traffic among Coast Indians of British Columbia in the 1860s." *Pacific Northwest Quarterly* 69, no. 4 (1978): 151–68.

Gough, Lyn. *As Wise as Serpents: Five Women and an Organization That Changed British Columbia, 1883–1939*. Victoria: Swan Lake, 1988.

Gowan, Herbert H. *Church Work in British Columbia*. London: Longmans, Green, 1899.

Granatstein, J. L. *Yankee Go Home? Canadians and Anti-Americanism*. Toronto: HarperCollins, 1996.

Granatstein, J. L., and Norman Hillmer. *For Better or For Worse: Canada and the United States to the 1990s*. Toronto: Copp Clark Pitman, 1991.

Grant, Ernest A. "The Liquor Traffic before the Eighteenth Amendment." *Annals of the American Academy of Political and Social Science* 163 (September 1932): 1–9.

Gray, James H. *Bacchanalia Revisited: Western Canada's Boozy Skid to Social Disaster*. Saskatoon SK: Western Producer Prairie Books, 1982.

———. *Booze: When Whiskey Ruled the West*. Western Canadian Classics. Saskatoon SK: Fifth House, 1995.

———. *The Roar of the Twenties*. Toronto: Macmillan, 1975.

Graybill, Andrew R. *Policing the Great Plains: Rangers, Mounties, and the North American Frontier, 1875–1910*. Lincoln: University of Nebraska Press, 2007.

Gray Line Tours. *Seattle, Gray Line: Guide to the Pacific Northwest*. Seattle: Gray Line Motor Tours, 1930.

———. *Travelogue: Timely Tips to Tourists*. Victoria: Gray Line Travel Bureau, 1925.

Great Northern Railway Company. *Western Trips for Eastern People, 1915*. St. Paul: Great Northern Railway, 1915.

Greene, Ruth. *Personality Ships of British Columbia*. West Vancouver BC: Marine Tapestry Publications, 1969.

Guide to the Province of British Columbia for 1877–78. Victoria: T. N. Hibbin, 1877.

Hacker, Louis M. "The Rise and Fall of Prohibition." *Current History* 36 (September 1932): 662–72.

Hamilton, Douglas L. *Sobering Dilemma: The Story of Prohibition in British Columbia.* Vancouver: Ronsdale Press, 2004.

Hannigan, Robert E. "Reciprocity 1911: Continentalism and American Weltpolitik." *Diplomatic History* 4 (Fall 1980): 1–18.

Hansen, Marcus Lee, and John Bartlet Brebner. *The Mingling of the Canadian and American Peoples.* New Haven CT: Yale University Press, 1940.

Hargrove, Erwin C. "On Canadian and American Political Culture." *Canadian Journal of Economics and Political Science* 33, no. 1 (1967): 107–11.

Harrington, Robert F. "The Kootenay Area of British Columbia." *Canadian Geographic Journal* 63 (December 1961): 193–201.

Hart, Edward J. *The Selling of Canada: The CPR and the Beginnings of Tourism.* Banff AB: Altitude Publishers, 1983.

Hawley, Lowell S., and Ralph Bushnell Potts. *Counsel for the Damned.* New York, 1953.

Hayman, Michael. "The Volstead Act as a Reflection of Canadian-American Relations." MA thesis, McGill University, 1971.

Haynes, Roy. *Prohibition Inside Out.* New York: Doubleday, 1923.

Henrickson, James E., ed. *Journals of the Colonial Legislatures of the Colonies of Vancouver Island and British Columbia, 1851–1871.* Vol. 5. Victoria: Provincial Archives of British Columbia, 1980.

Heron, Craig. *Booze: A Distilled History.* Toronto: Between the Lines, 2003.

Hiebert, Albert John. "Prohibition in British Columbia." MA thesis, Simon Fraser University, 1969.

Hines, H. K. *An Illustrated History of the State of Washington.* Chicago, 1893.

Hinken, Susan Elizabeth. "The Woman's Christian Temperance Union of Oregon, 1880–1916." MA thesis, University of Portland, 1987.

Hinman, George W. "Diplomatic Victory over Rum." *American Review* 3, no. 4 (1925): 418–25.

Hitchman, James H. *A Maritime History of the Pacific Coast, 1540–1980.* Lanham MD: University Press of America, 1990.

———. "Origins of Yacht Racing in British Columbia and Washington." *American Neptune* 36 (October 1976): 231–51.

———. *The Port of Bellingham, 1920–1970.* Bellingham: Center for Pacific Northwest Studies, Western Washington State College, 1972.

———. *The Waterborne Commerce of British Columbia and Washington, 1850–1970.* Bellingham: Center for Pacific Northwest Studies, Western Washington State College, 1976.

Hoagland, Edward. *Notes from the Century Before: A Journal from British Columbia*. New York: Random House, 1969.

Hobson, Richmond, Jr. *Grass beyond the Mountains*. Toronto: McClelland and Stewart, 1951.

Holbrook, Stewart H. *Far Corner: A Personal View of the Pacific Northwest*. New York: Ballantine Books, 1952.

———. *Holy Old Mackinaw: A Natural History of the American Lumberjack*. New York: Macmillan, 1940.

Holsinger, Paul M. "The *I'm Alone* Controversy: A Study in Inter-American Diplomacy, 1929–35." *Mid America* 50, no. 4 (1968): 305–13.

Horrall, S. W. "Sir John A. Macdonald and the Mounted Police Force for the Northwest Territories." *Canadian Historical Review* 53, no. 2 (1927): 179–200.

Hose, Reginald E. "Control of Liquor Traffic in British Columbia." *North American Review* 223, no. 832 (1926): 420–30.

———. *Prohibition or Control? Canada's Experience with the Liquor Problem, 1921–1927*. New York: Longmans, Green, 1928.

Howay, F. W. "The Introduction of Intoxicating Liquors amongst the Indians of the Northwest Coast." *British Columbia Historical Quarterly* 6, no. 3 (1942): 157–70.

Howay, F. W., and E. O. S. Scholefield. *British Columbia from the Earliest Times to the Present*. Vancouver: S. J. Clarke, 1914.

Huber, Armin Otto. *Looking for Danger*. London: Skeffington & Son, 1939.

Hunt, C. W. *Booze, Boats, and Billions: Smuggling Liquid Gold*. Toronto, 1988.

Hyde, Anne Farrar. "From Stagecoach to Packard Twin Six: Yosemite and the Changing Face of Tourism, 1880–1930." *California History* 69, no. 2 (1990): 154–69.

Inglis, Alex I. "The 'W.H. Eastwood' Affair." *External Affairs* 22, no. 2 (1970): 51–56.

Ireland, Willard E. "First Impressions: Letter of Colonel Richard Clement Moody, R.E., to Arthur Blackwood, February 1, 1859." *British Columbia Historical Quarterly* 15 (January–April 1951): 85–107.

Irving, Washington. *Astoria; or, Anecdotes of an Enterprise Beyond the Rocky Mountains*. 1836. Repr., Norman: University of Oklahoma Press, 1964.

Jensen, Merrill. *Regionalism in America*. Madison: University of Wisconsin Press, 1952.

Johnson, Benjamin, and Andrew R. Graybill, eds. *Bridging National Borders in North America: Transnational and Comparative Histories*. Durham NC: Duke University Press, 2010.

Johnston, Hugh J. M., ed. *The Pacific Province: A History of British Columbia*. Vancouver: Douglas and McIntyre, 1996.

Jones, Robert L. "Canada's Cooperation in Prohibition Enforcement." *Current History* 32, no. 4 (1930): 712–16.

———. *The Eighteenth Amendment and Our Foreign Relations*. New York: Thomas Y. Crowell, 1933.

Jones, Stephen. "The Cordilleran Section of the Canada–United States Borderland." *Geographical Journal* 89 (June 1937): 439–50.

Keenleyside, Hugh. *Canada and the United States: Some Aspects of Their Historical Relations*. New York: Knopf, 1952.

Kennedy, Margaret A. *The Whiskey Trade of the Northwestern Plains: A Multidisciplinary Study*. New York: Peter Lang, 1997.

Kerr, K. Austin. *Organized for Prohibition: A New History of the Anti-saloon League*. New Haven CT: Yale University Press, 1985.

Kett, Joseph F. "Temperance and Intemperance as Historical Problems." *Journal of American History* 67, no. 4 (1981): 878–85.

Kipling, Rudyard. *Letters of Travel, 1892–1913*. New York: Doubleday, Page, 1920.

Klug, Thomas A. "The Immigration and Naturalization Service (INS) and the Making of a Border-Crossing Culture on the US-Canada Border, 1891–1941." *American Review of Canadian Studies* 40, no. 3 (2010): 395–415.

Knight, Phyllis, and Rolf Knight. *A Very Ordinary Life*. Vancouver,: New Star Books, 1974.

Konrad, Victor. "The Borderlands of the United States and Canada in the Context of North American Development." *International Journal of Canadian Studies* 4 (Fall 1991): 77–95.

Kottman, Richard. "Volstead Violated: Prohibition as a Factor in Canadian-American Relations." *Canadian Historical Review* 43, no. 2 (1962): 106–26.

Kresl, Peter Karl. "Struggling in the Net." *American Review of Canadian Studies* 25, no. 2 (1994): 561–72.

Kyvig, David E. *Repealing National Prohibition*. Chicago: University of Chicago Press, 1979.

LaDow, Beth. *The Medicine Line: Life and Death on a North American Borderland*. New York: Routledge, 2000.

Langley, Harry. *Vancouver Island, a Crown Colony!* Victoria: J. Parker Buckle, 1934.

Laskin, Bora. *Canadian Constitutional Law: Cases, Text, and Notes: A Distribution of Legislative Power*. 2nd ed. Toronto: Carswell, 1966.

Leacock, Stephen. *Wet Wit and Dry Humour*. New York: Dodd, Mead, 1931.

Lecker, Robert, ed. *Borderlands: Essays in Canadian-American Relations*. Toronto: ECW Press, 1991.

Lee, Daniel, and Joseph Frost. *Ten Years in Oregon*. New York: J. Collord, 1844.

Lee, Erika. "Enforcing the Borders: Chinese Exclusion along the U.S. Borders with Canada and Mexico, 1882–1924." *Journal of American History* 89, no. 1 (2002): 54–86.

Legate, David. *Stephen Leacock*. Toronto: Doubleday Canada, 1970.

Legg, Herbert. *Customs Services in Western Canada, 1867–1925: A History*. Creston BC: Creston Review, 1962.

Lipset, Seymour Martin. *Continental Divide: The Values and Institutions of the United States and Canada*. Toronto: Canadian-American Committee, 1989.

Lonsdale, A. L. "Rumrunners on Puget Sound." *American West* 9, no. 3 (1972): 28–33, 70–71.

Lumsden, Ian, ed. *Close the 49th Parallel, etc.: The Americanization of Canada*. Toronto: University of Toronto Press, 1970.

MacDonald, Norbert. *Distant Neighbors: A Comparative History of Seattle and Vancouver*. Lincoln: University of Nebraska Press, 1987.

MacGregor, James G. *A History of Alberta*. Edmonton: Hurtig, 1972.

Marr, William L., and Donald G. Paterson. *Canada: An Economic History*. Toronto: Gage, 1980.

Marrus, Michael. *Samuel Bronfman: The Life and Times of Seagram's Mr. Sam*. Toronto: Penguin Books Canada, 1991.

Marshall, Don. *Oregon Shipwrecks*. Portland OR: Binfords & Mort, 1984.

Matthews, Geoffrey J. *Historical Atlas of Canada*. Toronto: University of Toronto Press, 1987.

Mattingly, Carol. *Well-Tempered Women: Nineteenth-Century Temperance Rhetoric*. Carbondale: Southern Illinois University Press, 2000.

Mattison, David. *Projected Image: Provincial Government Travel Films, 1920–1984*. Victoria: B.C. Studies Conference, 1986.

Mayne, R.C. *Four Years in British Columbia and Vancouver Island: An Account of Their Forests, Rivers, Coasts, Gold Fields, and Resources for Colonisation, with Map*. London: Murray, 1862.

McCrady, David G. *Living with Strangers: The Nineteenth-Century Sioux and the Canadian-American Borderlands*. Lincoln: University of Nebraska Press, 2006.

McCurdy, James G. *By Juan de Fuca's Strait: Pioneering along the Northwestern Edge of the Continent*. Portland OR: Metropolitan Press, 1937.

————. "Criss-cross over the Boundary: The Romance of Smuggling across the Northwest Frontier." *Pacific Monthly* 23 (February 1910): 182–93.

McDonald, Robert A. J. "Victoria, Vancouver, and the Economic Development of British Columbia, 1886–1914." In *British Columbia: Historical Readings*, edited by W. Peter Ward and Robert A. J. McDonald, 369–95. Vancouver: Douglas and McIntyre, 1981.

McDougall, John. *On Western Trails in the Early Seventies: Frontier Life in the Canadian Northwest*. Toronto: W. Briggs, 1911.

McEvoy, Bernard. *From the Great Lakes to the Wide West: Impressions of a Tour between Toronto and the Pacific*. London: Sampson Low, Marston & Company, 1902.

McGreevy, Patrick. "The End of America: The Beginning of Canada." *Canadian Geographer* 32, no. 4 (1989): 307–18.

————. *The Wall of Mirrors: Nationalism and Perceptions of the Border at Niagara Falls*. Orono ME: Borderlands Project, 1991.

McIntosh, Dave. *The Collectors: A History of the Canadian Customs and Excise*. Toronto: NC Press, 1984.

McKercher, B. J. C. "Between Two Giants: Canada, the Coolidge Conference, and Anglo-American Relations in 1927." In *Anglo-American Relations in the 1920s: The Struggle for Supremacy*, edited by B. J. C. McKercher, 81–124. Edmonton: University of Alberta Press, 1990.

McKinsey, Lauren, and Victor Konrad. *Borderlands Reflections: The United States and Canada*. Orono: Canadian-American Center, University of Maine, 1989.

McLean, Robert Irwin. "A Most Effectual Remedy: Temperance and Prohibition in Alberta, 1875–1915." MA thesis, University of Calgary, 1969.

McManus, Sheila. *The Line Which Separates: Race, Gender, and the Making of the Alberta-Montana Borderlands*. Lincoln: University of Nebraska Press, 2005.

———. "Mapping the Alberta-Montana Borderlands: Race, Ethnicity, and Gender in the Late Nineteenth Century." *Journal of American Ethnic History* 20, no. 3 (2001): 71–87.

Meinig, Donald W. "Continental America, 1800–1915: The View of a Historical Geographer." *History Teacher* 22, no. 2 (1989): 189–203.

———. *The Great Columbia Plain: A Historical Geography, 1805–1910*. 1968. Repr., Seattle: University of Washington Press, 1995.

Mendeville, Ernest W. "The Sources of the Booze Supply." *Outlook*, July 15, 1925, 400–402.

Merk, Frederick, ed. *Fur Trade and Empire: George Simpson's Journal*. Rev. ed. Cambridge MA: Harvard University Press, 1968.

Merrit, Chris. *Crossing the Border: The Canada–United States Boundary*. Orono ME: Borderlands Project, 1991.

Merz, Charles. *The Dry Decade*. New York: Doubleday, 1931.

Miles, Fraser. *Slow Boat on Rum Row*. Madeira Park BC: Harbour Publishing, 1992.

Mills, Randall V. "A History of Transportation in the Pacific Northwest." *Oregon Historical Quarterly* 47 (September 1946): 281–312.

Moffit, L. W. "Control of the Liquor Traffic in Canada." *Annals of the American Academy of Political and Social Science* 163 (September 1932): 188–96.

Moore, Stephen T. "Cross-Border Crusades: The Binational Temperance Movement in Washington and British Columbia." *Pacific Northwest Quarterly* 98, no. 3 (2007): 130–42.

———. "Defining the 'Undefended': Canadians, Americans, and the Multiple Meanings of Border during Prohibition." *American Review of Canadian Studies* 34, no. 1 (2004): 3–32.

———. "Refugees from Volstead: Cross-Boundary Tourism in the Northwest during Prohibition." In *The Borderlands of the American and Canadian Wests: Essays on Regional History of the Forty-Ninth Parallel*, edited by Sterling Evans, 247–61. Lincoln: University of Nebraska Press, 2006.

Morrissey, Katherine G. *Mental Territories: Mapping the Inland Empire*. Ithaca NY: Cornell University Press, 1997.

Neatby, H. Blair. *William Lyon Mackenzie King: The Lonely Heights, 1924–1932*. Toronto: University of Toronto Press, 1963.

Netboy, Anthony, ed. *The Pacific Northwest*. New York: Doubleday, 1963.

New, W. H. *Borderlands: How We Talk about Canada*. Vancouver: University of British Columbia Press, 1998.

Newman, Peter. *Bronfman Dynasty: The Rothschilds of the New World*. Toronto: McClelland and Stewart, 1978.

Newsome, Eric. *The Case of the* Beryl G. Victoria: Orca Book Publishers, 1989.

———. *Pass the Bottle: Rum Tales of the West Coast*. Victoria: Orca Book Publishers, 1995.

Noel, Janet. *Temperance Crusades before Confederation*. Toronto: University of Toronto Press, 1995.

Noel, Thomas J. *The City and the Saloon: Denver, 1858–1916*. Lincoln: University of Nebraska Press, 1982.

Northern Pacific Railway Company. *Opportunities along the Scenic Highway through the Land of Fortune*. St. Paul: Northern Pacific Railway, 1911.

Northwest Greyhound Lines. *To and through the Pacific Northwest by Greyhound: Washington, Oregon, Idaho, Montana, Western Canada*. Seattle: Craftsman Press, 1930.

Okrent, Daniel. *Last Call: The Rise and Fall of Prohibition*. New York: Scribner, 2010.

Ormsby, Margaret A. *British Columbia: A History*. Toronto: Macmillan, 1958.

Osoyoos Border Centennial Committee. *100 Years Customs Service at Osoyoos, British Columbia, 1861–1961*. Osoyoos BC: Osoyoos Times, 1961.

Palmer, Bryan D. *Working-Class Experience: The Rise and Reconstitution of Canadian Labour, 1800–1980*. Rev. ed. Toronto, 1983.

Palmer, Howard, and Tamara Palmer. *Alberta: A New History*. Edmonton: Hurtig, 1990.

Palmer, Richard F. "The Rum Runners." *Inland Seas* 45, no. 4 (1989): 246–49.

Parker, Marion, and Robert Tyrrell. *Rumrunner: The Life and Times of Johnny Schnarr*. Victoria: Orca Book Publishers, 1992.

Parks, W. S. *Tourists' Guide of Vancouver, British Columbia: The Sunset Doorway of the Dominion*. Vancouver: W. S. Parks, 1905. Available at British Columbia Archives, Victoria.

Patton, Janice. *The Sinking of the* I'm Alone. Toronto: McClelland and Stewart, 1973.

Piers, Sir Charles P. *Sport and Life in British Columbia*. London: Heath Cranton, 1923.

Playfair, W. E. "British Columbia's Fifty-Seven Varieties." *British Columbia Magazine*, September 1911, 903–15.

Pollard, Lancaster. "The Pacific Northwest." In *Regionalism in America*, edited by Merrill Jensen, 187–212. Madison: University of Wisconsin Press, 1952.

Popham, Robert E., and Wolfgang Schmidt, eds. *Statistics of Alcohol Use and Alcoholism in Canada, 1871–1956*. Toronto: University of Toronto Press, 1958.

Potts, Ralph Bushnell. *Seattle Heritage*. Seattle: Superior, 1955.

Powers, Madelon. *Faces along the Bar: Lore and Order in the Workingman's Saloon, 1870–1920*. Chicago: University of Chicago Press, 1998.

Puget Sounders and British Columbians Associated. *Evergreen Playground of Puget Sound and British Columbia*. N.p., 1927. Available at British Columbia Archives, Victoria.

Putman, Edison Klein. "The Prohibition Movement in Idaho, 1863–1934." PhD diss., University of Idaho, 1981.

R. "Neighbors: A Canadian View." *Foreign Affairs* 10, no. 3 (1932): 417–30.

Ramirez, Bruno. *Crossing the 49th Parallel: Migration from Canada to the United States, 1900–1930*. Ithaca NY: Cornell University Press, 2001.

Ramsay, Bruce. *Ghost Towns of British Columbia*. Vancouver: Mitchell, 1963.

Rannie, F. "Old Big, Colourful: The Distilling Industry." *Canadian Geographical Journal* 93 (December 1976/January 1977): 20–27.

Redekop, John H., ed. *The Star-Spangled Beaver*. Toronto: Peter Martin Associates, 1971.

Reiber, Paul. "The Old Whiskey Trail." *Big Smoke*, 1983, 12.

Rich, E. E., ed. *McLoughlin's Fort Vancouver Letters*. 3 vols. London: Hudson's Bay Record Society, 1941–44.

———. *Part of Dispatch from George Simpson Esq., Governor of Ruperts Land to the Governor & Committee of the Hudson's Bay Company, London*. London: Hudson's Bay Record Society, 1947.

———. *Peter Skene Ogden's Snake Country Journals, 1824–25 and 1825–26*. London: Hudson's Bay Record Society, 1950.

———. *Samuel Black's Rocky Mountain Journal, 1824*. London: Hudson's Bay Record Society, 1955.

Richard, Mark Paul. "'Why Don't You Be a Klansman?' Anglo-Canadian Support for the Ku Klux Klan Movement in 1920s New England." *American Review of Canadian Studies* 40, no. 4 (2010): 508–16.

Richardson, David. *Pig War Islands*. East Sound WA: Orcas, 1971.

Riddell, Walter A., ed. *Documents on Canadian Foreign Policy, 1917–1939*. Toronto: Oxford University Press, 1962.

Robbins, William G. *Colony and Empire: The Capitalist Transformation of the American West*. Lawrence: University Press of Kansas, 1994.

Robbins, William G., and Katrine Barber. *Nature's Northwest: The North Pacific Slope in the Twentieth Century*. Tucson: University of Arizona Press, 2011.

Robbins, William G., Robert J. Frank, and Richard E. Ross, eds. *Regionalism and the Pacific Northwest*. Corvallis: Oregon State University Press, 1983.

Robin, Martin. *The Rush for Spoils: The Company Province, 1871–1933*. Toronto: McClelland and Stewart, 1972.

Rogers, Will. *Rogers-isms: The Cowboy Philosopher on Prohibition; The Writings of Will Rogers*. Stillwater: Oklahoma State University Press, 1975.

Ronyk, Gwenn. "The United States in the Twenties as Seen by the Western Canadian Press." MA thesis, University of Regina, 1979.

Rose, Kenneth D. "The Labbe Affair and Prohibition Enforcement in Portland." *Pacific Northwest Quarterly* 77, no. 2 (1986): 42–51.

Roy, Patricia. *A White Man's Province: British Columbia Politicians and Chinese and Japanese Immigrants, 1858–1914.* Vancouver: University of British Columbia Press, 1989.

Roy, R. H. "The Early Defense and Militia of the Okanagan Valley, 1871–1914." *Pacific Northwest Quarterly* 57 (January 1966): 28–35.

Rutan, Gerard F. "British Columbia–Washington State Governmental Interrelations: Some Findings upon the Failure of Structure." *American Review of Canadian Studies* 15, no. 1 (1985): 97–110.

Sage, Walter N. "British Columbia Becomes Canadian, 1871–1901." *Queen's Quarterly* 52, no. 2 (1945): 168–83.

Sanford, E. P. "The Illegal Liquor Traffic." *Annals of the American Academy of Political and Social Science* 163 (September 1932): 39–45.

Schonberger, Howard B. *Transportation to the Seaboard: The Communication Revolution and American Foreign Policy, 1860–1900.* Westport CT: Greenwood, 1971.

Schultz, John A. "Whose News: The Struggle for Wire Service Distribution, 1900–1920." *American Review of Canadian Studies* 10, no. 1 (1980): 27–38.

Schwantes, Carlos A. *The Pacific Northwest: An Interpretive History.* Lincoln: University of Nebraska Press, 1989.

———. "Perceptions of Violence on the Wageworkers' Frontier: An American-Canadian Comparison." *Pacific Northwest Quarterly* 77, no. 2 (1986): 52–57.

———. *Radical Heritage: Labor, Socialism, and Reform in Washington and British Columbia, 1885–1917.* Seattle: University of Washington Press, 1979.

Scott, A. D. "Notes on a Western Viewpoint." *BC Studies* 13 (Spring 1972): 3–15.

Scott, James W., and Roland L. De Lorme. *Historical Atlas of Washington.* Norman: University of Oklahoma Press, 1988.

Seager, Allen. "The Resource Economy, 1871–1921." In *The Pacific Province: A History of British Columbia,* edited by Hugh J. M. Johnston, 205–51. Vancouver: Douglas & McIntyre, 1996.

See, Scott W. "Nineteenth-Century Collective Violence: Toward a North American Context." *Labour/Le Travail* 39 (Spring 1997): 13–38.

Shah, Nayan. *Stranger Intimacy: Contesting Race, Sexuality, and the Law in the North American West.* Berkeley: University of California Press, 2011.

Sharp, Paul. *Whoop-Up Country: The Canadian-American West, 1865–1885.* Minneapolis: University of Minnesota Press, 1955.

Sheehan, Nancy M. "Temperance, the WCTU and Education in Alberta, 1905–1930." PhD diss., University of Alberta, 1981.

―――. "The WCTU on the Prairies, 1886–1930: An Alberta-Saskatchewan Comparison." *Prairie Forum* 6, no. 1 (1981): 17–33.

―――. "Women Helping Women: The WCTU and the Foreign Population in the West, 1905–1930." *International Journal of Women's Studies* 6, no. 5 (1983): 395–411.

Shi, David E. "Seward's Attempt to Annex British Columbia, 1865–1869." *Pacific Historical Review* 47, no. 2 (1978): 217–38.

Siener, William H. "'A Barricade of Ships, Guns, Airplanes and Men': Arming the Niagara Border, 1920–1930." *American Review of Canadian Studies* 38, no. 4 (2008): 429–50.

Sinclair, Andrew. *Prohibition, the Era of Excess.* 1962. Repr., Norwalk CT: Easton Press, 1985.

Sloan, R. W. "The Canadian West: Americanization or Canadianization?" *Alberta Historical Review* 16, no. 1 (1968): 1–7.

Smiley, Donald V., ed. *The Rowell-Sirois Report: An Abridgement of Book One of the Royal Commission Report on Dominion-Provincial Relations.* 1963. Repr., Toronto: Macmillan, 1978.

Smith, Dorothy Blakey, ed. *The Reminiscences of Doctor John Sebastian Helmcken.* Vancouver: University of British Columbia Press, 1975.

Smith, Goldwin. *Essays on Questions of the Day, Political and Social.* New York: Macmillan, 1893.

―――. "Prohibitionism in Canada and the United States." *Macmillan's Magazine,* March 1889, 338–41.

Smith, Robert L. "Bibles and Booze: Prohibition in Chilliwack in the Late 1800's." *British Columbia Historical News* 12, no. 3 (1979): 2–9.

Smith, W. H. *The Liquor Traffic in British Columbia.* Toronto: Board of Home Missions and Social Service, Presbyterian Church in Canada, 1922.

Soberg, Ralph. *Confessions of an Alaska Bootlegger.* Walnut Creek CA: Hardscratch Press, 1990.

Soden, Dale E. "Billy Sunday in Spokane: Revivalism and Social Control." *Pacific Northwest Quarterly* 79 (January 1988): 10–17.

―――. "The Woman's Christian Temperance Union in the Pacific Northwest: A Different Side of the Social Gospel." In *Gender and the Social Gospel,* edited by Wendy J. Deichmann Edwards and Carolyn De Swarte Giffort, 103–16. Urbana: University of Illinois Press, 2003.

Soule, A. Bradley. "The United States Customs Boat Patrol on Lake Champlain during the Prohibition Era." *Vermont History* 48, no. 3 (1980): 133–43.

Spence, Ben H. *Liquor Control in Canada.* Toronto: Canadian Prohibition Bureau, 1930.

―――. "Prohibitory Legislation in Canada." *Annals of the American Academy of Political and Social Science* 109 (September 1923): 230–64.

Spence, F. S. *The Facts of the Case: A Summary of the Most Important Evidence and Argument Presented in the Report of the Royal Commission on the Liquor Traffic.* Toronto: Newton & Treloar, 1896.

Spinelli, Lawrence. *Dry Diplomacy: The United States, Great Britain, and Prohibition.* Wilmington DE: Scholarly Resources, 1989.

Splitstone, Fred John. *Orcas: Gem of the San Juans.* Sedro-Wooley WA: Courier-Times Press, 1946.

Stacey, C. P. *The Undefended Border: The Myth and the Reality.* Ottawa: Canadian Historical Association, 1967.

Starkins, Ed. "Rum Running." In *Raincoast Chronicles: First Five,* edited by H. White, 10–19. Madeira Park BC: Harbour, 1976.

Stayton, W. H. "Our Experiment in National Prohibition: What Progress Has It Made?" *Annals of the American Academy of Political and Social Science* 109 (September 1923): 26–38.

Stegner, Wallace. *Wolf Willow.* New York: Viking, 1962.

Stevenson, J. A. "Sectional Factors in Canadian Foreign Policy." *Foreign Affairs* 16 (July 1938): 667–78.

Stewart, Gordon T. *The American Response to Canada since 1776.* East Lansing: Michigan State University Press, 1992.

———. *The Origins of Canadian Politics: A Comparative Approach.* Vancouver: University of British Columbia Press, 1986.

Stokes, Charles W. "Prohibition's Decline and Fall in Canada." *American Review of Reviews* 77, no. 2 (1928): 169–74.

Stone, Leroy. *Urban Development in Canada.* Ottawa: Dominion Bureau of Statistics, 1967.

Stretch, Dianne Kathryn. "From Prohibition to Government Control: The Liquor Question in Alberta, 1909–1929." MA thesis, University of Alberta, 1980.

Stuart, Reginald C. "Anti-Americanism in Canadian History." *American Review of Canadian Studies* 27, no. 2 (1997): 293–310.

———. "Continentalism Revisited: Recent Narratives on the History of Canadian-American Relations." *Diplomatic History* 18, no. 3 (1994): 405–14.

———. *Dispersed Relations: Americans and Canadians in Upper North America.* Washington DC: Woodrow Wilson Center Press, 2007.

———. Review of *Canada and the United States: Ambivalent Allies,* by John Herd Thompson and Stephen J. Randall. *Canadian Review of American Studies* 25, no. 2 (1995): 118–20.

Sunset Magazine. "Trails to Two Cities." May 1933, 22–24.

Swanson, Roger F., ed. *Canadian-American Summit Diplomacy, 1923–1973: Selected Speeches and Documents.* Toronto: McClelland and Stewart, 1975.

Talbot, Frederick Arthur Ambrose. *The New Garden of Canada: By Pack-Horse and Canoe through Undeveloped New British Columbia.* New York: Cassell, 1911.

Thompson, John Herd, and Stephen J. Randall. *Canada and the United States: Ambiva-lent Allies*. Athens: University of Georgia Press, 1994.

Thompson, John Herd, and Allen Seager. *Canada 1922–1939: Decades of Discord*. Toronto: McClelland and Stewart, 1985.

Thompson, Retta L. B. *A Synoptic View of the History of the Woman's Christian Temper-ance Union of Saskatchewan, Canada: A Goodly Heritage, 1913–1973*. Saskatoon SK: Early Mailing Service, 1975.

Thompson, Wayne C. *Canada 2001*. Harper's Ferry WV: Stryker-Post, 2001.

Thornton, Mark. *The Economics of Prohibition*. Salt Lake City: University of Utah Press, 1991.

Timberlake, James H. *Prohibition and the Progressive Movement, 1900–1920*. Cambridge MA: Harvard University Press, 1963.

Tremayne, Russell M. "Western Canada: The West beyond the Pacific Northwest." *Pacific Northwest Quarterly* 86 (Summer 1995): 118–120.

Triangle Tours. *Sightseeing: Banff, Vancouver, Victoria, Seattle, Rainier National Park*. Seattle: Triangle Tours, 1922.

Turnbull, Elsie G. *Trail between Two Wars: The Story of a Smelter City*. Victoria: Mor-riss, 1980.

Tyrrell, Ian. "Prohibition, American Cultural Expansion, and the New Hegemony in the 1920s: An Interpretation." *Social History* (Canada) 27, no. 54 (1994): 413–45.

———. *Sobering Up: From Temperance to Prohibition in Antebellum America, 1800–1860*. Westport CT: Greenwood Press, 1979.

———. *Woman's World/Woman's Empire: The Woman's Christian Temperance Union in International Perspective, 1880–1930*. Chapel Hill: University of North Carolina Press, 1991.

Union Pacific Railroad Company. *The Pacific Northwest and Alaska*. Omaha: Union Pacific System, 1924. Available at British Columbia Archives, Victoria.

Union Steamships, Ltd. *Bowen Island, Summer Play—Shores of Howe Sound*. Vancou-ver: Union Steamships, 1925.

United States. Wickersham Commission. *Enforcement of Prohibition Laws of the United States*. Washington DC: GPO, 1931.

U.S. Bureau of the Census. *Foreign Commerce and Navigation of the United States*. Washington DC: GPO, 1915–35.

———. *Statistical Abstract of the United States*. Washington DC: GPO, 1915–35.

U.S. Bureau of Prohibition. *Laws Relating to National Prohibition Enforcement, November 1929*. Washington DC: GPO, 1930.

———. *Statistics Concerning Intoxicating Liquors*. Washington DC: GPO, 1923–30.

U.S. Congress. *Congressional Record*.

U.S. Department of Justice. *Annual Report of the Attorney General of the United States*. Washington DC: GPO.

U.S. Department of State. *Foreign Relations of the United States*. Washington DC: GPO.

U.S. Department of the Treasury. *Annual Report of the Secretary of the Treasury*. Washington DC: GPO.

U.S. Supreme Court. *Reports*.

United States Brewers' Association. *The Year Book of the United States Brewers' Association*. New York: United States Brewers' Association, 1919, 1920–21.

Urquhart, M. C., ed. *Historical Statistics of Canada*. Ottawa: Statistics Canada, 1965.

Vancouver Board of Park Commissioners. *Handbook of Parks, Playgrounds, and Bathing Beaches*. Vancouver: Sun, 1925.

Vancouver Publicity Bureau. *Beauty Spots at Vancouver, Canada: The Lion Guarded City*. Vancouver: Sun, 1923–24.

Vassilopoulos, Peter. "Fast Rumrunner—Albi Wahoo." *Pacific Yachting* 9 (January 1975): 33–35.

Victor, Frances Fuller. *River of the West: Life and Adventures in the Rocky Mountains and Oregon*. Hartford CT: R. W. Bliss, 1870.

Victoria & Island Development Association. *The Call of Victoria*. Victoria: Buckle & Neill, 1918. Available at British Columbia Archives, Victoria.

———. *A Guide to Your Wanderings through the Port of Victoria, B.C.: The Delightful Old-World City on the Shores of the Pacific*. Victoria: Colonist Presses, 1918.

———. *Tourists' Map and Guide to Victoria*. Victoria: The Association, 1918. Available at British Columbia Archives, Victoria.

Victoria & Island Publicity Bureau. *Vancouver Island and Its Holiday Resorts*. Victoria: Victoria & Island Publicity Bureau, 1920, 1925. Available at British Columbia Archives, Victoria.

Wadewitz, Lissa K. *The Nature of Borders: Salmon, Boundaries, and Bandits on the Salish Sea*. Seattle: University of Washington Press, 2012.

Walker, Anna Sloan. "History of the Liquor Laws of the State of Washington." *Pacific Northwest Quarterly* 5, no. 2 (1914): 116–20.

Wallace, W. Stewart, ed. *The Macmillan Dictionary of Canadian Biography*. Toronto: Macmillan, 1978.

Warburton, Clark. *The Economic Results of Prohibition*. New York: Columbia University Press, 1932.

Warner, Donald F. *The Idea of Continental Union: Agitation for the Annexation of Canada to the United States, 1849–1893*. Lexington: University of Kentucky Press, 1960.

Warsh, Cheryl Krasnick, ed. *Drink in Canada: Historical Essays*. Montreal: McGill-Queen's University Press, 1993.

Washington State Advisory Liquor Control Commission. *Report of State Advisory Liquor Control Commission*. Olympia WA: State Printing Plant, 1933.

Washington State Liquor Control Board. *Report*. Olympia WA: State Printing Plant, 1934.

Waters, Harold. *Smugglers of Spirits: Prohibition and the Coast Guard Patrol.* New York: Hastings House, 1971.

Watson, George. *Pioneer Breweries of British Columbia: A Look at B.C. Breweries from a Collector's Point of View.* Nanaimo BC: Westward Collector, 1974.

Wheeler, Wayne B. "Liquor in International Trade." *Annals of the American Academy of Political and Social Science* 109 (September 1923): 145–54.

Widdis, Randy William. *With Scarcely a Ripple: Anglo-Canadian Migration into the United States and Western Canada, 1880–1920.* Montreal: McGill-Queen's University Press, 1998.

Wilbur, Richard. *H. H. Stevens, 1878–1973.* Toronto: University of Toronto Press, 1977.

Wilgus, William J. *The Railway Interrelations of the United States and Canada.* New Haven CT: Yale University Press, 1937.

Willard, Frances S. *Woman and Temperance: Or the Work and Workers of the Woman's Christian Temperance Union.* Chicago: The Temple, 1897.

Willebrandt, Mabel Walker. *The Inside of Prohibition.* Indianapolis: Bobbs-Merrill, 1929.

Williams, William Appleman. "Backyard Autonomy." *Nation,* September 5, 1981, 161, 179–80.

———. "Radicals and Regionalism." *Democracy* 1, no. 4 (1981): 87–98.

Willoughby, Malcolm Francis. *Rum War at Sea.* Washington DC: GPO, 1967.

Wills, Jocelyn. "Divided Loyalties: Private Ambition, Nation-Building, and the Railroad Racket along the Northwestern Borderlands, 1877–1883." *Journal of the West* 39, no. 2 (2000): 8–16.

Wilson, Gary A. *Honky-Tonk Town: Havre's Bootlegging Days.* Helena MT: Highline Books, 1985.

Winks, Robin W. *The Relevance of Canadian History.* Lanham MD: University Press of America, 1988.

Women's Christian Temperance Union. *W.C.T.U. Songs.* Evanston IL: National Women's Christian Temperance Union Publishing House, 1928.

Wood, Ruth K. *The Tourist's Northwest.* New York: Dodd, Mead, 1916.

Zolo, Serge. *Sentenced to Adventure: An Autobiography by Serge Zolo.* London: George G. Harrap, 1936.

Index

Borah, William, 157

border (Canadian-American): challenges in patrolling, 68–69, 77, 143; different meanings of, xiv–xv, 135–36, 168–69; effect of the automobile on, xiv; as interface, 23, 43, 152–53; as margin, 135–36; perils of, 117; permeability of, 11, 29–31, 56; physical demarcation of, ix; statistics of crossings, 47; as symbol of sovereignty and identity, xii–xiii, 82–83; as symbol of unique relationship, xiii, 146–47

border patrol, proposed, 146–47

Borquin, George, 148

Boston Globe (newspaper), 155

Brandeis, Louis, 64

Brebner, John Bartlet, 47

brewing industry, 39, 57, 90–91, 92–93, 163, 181n61

British Columbia: America's role in economic development of, 4–5; confederation with Canada, 12–14, 176n62; cooperation in enforcement, 102, 117, 133–34, 136, 138–39, 169–70; cultural identity, 9–10; cultural ties to Great Britain, 6–8; demographics of, 6, 10–11, 37, 175n45, 180n51; drinking rates in, 26; federal-provincial jurisdictional conflicts, 139–42; geography and demographics of, 2–5, 8–9, 173n4; government control system, 36–38, 154–61; lack of national identification, 10–14; liquor consumption in, 178n14; Peace Arch, xi; perceptions of Americans in, 52–54; prohibition in, 33, 35–36; reasons for abandoning prohibition, 34–35, 39–40; settlement patterns in, 9;

175n36; social reform in, 32; tourism industry, 43–46, 48–51. *See also Beryl G* hijacking

British Columbia-American relations: cultural differences, 6–10; cultural interactions, 5; effect of the *Beryl G* hijacking on, 114–16; governmental cooperation, 162–64; Great Britain's role in, 7–8; nationalism and marginalization, 12–15; proposed border patrol and, 146–47; role of Rocky Mountains in, 10–11; smuggling's role in, 15–17, 21; special nature of, 137–38; during temperance movement, 30–31; tourism, 167. *See also Beryl G* hijacking

British Columbia Distillery, 128, 130

British Columbia Hotelman's Association, 50–51

British Columbia Liquor Control Board, 130, 140, 156, 163

British Columbia Prohibition Act (1917), 36

British Columbia Prohibition Association, 167

British Columbia Temperance League, 167

British North America Act, 33

Brown, Russell, 52

Bryan, William Jennings, 55

Bureau, Jacques, 122

Bureau of Prohibition, 77–78, 150

Butler, Nicholas Murray, 65

Butler, Pierce, 64

Calgary Albertan (newspaper), 115

Calgary Brewing and Malting Company, 39

Cameron, Slim, 66, 76

campaign donations, 131–33

Canada: abandonment of prohibition, 36–41; acceptance of rumrunning trade, 58–59; American tourism in, 49–51; demographics and geography, 172n8; diplomatic relations with United States, 84–90, 97, 145; government control in, 153–61; as linchpin in Anglo-American relations, 138–39, 198n14; liquor consumption in, 178n14; national identity of, xii–xiii, 52, 84; passage of prohibition laws, 36; public opinion on enforcement cooperation, 91, 96–97, 98–102, 143–44; as sanctuary for American refugees, 46–47; special relationship with United States, x–xi, xiii; temperance organizations in, 29–32
Canadian-American border. *See* border (Canadian-American)
Canadian-American relations: border's importance in, 135–36, 172n14; Canadian views of Americans, 52–54, 94–98, 114–16; fears of cultural intrusion, 30, 98; First World War and, 7–8; role of geography in, xi–xii, 2–5; special relationship, x–xi, xiii. *See also* British Columbia-American relations
Canadian-American treaty (1924), 89–90, 97, 142–43
Canadian customs: border crossing statistics, 47; cooperation between countries, 97; corruption in, 122, 124; issuing clearances, 86–87; liquor traffic and, 68–69, 119–20; required courteous behavior, 48, 52, 53–54. *See also* parliamentary commission; Royal Commission on Customs and Excise
Canadian foreign policy, xiv, 84, 168

Canadian Forum (newspaper), 95, 96–97
Canadian justice system: *Beryl G* hijacking case, 110, 113; compared to American, 115–16
Canadian Pacific Railway, 3, 14, 93
Canadian Press, 5
Canadian Temperance Act (1878), 32–33, 139, 141
Caoba (ship), 100–102
Carmichael, William, 19
Carr, Emily, 26
cars. *See* automobiles
Chicago Tribune (newspaper), 12
Chilton, H. G., 86–88, 87
Chinese immigrants, 11, 17
Chris Moeller (ship), 129–30
Christian Guardian (newspaper), 36
Chronicle Telegraph (newspaper), 146
Clark, Champ, 82
Clark, Norman, 26, 78
Clausen, Al, 106–7
clearances. *See* liquor clearances
Cleveland, Grover, 18, 20
Coast Guard: approaches to enforcement, 148–50; challenges in smuggling enforcement, 18–20, 78–80; questionable seizures, 76, 98–102
Coates, Ken, 9
Coleman, Herbert, 138–39
Colonist (newspaper), 26
commercial goods smuggling, 89, 119–20, 124, 126, 176n68
Commercial Protective Association (CPA), 119–20
Conservative party (Canada), 121–22, 124–25, 132–33, 136
Consolidated Exporters Corporation, 69–73, 99–100, 127–28, 131, 132–33, 140
Coolidge, Calvin, 102
Cosmos, Amor de, 13

courts. *See* justice systems

Cox, Ross, 23

Cross, A. E., 39

Cruickshank, Forbes, 105–7, 108–9, 109–10, 113

Cunard Steamship Company, Ltd. v. *Mellon*, 87, 88

customs. *See* Canadian customs; United States customs

customs scandal. *See* parliamentary commission; Royal Commission on Customs and Excise

Daily Chronicle (newspaper), 55, 156

Daily News-Advertiser (newspaper), 31

Daily Province (newspaper), 31, 137–38, 142, 146

D'Arcy Island, 72

Dashaways, 28, 29

Daughters of Temperance, 28

de Brisay, Richard, 40

De Lorme, Roland, 20

Denman No. 11 (ship), 107, 111–12

distilling industry, 39, 57, 90–91, 92–93, 163, 181n61

dollar-bill method of exchange, 72

Dominion Hotel (Victoria BC) guest book poem, 45–46

Doran, James, 143

drunkenness, 25–26, 53, 156, 160–61

Dunwoody, W. R., 108

economy (Canadian): commercial goods smuggling and, 119; effect of America's repeal on, 163; example of as reason for American repeal movement, 161–62; government control benefits for, 159–60; liquor traffic and, 90–92, 130, 131; tourism and, 47–48, 49–51, 53–54

Eighteenth Amendment: flaws in, 75; irony of, 40–41; jurisdictional challenges, 81; liquor trials under, 64; passage of, x, 34; public opinion of, 65, 75–76, 94–96; repeal movement, 161–62; repeal of, 162–64, 201n5. *See also* prohibition; prohibition enforcement

enforcement. *See* prohibition enforcement

England. *See* Great Britain

Erickson, William, 103

Euler, W. D., 118, 143

export companies. *See* liquor export companies

exports. *See* liquor exportation

extradition, 87, 88

Federalship (ship), 148

financing of liquor traffickers, 70

Finch, Jerry, 64

First World War, 7–8, 35–36, 37, 152

fishing industry, 59, 89

foreign vessel registry, 84–85

Fraser River gold rush, 4

Frye, Northrop, 52

fur traders, 3, 23–25

Geddes, Auckland, 86

geography (north-south alignment), xi–xii, 2–5, 169–70, 173n7

Gillis, William, 104, 105, 106, 107, 112

Gillis, William, Jr., 104, 106, 107, 112

goods smuggling, 89, 119–20, 124, 126, 176n68

Gordon's Digest of the Revenue Laws, 20

government: differing beliefs on role of, 40; jurisdictional conflicts within, 38–39, 139–42

law enforcement agencies, 72, 75–76, 80, 147–50. *See also* prohibition enforcement

Leacock, Stephen, xiii, 1, 152

legislation: Canadian liquor permits, 48; Canadian prohibition, 36; local option, 32–33; regulating morality, 95–96. *See also* Eighteenth Amendment

Liberal party (Canadian), 120, 121–23, 125, 127, 132–33, 136

Lipset, Seymour Martin, xii, xiii, 172n14

liquor: as a commodity, 24; cultural role of in the Northwest, 25–27; dangerous alternatives to, 57–58; effects of, 35–36; miners use of, 35

liquor caches, 111

liquor clearances, 86–87, 88, 89, 129–30, 143. *See also* liquor export ban

liquor control boards, 130, 140, 156, 162–63

liquor exportation, 58, 73, 86–87, 90–93

liquor export ban, 142–47, 151. *See also* liquor clearances

liquor export companies: Consolidated Exporters Corporation, 69–73, 99–100, 127–28, 131, 132–33, 140; Joseph Kennedy Ltd., 69–70, 127–29, 131, 132–33, 140, 187n54; lobbying of, 92–93; royal commission hearings, 127–29

liquor industry: effect on Canadian government, 92; effect on economy, 90–91; lobby efforts of, 39, 92–93; tax revenue from, 91–92

liquor labels, forgery of, 130–31

liquor traffic: dangers in, 117; effect of Canadian-American treaty on, 89–90; effect on Canadian economy, 90–92; enforcement problems,

73–81; fur trade and, 23–25; jurisdiction over, 38–39; opposition to, 59; Pacific Northwest problems with, 22–23; professionalizing of, 60–61, 69–73; profits in, 59–60, 185n27; reasons for success of, 58–59, 59–60; relations with law enforcement, 75–76; royal commission on, 124, 126–31; smuggling methods, 65–73; suppliers, 56–57. *See also Beryl G* hijacking

Literary Digest (newspaper), 43, 47

local option laws, 32–33

London Times (newspaper), 12

Lonsdale, Lorenz A., 79–80

Lord's Day Act (1906), 38

Lowman, Seymour, 54

lumber industry, 4–5, 26

Lyle, Roy C., 77–78, 140, 150

M-220 (ship), 79–80

M493 (ship), 105–6

Macdonald, John A., 14

MacDonald, Norbert, 175n36

Maclean's Magazine, 4

Majewski, John, 111

Manitoba Refineries, 69–70

Manson, Arthur, 140–41

Marechal Foch (ship), 71

margins, borders as, 10, 13–14, 135, 168

Marinoff, Pete, 106, 108, 111–12

Marmaduke, James Crawford, 161

Martin, Clarence, 162, 163

McCarthy Act, 33

McDonald, Donald A., 74

McDonald, Robert, 5

McFatridge, A. E., 76

McLoughlin, John, 25, 27

McQuarrie, William Garland, 49

Meighen, Arthur, 122, 125, 139

politics: illegal campaign contributions to, 132–33; role in
abandonment of prohibition in
Canada, 38–39, 40–41; role in transnational cooperation, 121–23; royal
commission and, 120, 124–25, 127
Pooley, R. H., 141–42
populist movements, 15
Portland (OR), 101–2, 181n57
Presbyterian synod, 26
Progressive party (Canadian), 122, 123,
124–25
prohibition: alternatives to, 153–54;
British Columbia-American relations during, 169–70; changing
public opinion of, 65, 75–76, 152–53;
economic consequences of, 34–35;
effect on Canadian government,
92; functions of the border during,
168–69; Hudson's Bay Company's
liquor ban, 24–25; influence of
war on, 35–36, 37; national vs local
option, 32–33, 34, 36–41; post-repeal
activity, 167; problems with legislating morality, 95–96; prohibition
movements, 41. *See also* government
control; prohibition enforcement;
temperance reform movements
prohibition agents, 62–65, 76, 77–78
Prohibition Bureau, 57, 63–65, 77, 81
prohibition enforcement: American
excesses of, 143–44; approaches to,
147–50; British Columbia's role
in, 137–42; Canadian cooperation, 83, 84–90, 136, 137–38, 144–47;
challenges of, 19–20, 38–39, 73–81,
83–86, 96; disorganization in,
80–81; institutional reform, 150–51;
jurisdiction problems, 83; political
difficulties with, 91–94

prohibition rallies, 22, 31, 167
Puget Sound, 61–65, 74, 79

Quadra (ship), 99–100
Quebec (province), 137, 159

railroad camps, 26
railroads, 3, 14, 93
Reciprocity Treaty, 82
registry of ships, 84–85
Reifel, George C., 128–29, 131, 166
Reifel, Henry, Jr., 128–29
Reifel, Henry, Sr., 128–29, 131–32, 166,
187n54
Revuocnav (ship), 72
roads, 3–4, 45, 67–68, 74, 174n11
Robbins, William, 9
Robinson, Lucy, 45
Rocky Mountains, 10–11
Rodman, Hugh, 160
Rogers, Will, 65, 67
Ronyk, Gwen, 7
Ross, Herbert, 109–10, 114
Rowell, Newton, 126–27, 128, 132
Royal Commission on Customs and
Excise: challenges faced by, 127–29;
focus and criticisms of, 125–27;
major issues investigated by, 129–
33; recommendations of, 141, 142;
role in changing public opinion
on liquor traffic, 133–34
Royal Commission on the Liquor Traf-
fic, 33–34
rum-running industry: challenges to, 72,
79–80, 147–50; dangers in, 105, 117;
defined, 184n2; early respectability
of, 60–61, 63; effect of Canadian-
American treaty on, 89–90; effect
of liquor export ban on, 151;
Olmstead's contributions to, 61–65;

post-repeal activity, 165–67; profits in, 59–60, 185n27; public opinion on, 57; reasons for success of, 58–59, 59–60; relations with law enforcement, 75–76; royal commission on, 126–31; smuggling methods, 65–73. *See also Beryl G* hijacking

Russian Fur Company, 25

saloons, 26–27, 28, 186n42
Saturday Sunset (newspaper), 34
Sawyer, H. L., 48
Schnarr, Johnny, 61, 70, 71–72, 76, 165–66
Schwantes, Carlos, 8, 40
Scott Act (1878), 32–33, 139, 141
search and seizure policy, 84, 85–86, 87, 88. *See also* waterborne liquor traffic
Seattle (wa), 34–35, 61–65
Seattle Argus (newspaper), 65, 116
Seattle Post-Intelligencer (newspaper), 41, 46, 63, 74–75, 81, 114, 153
Seattle Times (newspaper), 174n11, 175n45
Shawnee (ship), 99–100
ships, smuggling method, 70–73, 84–86, 166–67
short-circuiting process, 130
Simpson, George, 23–24, 25, 27
Sinclair, Andrew, 55
Smith, C. D., 42
smuggling: of Chinese immigrants, 17; difficulties in preventing, 18–21, 118; fishing industry, 176n68; government corruption in, 119–20, 123–24; of narcotics, 17–18; reasons for and perceptions of, 15–18; royal commission on, 126–31; seizure and use of vessels used in, 148–49. *See also* commercial goods smuggling; waterborne liquor traffic
social reform, 28–29, 32, 40

Sons of Temperance, 28, 29
sovereignty (Canadian), 82–83, 84, 137–38, 144
Sowash, Harry, 107–9, 110–13, 115
Sparks, R. Percy, 119–20
speakeasies, 158–59, 186n42
Spokane Daily Chronicle (newspaper), 45, 155
Spokesman-Review (newspaper), 55, 80, 155
Stadacona (ship), 71
Starwich, Matt, 66, 106, 107
Steele Act, 162–63
Stegner, Wallace, 46–47
Stevens, Henry Herbert, 120–21, 122–24, 140
Stevens customhouse inquiry: background to, 118–23; findings and results of, 123–25
St. Leonard Hotel, 48
Stone, Harlan, 64
Stowe, Harriet Beecher, 46
Strompkins, Paul, 107, 110–12
suffrage, 29, 32
Sunday, Billy, 22, 31–32
Sunday-closing law (1906), 38
Swanson, Robert, 131, 149

Taft, William Howard, 64
Talbot, Frederick, 1, 2, 11
temperance: under government control, 158–59, 160–61; legislating, 154–55; moderation as "true," 38; prohibition's effect on, 36–37
temperance organizations, 28, 29–31
temperance reform movements, ix, 27–32, 32–36
Templars, 28, 29–30
Tewell, Harold, 133, 134
Three Deuces (ship), 71

three-mile international water boundary, 83, 84, 85–86, 88, 190n21
timber industry, 4–5, 26
tin corsets, 65–66
tobacco industry, 119
Tolmie, Simon Fraser, 48
Toronto Mail and Empire (newspaper), 96, 98, 123
Toronto Saturday Night (newspaper), 96
tourism: border crossing statistics, 47; Canadians' view of American tourists, 42; cultural transmission and, xiv; economic effects of, 47–48, 49–51, 159–60; influence on Canadian-American relations, 51–52; lost revenue for America, 161; negative effects of, 52–55; post-repeal flow reversal, 167–68; transnational efforts to promote, 43–46, 48–49
trade reciprocity, 82
traffic laws, 44
Trane, Henry, 76
travel. *See* tourism
treaty, Anglo-American, 88–90
Treaty of Washington (1871), 87
Turner, Ballard, 78
Turner, Frank, 72
Twenty-first Amendment, 162–64

Uncle Tom's Cabin (Stowe), 46
United Distillers of Vancouver, 130
United States: adoption of prohibition, 34; Canadians' perceptions of, 52–54, 115–16; Canadian treaty, 84–90; investments in British Columbia's economy, 4–5; looking at government control as example, 153–61; public opinion on prohibition, 58–59; settlement patterns in, 9, 175n36; temperance organizations in, 29–31. *See also* Canadian-American relations; prohibition enforcement
United States Congress, 34, 77, 78–79, 148, 149, 160
United States customs: border crossing statistics, 47; challenges faced by, 18–20; cooperation between countries, 97; establishment of in Pacific Northwest, 15–16
United States Supreme Court, 64
Upshaw, William D., 167
Ure, Benjamin, 17

Valsich, Ernest, 78
Vancouver (BC), 70, 126
Vancouver Breweries, 128
Vancouver Brewing Company, 131–32
Vancouver Daily Province (newspaper), 55, 101, 134
Vancouver Province (newspaper), 53, 125, 133
Vancouver Sun (newspaper), 95, 115, 138, 152, 157
Vancouver World (newspaper), 22, 132
Vanderbilt, Cornelius, Jr., 153, 158, 159
vessels, 70–73, 84–86, 148–49, 166–67
Victoria (BC), 45–46, 70, 126
Victoria Chronicle (newspaper), 18
Victoria Daily Colonist (newspaper), 34–35, 95, 157–58
Victoria Daily Times (newspaper), 39
Volstead Act, x, 75, 76–77, 150. *See also* Eighteenth Amendment; prohibition enforcement

Warner, Donald, 173n7
Washington (state): adoption of prohibition, 34; Peace Arch, xi; post-repeal tourism in, 167; repealing

www.ingramcontent.com/pod-product-compliance
Lightning Source LLC
Chambersburg PA
CBHW021934180725
29816CB00015B/98/J